MAGHREB REGIONAL AND GLOBAL INTEGRATION:
A Dream to Be Fulfilled

Gary Clyde Hufbauer and Claire Brunel, editors

PETERSON INSTITUTE
FOR INTERNATIONAL ECONOMICS
Washington, DC
October 2008

Gary Clyde Hufbauer has been the Reginald Jones Senior Fellow at the Peterson Institute for International Economics since 1992. He was the Marcus Wallenberg Professor of International Finance Diplomacy at Georgetown University (1985–92), senior fellow at the Institute (1981–85), deputy director of the International Law Institute at Georgetown University (1979–81); deputy assistant secretary for international trade and investment policy of the US Treasury (1977–79); and director of the international tax staff at the Treasury (1974–76). He has written extensively on international trade, investment, and tax issues. His publications include *Economic Sanctions Reconsidered,* 3rd edition (2007), *US Taxation of Foreign Income* (2007), *Toward a US-Indonesia Free Trade Agreement* (2007), *US-China Trade Disputes: Rising Tide, Rising Stakes* (2006), *The Shape of a Swiss-US Free Trade Agreement* (2006), *NAFTA Revisited: Achievements and Challenges* (2005), *Reforming the US Corporate Tax* (2005), *Awakening Monster: The Alien Tort Statute of 1789* (2003), *The Benefits of Price Convergence* (2002), *The Ex-Im Bank in the 21st Century* (2001), *World Capital Markets* (2001), *Fundamental Tax Reform and Border Tax Adjustments* (1996), and *US Taxation of International Income* (1992).

Claire Brunel is a research assistant at the Peterson Institute for International Economics, where she works on trade issues, particularly regarding North Africa, North America, and the European Union. Before joining the Institute, she worked at the European Commission in the Economics and Financial Affairs DG, for BNP Paribas in macroeconomic studies, and for Schroeder Salomon Smith Barney in mergers and acquisitions. She obtained a bachelor of science degree in mathematics and economics from Georgetown University and an MPhil in economics from the University of Oxford.

PETER G. PETERSON INSTITUTE
FOR INTERNATIONAL ECONOMICS
1750 Massachusetts Avenue, NW
Washington, DC 20036-1903
(202) 328-9000 FAX: (202) 659-3225
www.petersoninstitute.org

C. Fred Bergsten, *Director*
Edward Tureen, *Director of Publications, Marketing, and Web Development*

Typesetting by BMWW
Printing by Edwards Brothers, Incorporated

Printed in the United States of America
10 09 08   5 4 3 2 1

Library of Congress Cataloging-in-Publication Data

Maghreb regional and global integration : a dream to be fulfilled / Gary Clyde Hufbauer and Claire Brunel, editors.
    p. cm.
    1. Africa, North—Economic integration.   2. Africa, North—Economic conditions.   3. Africa, North—Commerce.   4. Africa, North—Foreign economic relations.   I. Hufbauer, Gary Clyde.   II. Brunel, Claire.

HC805.M339 2008
337.1'61—dc22

2008039564

Table of Contents

Preface

In recent years, the need to achieve stability in the Middle East North Africa region has become the main driver of US security and trade policy in this part of the world. Reflecting this background of high politics, the Institute has already published studies on trade relationships with the region, and on the political economy of the Middle East, notably by Robert Lawrence, *A US–Middle East Trade Agreement: A Circle of Opportunity?*, and by Marcus Noland and Howard Pack, *The Arab Economies in a Changing World*.

This study differs from earlier Institute work by concentrating exclusively on the Maghreb region: Algeria, Libya, Mauritania, Morocco, and Tunisia. Historically, the political, social, and economic background of the Maghreb distinguishes it from the greater Middle East. Moreover, US trade agreements with the Maghreb countries (building on the example of the US-Morocco FTA) could act as stepping stones towards the greater goal of a US–Middle East free trade agreement.

This study explores the economic prospects for greater regional and global integration for the Maghreb—between the countries in the region itself and with the United States and the European Union. To achieve meaningful results, economic and political reforms should go hand in hand, complementing each other to improve stability and standards of living in the region. Trade and investment relationships between the countries are currently very low. Political tensions are high. Yet significant benefits for all Maghreb countries would flow from enhanced economic engagement with their immediate neighbors and the outside world. Greater unity would confer on the Maghreb region a stronger bargaining position in dealing with its trading partners, and a more compelling voice in global councils. Perhaps most important, economic integration would raise levels of trade, investment, employment, output, and economic growth.

This study analyzes the payoff to the Maghreb region from pursuing economic ties with the European Union and the United States. It then proposes concrete steps to accelerate integration. Many of those steps can be taken by the Maghreb countries themselves, to improve ties between individual sectors of the regional economy.

The recommendations also emphasize the role that the United States and the European Union can play in promoting regional integration. Important measures can be built into the text of bilateral trade and investment agreements or in companion pacts. On topics such as tariff barriers, rules of origin, and technical assistance, the study suggests constructive measures that could realistically be achieved in the medium term. Those steps would contribute to the integration process in the Maghreb and help transform the economies to create more jobs, better living conditions, and faster growth.

The Peter G. Peterson Institute for International Economics is a private, nonprofit institution for the study and discussion of international economic policy. Its purpose is to analyze important issues in that area and to develop and communicate practical new approaches for dealing with them. The Institute is completely nonpartisan.

The Institute is funded by a highly diversified group of philanthropic foundations, private corporations, and interested individuals. About 22 percent of the Institute's resources in our latest fiscal year were provided by contributors outside the United States, including about 9 percent from Japan. This study was supported by the Office Chérifien des Phosphates, the national Moroccan phosphates company and one of the world's largest exporters of phosphates and derivatives.

The Institute's Board of Directors bears overall responsibilities for the Institute and gives general guidance and approval to its research program, including the identification of topics that are likely to become important over the medium run (one to three years) and that should be addressed by the Institute. The director, working closely with the staff and outside Advisory Committee, is responsible for the development of particular projects and makes the final decision to publish an individual study.

The Institute hopes that its studies and other activities will contribute to building a stronger foundation for international economic policy around the world. We invite readers of these publications to let us know how they think we can best accomplish this objective.

C. Fred Bergsten
Director
July 2008

Executive Summary

STUART EIZENSTAT and GARY CLYDE HUFBAUER

Economic integration among the countries of the Maghreb region of North Africa, as well as closer economic ties between the region and the broader world economy, are vital to the prosperity and stability of the region. Currently, the Maghreb countries—Morocco, Algeria, Tunisia, Mauritania, and Libya—trade little with each other. In fact, the rate of trade is one of the lowest in the world. The countries have many nontariff and regulatory barriers in place that impede trade and investment flows. Unemployment is high and, unless action is taken, promises to increase because of a burgeoning demographic bulge in the region. Extremism threatens to further limit economic growth and foreign investment. Economic integration in the Maghreb can help address these challenges by capitalizing on economies of scale, attracting increased investment, and turning the region into a more prosperous and stable economic zone with an improved standard of living for its inhabitants.[1]

The Maghreb countries will need to work together to break down barriers to trade and investment in the region by strengthening the free trade

Stuart E. Eizenstat heads the international practice of Covington & Burling LLP. He has held a number of key senior positions in US administrations, including chief White House domestic policy adviser to President Jimmy Carter (1977–81), US ambassador to the European Union, undersecretary of commerce for international trade, undersecretary of state for economic, business, and agricultural affairs, and deputy secretary of the Treasury in the Clinton administration (1993–2001). Gary Clyde Hufbauer has been the Reginald Jones Senior Fellow at the Peterson Institute for International Economics since 1992.

1. Speaking at the Peterson Institute for International Economics on May 29, 2008, Deputy US Trade Representative John Veroneau and Assistant Secretary of State Daniel Sullivan both endorsed Maghreb regional integration as a promising path to economic progress and political stability.

agreements (FTAs) already in place. However, the United States, the European Union, and international institutions, such as the International Monetary Fund (IMF) and the World Bank, are also important to promote economic integration in the Maghreb. Recently, the United States expanded its economic engagement in the region, including through a trade and investment dialogue with Libya and the recent Millennium Challenge Corporation (MCC) grant to Morocco. The European Union already is involved deeply in the Maghreb through the Euro-Mediterranean Partnership. The IMF and World Bank also have valuable experience in the region and continue to facilitate regional economic dialogue. Such efforts have well positioned the United States, the European Union, and international institutions to assist the Maghreb countries in integrating their economies and developing closer ties with the world economy. Now is the time for further decisive action to promote stability and prosperity. The United States and the European Union should complement their bilateral programs with regional initiatives, as there is an opportunity for such initiatives to provide a road map, incentives, and technical assistance to the Maghreb to promote regulatory harmonization and reduce barriers to trade and investment. As the studies described in this book demonstrate, large benefits would flow to the region from such integration efforts—and the costs of nonintegration are high.

This book provides general and sector-specific recommendations as to how the potential benefits of regional integration could best be achieved. It has a dual focus. First it analyzes the gains from closer economic integration among the Maghreb countries. Second it examines the additional benefits from closer economic ties between the region and the world economy, in particular the United States and European Union. The study underlines the need for economic reforms that reduce tariff and nontariff barriers, create a better investment climate, and foster regulatory harmonization, both to increase intraregional economic ties and to enhance the region's attractions for global firms. The study also examines specific economic sectors that may particularly benefit from Maghreb integration.

Political Economy:
The Maghreb without Economic Integration

The Maghreb experienced average annual GDP growth of 2.5 percent between 2001 and 2005, a disappointing record compared with that of South and East Asia. Among the various explanations that can be offered, constraining features include rigid economic structures, slow productivity growth, and modest investment levels. Agriculture remains important, especially in Morocco and Tunisia, but agricultural productivity shows few gains. Libya and Algeria derive substantial revenue from oil and gas, a blessing when the price of oil is $140 per barrel but not a source of gainful employment for millions of new entrants to the labor market. Other constraints are very meager levels of cross-border trade and investment within the region. Intraregional trade among the Maghreb countries was only 1.3 percent of their total merchandise trade in 2007, one of the lowest rates in the world. Cross-border investment figures are not reported, but the amounts are small. Tariffs within the Maghreb have been sharply reduced, but individual countries still maintain nontariff and regulatory barriers that impede regional trade and investment flows. Moreover, Maghreb countries do not view their immediate neighbors as markets or sources of supply, largely because each country has its own historical links to the rest of the Arab world, the rest of Africa, and Europe. Political tensions between Algeria and Morocco—which together represent 77 percent of the region's population and 66 percent of the region's GDP—are a major obstacle to economic cooperation in the region.

Unemployment is high, often above 20 percent. Population growth is expected to be high in coming decades, adding more pressure to unemployment figures. The challenge created by this demographic bulge would be better met if tackled at the regional level with the help of international players. Economic opportunities for the growing population of young urban men are few, which can make radical ideologies appealing. Terrorism and extremism are on the rise, and if unchecked, they will undermine political stability—which, along with feeble economic performance, damages the region's ability to attract trade and foreign direct investment (FDI).

To combat the terrorist threat, countries in the region have tightened border restrictions on the movement of people and goods, further reducing commerce and depressing economic activity. The United States and the European Union have encouraged the Maghreb countries to focus on antiterrorism measures, which has had the unintended consequence of taking the spotlight off economic reform. Without faster growth, long-term political stability will remain elusive.

Regional Integration

There have been numerous political attempts to achieve Maghreb integration (see table 3.1 and figure 3.1 in chapter 3). Unfortunately most have not realized their objectives.

The Arab Maghreb Union (AMU), the only initiative that includes all five Maghreb countries, reached a stalemate in 1994 because of cumbersome decision-making rules and political tensions among members. There are recent signs of better cooperation, but much remains to be done.

The Greater Arab Free Trade Area (GAFTA), which includes Libya, Morocco, and Tunisia, has made the most progress. In 2005 the countries created a duty-free zone for all industrial and agricultural goods. Services and investment are excluded, however, and nontariff barriers remain high.

EU association agreements with Algeria, Morocco, and Tunisia have made good progress in liberalizing merchandise trade (excluding agriculture), but little headway in services and investment. The partners agreed to a series of trade facilitation measures, now in the process of implementation. Libya and Mauritania do not have association agreements, although each country benefits from a special status relative to the European Union.

The Agadir Agreement of 2004 among Tunisia, Morocco, Egypt, and Jordan builds upon other agreements, such as the GAFTA and Euro-Med association agreements, and remains open to countries that sign Euro-Med association agreements and are GAFTA members.

Comparison with Other Regional Initiatives

In both Southeast Asia and Central America, an acute need for regional political stability was decisive in promoting integration. Among the results were the Association of Southeast Asian Nations (ASEAN) followed by the ASEAN Free Trade Area (AFTA), while in Central America, the Central American Common Market (CACM) served as a precursor to the Central American Free Trade Agreement (CAFTA) with the United States. Similar forces are at play in the Maghreb. If it becomes a unified economic region, the Maghreb stands to enjoy enhanced bargaining power regionally and worldwide, particularly with respect to the United States and the European Union.

Both the Southeast Asian and Central American agreements coped with different economic levels among their members and surmounted internal resistance to liberalization. Both regions successfully confronted differences in internal political systems and differences in relative power. That said, external assistance with institution building and trade facilitation was important to advancing the integration process of both regions.

Gravity Model Analysis

Given the Maghreb's small economic size, a gravity model analysis suggests that a full-fledged free trade area among the Maghreb countries would yield a gain in total merchandise trade of some $1 billion. Even this modest figure would almost double the extent of commercial relations within the region and might pave the way for a future deepening of ties. Moreover, the calculated impact on Mauritania's total trade ($122 million) and Libya's total imports (also $122 million) are significant as standalone gains.

FTAs between the European Union or the United States on one hand and the major Maghreb countries (Algeria, Morocco, and Tunisia) on the other seem the most feasible from a political economy standpoint and would generate much larger gains. Based on gravity model calculations, total Maghreb trade would expand by $4 billion to $5 billion (3.0 to 4.5 percent) if the European Union and the United States were to separately establish free trade areas with the AMU countries, and by nearly $9 billion (nearly 8 percent) if both were to establish regional FTAs with the AMU countries. This includes increases in exports from the Maghreb to the US and EU markets as well as increased imports from the United States and Europe.

Inward FDI stocks likely would increase substantially if closer economic ties were pursued with the European Union or the United States rather than simply within the Maghreb. In the most ambitious scenario of a possible EU-US-Maghreb free trade area, total Maghreb inward FDI stocks increase by $5.8 billion (75 percent) and total Maghreb outward FDI stocks rise by $3.9 billion. The significant outward FDI stocks indicate that the Maghreb countries would not alone reap the benefits of trade; both the US and European economies stand to gain as well from enhanced integration with the Maghreb region.

If the agreements depicted in these scenarios are implemented, the trade and FDI impacts of Maghreb economic integration can be expected to materialize over horizons of two to five years.

Mirage Model Analysis

The Mirage model is a computable general equilibrium (CGE) model that represents the structure of production and trade in the Maghreb countries and their external partners. The static version of this model (covering only merchandise trade) suggests that free trade, fully implemented only among the Maghreb countries, would only create a small amount of new commerce. However, a regional agreement between the Maghreb countries and the European Union would have a much larger payoff: A regional FTA could increase the exports of Morocco and Tunisia by around 40 percent, and a regional agreement with the United States would have substantial but smaller payoffs.

However, the static Mirage model does not account for the benefits of greater competition and possible returns to scale. A dynamic Mirage model was therefore devised to assess the role of policies that complement merchandise trade liberalization, namely the liberalization of services and trade facilitation, plus the effects of reducing monopolistic barriers and increasing domestic investment. In the most ambitious scenario, an EU-US-Maghreb FTA, the model predicts dramatic changes. Terms of trade losses for the Maghreb countries are offset by productivity gains, resulting in larger exports and higher GDP. The positive GDP impact reaches 10 percent in Libya, nearly 8 percent in Tunisia, 6 percent in Algeria, and around 4 percent in both Morocco and Mauritania. The gains from complementary policies and the dynamic payoff from enhanced investment benefit oil-exporting countries to the greatest extent. However, Morocco and Tunisia realize the largest export increases.

Recommendations

This book begins by examining the potential for integration within specific sectors that are particularly important to all five economies: energy, banking and insurance, transport, and food. Then global recommendations are made related to the role of the United States and the European Union in working with any Maghreb partner to promote regional integration through trade and investment agreements.

Sector-Specific Recommendations

Achieving progress on a sector-by-sector basis should prove feasible in the short term and prepare the ground for full liberalization in the medium term. The sector studies contain limited reference to Libya and Mauritania because data are not available, but the recommendations should apply to those two countries as well.

Energy

Energy remains the Maghreb's most significant strategic sector. Sonatrach, Algeria's state oil and gas company, could agree to sell greater quantities of gas to Morocco through the Maghreb-Europe Pedro Duran Farell Pipeline, which runs from Algeria to the Iberian peninsula. Currently Morocco levies a 7 percent transit fee, paid in kind, on the throughput of Algerian gas. At first Morocco sold the gas received as its transit fee to Spanish companies; today Morocco uses some of this gas (about 0.5 billion cubic meters annually) for the Tahaddart combined-cycle thermal plant. Soon Morocco will use all the transit fee gas when the combined-cycle thermal plant at Aïn Beni Mathar is completed. As a confidence-building measure, the state-owned Algerian gas company Sonelgaz should be invited to invest capital in this new venture. If the capacity of the pipeline were increased—thereby increasing the levies—and Morocco were allowed to contract gas from Algeria, Morocco could receive 50 to 70 percent of its estimated gas needs from Algeria by 2020. To boost confidence further, Sonatrach could be invited to invest capital in the underwater section of the Pedro Duran Farell Pipeline. Sonatrach already holds a 50 percent stake in the underwater section of the Trans-Med Pipeline (Enrico Matteï), which has carried gas from Algeria to Italy through Tunisia and under the strait of Sicily since 1983. Office National de l'Electricité, the state-owned Moroccan electricity company, had envisaged building a combined-cycle plant to produce electricity at Al Wahda. It proposed to buy gas from the pipeline and pay the same cost and freight that Spanish buyers pay when receiving liquefied natural gas from Algeria. Algeria refused, but this project could be revived and would lead to greater economic efficiencies.

Multiproduct pipelines carrying liquefied petroleum gas, gasoline, and diesel could link different centers of gas bottling and distribution situated on either side of the Algeria-Morocco border. This would not only help to meet local energy needs, but also diminish the extensive smuggling trade in oil and gas products. Pipelines feeding off the current Maghreb-Europe pipeline could be built to supply major Moroccan cities, such as Fez.

Finally, connecting the different north-south gas lines, both current and under construction, could increase by 2020 the volume of trade in the western Mediterranean to 18 million tons of oil equivalent, or 20 percent of all energy requirements in the region.

Banking and Insurance

Maghreb banks currently hold large amounts of unused liquidity and some of this could be put to productive use. New financial instruments could be created that are recognized and traded in the three countries (Algeria, Morocco, and Tunisia). Inspiration could be drawn from the Asian Bond Initiative and Asian Bond Funds created by ASEAN+3. A North African equivalent to the United Kingdom's Financial Times Stock Exchange (FTSE) index or France's Continuous Assisted Quotation (CAC 40) would help draw financial markets closer. Beyond this, ensuring full currency convertibility, at least for Algeria, Morocco, and Tunisia, would ensure greater transparency and bolster capital markets.

Following the above steps, the reform process could build upon the inevitable privatization of the Algerian banking system, an event that could spark the creation of two or more private regional banks with shareholdings in the three countries. A prime task of these banks would be to encourage and engineer mergers and acquisitions across North Africa. Finally, a Mediterranean financial agency, adequately financed to be triple-A rated, would help to bring these and other initiatives under one roof. EU and US support for the new agency would signal a keen interest in promoting economic development.

Transport

The most obvious measure to promote regional integration is to reopen road and rail services between Algeria and Morocco, which would require only a few weeks' work. The frequency of flights between Algiers and Casablanca should also be increased. These steps would turn the border into a manageable line of demarcation, as opposed to the unmanaged area that it is today.

The motorways being built in all three countries need to be connected, both near the coast and inland. Such links would boost trade and investment. Ports could cooperate far more than they do today and promote transshipment, which would insert them more fully in the global value chain.

Regarding air traffic, a joint air safety regulation authority would be a good start. Morocco has adopted an open skies policy. Tunisia is receptive to low-cost carriers. Persuading Algeria to join these efforts would reinforce what is already a very active north-south volume of traffic. Casablanca could become a hub serving West Africa and South America. Algiers could become a hub for North America and the Far East. Meanwhile, the Tunis/Monastir airport could become a favored destination for the mass tourism market.

Agribusiness

Agribusiness offers many opportunities for cooperation in the Maghreb, where patterns of production and consumption are similar and proximity is a potential asset. Economies of scale could be exploited. Vertical integration could draw upon the relative advantages of each country: water in Morocco, energy in Algeria, food processing in Tunisia. Multinational companies already consider the Maghreb as a whole; private food companies operating in the region could be merged. Greater value could be added to luxury products such as dates, olive oil, and camel milk.

Opening up borders would also help to rid the region of smuggling and encourage each government to rationalize product standards as well as subsidies designed to foster food production. Joint policies could be enacted, especially regarding the conservation of water, the protection of a fragile and often overfished coastline, and the further development of agriculture and tourism.

Global Recommendations

EU relations with Maghreb countries are currently governed by the Barcelona Process. The new Union for the Mediterranean is meant to freshly spur regional integration, but the project has been widely criticized. The main concerns focus on the possible duplication of institutions and the dual presidency concept.[2]

---

2. The dual presidency concept of the Mediterranean Union calls for a representative of a country from the Mediterranean's northern bank (a member of the European Union) and a representative of the southern bank (including the Maghreb) to share the presidency.

The United States provides financial and technical assistance to the Maghreb through the Middle East Peace Initiative and the MCC. US relations with the Maghreb are summarized in table 13.1 in chapter 13.

Without delving into institutional details, it seems evident that US-EU-Maghreb integration could transform the Maghreb economies by creating new industries and service activities, promoting faster growth and more jobs. We recommend that the United States and the European Union work with their Maghreb partners, flexibly with respect to institutions, but in a manner designed to enhance regional integration. Bilateral trade and investment agreements or regional arrangements can provide the appropriate vehicles.

Tariff Barriers

A Maghreb partner of the United States or European Union should eliminate its own tariffs on selected products imported from other Maghreb countries. Within the General Agreement on Tariffs and Trade, the Enabling Clause could be used to defend the World Trade Organization (WTO) consistency of these provisions.[3] Ideally, tariff preferences granted by a Maghreb country to the United States or the European Union through a trade agreement would be extended fully by that Maghreb partner to its Maghreb neighbors. In practice, however, the Maghreb preferences might be limited to a subset of products covered by a US or EU bilateral FTA.

Rules of Origin

Rules of origin for shipping merchandise through cross-border supply chains can be particularly cumbersome when a country is a partner to several bilateral trade agreements. In the context of the Euro-Med Partnership, Algeria, Morocco, and Tunisia apply full cumulation among themselves and diagonal cumulation with the other pan-European countries. Those provisions should be extended to Libya and Mauritania as well.

The United States and any of its Maghreb partners, starting with Morocco, could negotiate agreements similar to the qualified industrial zone (QIZ) program that the United States has with Egypt and Jordan. The QIZ agreement allows duty-free entry to the United States for Egyptian goods

---

3. In a decision titled "European Communities—Conditions for the Granting of Tariff Preferences to Developing Countries," the Appellate Body ruled that the Enabling Clause did not require countries to grant identical tariff preferences to all developing countries, but instead required that the level of preference be based on the specific development, financial, and trade needs of the developing countries in question. Available at www.ejil.org (accessed April 15, 2008).

produced in a QIZ that uses Jordanian inputs.[4] In the same spirit, QIZs for other Maghreb countries, starting with an extension of the US-Morocco FTA, could help the Maghreb integrate regionally and with the global economy.

As a larger-scale version of the QIZ concept, the United States could allow for the cumulation of inputs across the Maghreb in meeting rules of origin. This approach could be coupled with a requirement that Maghreb countries lower their own tariff barriers for shipments within the region.

Aid for Technical Assistance and Capacity Building

In a World Bank study, Allen Dennis shows that the benefits of a regional trade agreement among Middle East and North Africa countries could be tripled if accompanied by meaningful trade facilitation measures;[5] detailed models for Morocco and Tunisia suggest that flexibility in capital, labor, and land markets would increase the payoff from trade liberalization six-fold.[6] Existing rigidities in factor markets include delays in securing finance, controls on land and construction, and restrictions on majority ownership by foreign firms. These econometric findings reflect the poor business climate that prevails throughout the Maghreb. According to the World Bank report, *Doing Business 2008*, which compares regulation and reforms in 178 economies, the Maghreb does not shine: Algeria, Morocco, and Mauritania rank in the bottom third and Tunisia barely makes the top half.[7] Mauritania is the lowest ranked Maghreb country. Among Mauritania's business handicaps are an inflexible labor market, low educational attainment, and extreme corruption and taxation levels.[8]

By emphasizing reform, the European Union has done a great deal to improve the business climate in Eastern Europe. Through the framework of the Union for the Mediterranean, it might do the same for the Maghreb.

---

4. To qualify, a good must be "substantially transformed" and must have at least 35 percent of its value added in the QIZ factories.

5. Allen Dennis, *The Impact of Regional Trade Agreements and Trade Facilitation in the Middle East North Africa Region*, World Bank Policy Research Working Paper 3837 (Washington, February 2006).

6. Allen Dennis, *Trade Liberalization, Factor Market Flexibility, and Growth: The Case of Morocco and Tunisia*, World Bank Policy Research Working Paper 3857 (Washington, March 2006).

7. Libya is not included in the World Bank report.

8. Enterprise Surveys Country Profile: Mauritania, *World Bank Enterprise Surveys*, 2006, available at www.enterprisesurveys.org (accessed April 20, 2008).

Bilateral US and EU trade agreements with individual countries could likewise contribute. A modest starting point would be systems for independent administrative and judicial review of customs determinations.

Investment and service-sector reforms are particularly important.[9] To this end, the United States and the European Union should encourage harmonization of regulatory regimes throughout the region to the highest possible standards. One practical step might be to create an institution to coordinate regulation across the region. This institution would seek to ensure that rules established by each Maghreb country meet minimum criteria, paving the way for a process of either mutual recognition by neighboring countries or general harmonization.[10]

In addition, the United States and the European Union should promote sector-specific investment and regulatory reforms, for service sectors in particular. The Euro-Med Partnership is seeking to complete the integration of electricity markets in the Maghreb.[11] As of now, only a few countries (Algeria and Tunisia) have linked their electricity grids. Morocco and Algeria are setting up a joint venture that would link the Algerian power grid to the European Union via Morocco.[12] The ultimate goal is to connect all North African countries to the single EU energy market. The project would facilitate electricity generation at low-cost plants and reduce outlays for spare capacity. A trans-Maghreb power grid would also provide energy security for the region. Similar benefits could be achieved for natural gas in both production and distribution.

Maghreb partners also could be asked to open their insurance and leasing sectors, not only to US and EU firms, but also to other Maghreb countries. To this end, regulatory regimes for insurance and leasing should be harmonized across the Maghreb.

---

9. Paloma Anós Casero and Ganesh Kumar Seshan, *Is There a New Vision for Maghreb Economic Integration?* World Bank Report 38359 (Washington, November 2006).

10. For details on a worldwide version of this institution, see Mike R. Gadbaw, Proposal to Create a WTO Center for Global Regulatory Excellence (paper presented at the Eight Annual WTO Conference by the British Institute of International and Comparative Law, London, May 13–14, 2008).

11. In December 2003 in Rome, Algeria, Morocco, Tunisia, and the European Commission (as nonparticipant promoter) signed a protocol of agreement for the progressive integration of the electricity markets of the three Maghreb countries into the EU electricity internal market. The long-term objective is to sign a Euro-Maghreb energy community treaty that would also include Libya and Mauritania. See "Establishment of the 'Rome Euro-Mediterranean Energy Platform' within the Framework of the Euro-Mediterranean Energy Cooperation," decree of the Ministry of Productive Activities of the government of Italy, October 15, 2004, available at http://ec.europa.eu (accessed on March 23, 2008).

12. "Algeria Plans Power Export to Spain Via Morocco," Reuters, May 10, 2008.

The United States and the European Union could extend so-called fifth freedom rights to air carriers based in the region,[13] provided the home nations accorded similar rights to other carriers based in the region.

Capacity-building efforts and technical cooperation could be done through instruments similar to the Economic and Technical Cooperation (Ecotech) agenda of the Asia Pacific Economic Cooperation (APEC) arrangement. The Ecotech agenda was created to support the Bogor Goals for open trade and investment.[14] The United States and the European Union could provide assistance for a similar harmonization of standards throughout the Maghreb. One possible precedent is the US-ASEAN trade and investment framework arrangement (TIFA) applied to pharmaceutical and agricultural products.

While much of the Maghreb transportation infrastructure is good, the United States and the European Union could encourage the World Bank to launch selected projects to improve ports, airports, roads, and pipelines. Technical and financial assistance for transportation infrastructure should focus on transnational networks. In this spirit, in April 2008 the 10 Western Mediterranean countries—Portugal, Italy, Spain, France, Malta, and the five AMU members—signed a memorandum of understanding introducing a series of infrastructure projects, including a high-speed train and a motorway across North Africa.[15]

Improving the Efficiency of Intraregional Shipments

A final significant issue to be addressed is the need to decrease the time and cost of shipments between Maghreb neighbors and with the rest of the world. With US or EU encouragement and assistance a Maghreb country might agree to streamline its customs procedures to ensure faster release of goods, not only for goods arriving from the United States or Europe, but also for goods arriving from Maghreb neighbors. New procedures should strictly follow the principles of the Kyoto Convention, which state that customs authorities must maintain formal consultative relationships with importers and that custom formalities must be specified in national legislation and be as simple as possible. Consistent with these principles, Maghreb customs authorities should permit express shipments by qualified traders

---

13. Fifth freedom rights are the rights of an airline based in one country to land in another country, drop off some passengers and pick up others, and continue traveling to a third country, rather than returning to the home country.

14. Six priorities were identified: developing human capital, fostering safe and efficient capital markets, strengthening economic infrastructure, harnessing technologies of the future, promoting environmentally sustainable growth, and encouraging the growth of small and medium enterprises.

15. "Transport Infrastructure in Western Mediterranean," Agence Europe, April 19, 2008.

and open all borders for certified truckers. The authorities should publish applicable laws and regulations on the Internet and permit electronic submission of customs information before shipments arrive, whether by land, sea, or air. Maghreb partners should apply risk management principles for customs control so that officers only inspect shipments that are considered medium or high risk. In addition, the Maghreb partners should allow broker guarantees to cover potential duties and taxes while goods are in transit through a country. This element is essential if firms are to take advantage of improved transportation management across the region. Were goods to be diverted or lost, the issuer of the guarantee could compensate the host country for duties or taxes that ought to have been paid.

Conclusion

Economic integration would allow Maghreb countries to reap significant trade, investment, and welfare benefits. Some measures to promote integration can be implemented relatively easily in a short period of time and would provide immediate gains for each of the Maghreb countries. Others will need to be approached with a longer time frame and with help from third parties through technical and financial assistance. The starting point is for Maghreb countries to work together, and with their trading partners and international organizations, to build an integrated and stable regional economy.

Acknowledgments

We would like to thank Stuart Eizenstat, Marney Cheek, and David Shuford for their many thoughtful comments and help throughout the process. We are particularly grateful to Madona Devasahayam, Susann Leutjen, David Roth, and Edward Tureen for preparing this manuscript for publication.

1

Introduction

The Maghreb—Algeria, Libya, Mauritania, Morocco, and Tunisia—faces multiple political and economic challenges as both feeble economic performance and lurking political instability damage the region's ability to attract trade and investment.

Average annual GDP growth in the region was 2.5 percent in 2001–05, a disappointing record compared with South and East Asia. Constraints include rigid economic structures, slow productivity growth, and modest investment levels. Intraregional trade among the Maghreb countries was only 1.3 percent of their total merchandise trade in 2007, one of the lowest rates in the world. Intraregional investment is similarly low. While many tariffs have been reduced, Maghreb countries still have numerous nontariff and regulatory barriers that impede trade and investment flows. Moreover, the countries do not look to their immediate neighbors as markets or sources of supply, largely because each nation has its own historical links to the rest of the Arab world, the rest of Africa, and Europe. Political tensions between Algeria and Morocco—which together account for 77 percent of the region's population and 66 percent of the region's GDP—are a major obstacle to economic cooperation.

Unemployment is high and terrorism is on the rise; both forces undermine confidence and stability. To combat the terrorist threat, countries have tightened border restrictions on the movement of people and goods, further reducing commerce and depressing economic activity. The United States and the European Union have encouraged the Maghreb countries to escalate their antiterrorism efforts; this focus has had the unintended consequence of taking the spotlight off economic reform. Without substantially faster growth, long-term political stability will remain elusive.

The Maghreb countries could reap significant benefits by pursuing enhanced integration, both within the region and with the global economy.

There have been numerous political attempts to achieve Maghreb integration, but most have failed. Political tensions between members, internal resistance to liberalization, and differences in political systems are all factors that limit progress. However, this study emphasizes that similar hurdles were surmounted by regional integration initiatives in Central America and Southeast Asia. As in those areas, international technical assistance may be essential to success in the Maghreb.

This study has a dual focus. First, it analyzes the gains from closer economic integration among the Maghreb countries. Second, it examines the additional benefits of closer economic ties between the region and the world economy, in particular the United States and European Union. The modeling is carried out with two econometric tools: a gravity model and a computable general equilibrium model. In addition, the study examines four key economic sectors: energy, banking and insurance, transport, and food.

In 2008 the Maghreb countries are trying to put their differences aside and work together to address common challenges. To that end, the authors outline a series of recommendations to accelerate the integration process. Maghreb countries need to cooperate not only in reducing tariff barriers—which they have done—but also in eliminating nontariff barriers and harmonizing regulatory regimes. The authors propose sector-specific measures that could realistically be achieved in the short term and yield significant benefits.

The authors also urge the United States and European Union to work with their Maghreb partners, in a flexible fashion with respect to institutions, but in a manner designed to enhance regional integration. Bilateral trade and investment agreements, regional arrangements, and financial assistance are all potentially appropriate vehicles. The Maghreb countries stand to benefit from working with the United States and the European Union to transform their economies, fostering new industries and service activities with the goals of creating more jobs and promoting faster growth.

Political Economy of the Maghreb

CLAIRE BRUNEL

The Maghreb is often characterized as a region of political instability and mediocre growth. Economic reforms have taken place in recent years, with Morocco and Tunisia leading the way, but the political systems vary from a democratic republic in Mauritania to an authoritarian state in Libya. Internally, the countries suffer from divisions between state and society, urban and rural areas, and secular and religious movements.

Social unrest is high in Algeria and the threat of terrorism is rising throughout the region. Several terrorist attacks have already occurred in Algeria, Morocco, and Mauritania. Whereas violence in Morocco has been the work of pockets of opposition, other countries—particularly Algeria—are faced with nationwide terrorist networks. The Groupe Salafiste de la Prédication et du Combat (GSPC), an opposition group in Algeria, adopted al Qaeda's brand name in January 2007. Under its new name of al Qaeda in the Islamic Maghreb (AQIM), the group has become more deadly, using methods—particularly suicide bombings—that had not been used in the region for decades.[1] AQIM has claimed responsibility for a large number of attacks throughout Algeria in the past year, and in early February 2008, the group assaulted the Israeli embassy in Mauritania. This was the first instance of cross-border action from AQIM and may

Claire Brunel is a research assistant at the Peterson Institute for International Economics.

1. Craig Whitlock, "Algiers Attacks Show Maturing of Al-Qaeda Unit," *Washington Post*, December 13, 2007.

presage an evolving pattern of terrorism for the group. Since then, most acts of terror in the Maghreb have been attributed to AQIM. It remains unclear whether the authors of these attacks truly have links to al Qaeda, whether they simply use the name for dramatic effect, or whether third parties attribute the brand to them. Whatever the case, the wave of violence is growing increasingly worrisome.

Among other costs, the perception of terrorism could hurt the region's efforts to attract foreign direct investment (FDI) and tourism. French companies are repatriating some of their employees and families. The Dakar rally, an annual off-road vehicle race that passes through Mauritania, was cancelled for the first time in 2008. The government of the United Kingdom has advised against travel to Algiers. In response to these and other developments, Algerian security forces are stepping up efforts to combat AQIM. In March 2008 security forces killed 25 suspected terrorists linked to al Qaeda.[2] Nevertheless, foreign governments question Algeria's capacity to contain the threat and fear that AQIM might spread across the Maghreb. Morocco, Tunisia, and Mauritania are also increasing arrests of suspected terrorists with alleged links to al Qaeda.[3]

Maghreb countries increasingly are collaborating on security matters. For the moment, concrete steps have been limited to information sharing—in January 2006 Algeria and Mauritania signed a bilateral information-sharing agreement to combat smuggling—but at a meeting in Tunis in late January 2008, Arab ministers of the interior called for greater cooperation.[4] North African countries are talking about creating pan-African forces specifically to combat terrorism.[5]

The threat of terrorism also has led to tighter restrictions on the movement of people and merchandise through the Maghreb. Border controls are stringent. Crossing points between Algeria and Tunisia are highly congested. Travel from Algeria into Mauritania by road has become incredibly difficult, especially due to the presence of members of the Polisario Front in a city close to the frontier (Tindouf). The Algeria-Morocco border is effectively closed to truck traffic because of political disputes between the two countries over Western Sahara. (See chapter 3 for more on the Polisario Front and Western Sahara.) In February 2007 Libya decided to

2. "Papers: Terrorists Killed in Algeria," *Chicago Tribune*, March 3, 2008.

3. Angela Doland, "Morocco Arrests 32 Over Suspected Terrorism Plots," *Virginia Pilot*, February 23, 2008; Ahmed Mohamed, "7 Charged in Attack on Israeli Embassy in Mauritania," Associated Press Newswires, February 24, 2008; "Tunisia Jails 17 for al Qaeda Links," Reuters, February 27, 2008.

4. "Arab Ministers Urge More Cooperation on Terrorism," Reuters, January 31, 2008.

5. "North Africa Made Great Strides towards Building Pan-African Forces—Minister," BBC Monitoring Middle East, January 6, 2008.

impose visa requirements on all citizens of Arab countries except Tunisia, which has seriously hampered the free movement of people and blocked regional integration. A strong reaction from the Algerian government led Libya to agree to the free movement of people and vehicles from Algeria effective as of January 31, 2008, but other countries remain stymied.

To summarize, in recent years, Maghreb countries have focused their collaboration on antiterrorism measures rather than economic integration. Internal economic reform lately has been neglected. As the United States and European Union likewise seek to eliminate terrorist activities in the Maghreb, their encouragement of security cooperation has unwittingly contributed to downgrading the economic agenda in priority. Security and economic measures, however, must be complementary. Stability in the region could help economic integration, but equally important, reforms leading to a stronger economy could promote peace in the region.

In economic performance, the Maghreb has experienced average annual growth of 5.6 percent over the past five years. This figure represents an average annual improvement of around 4.1 percent in per capita income for the region, as population growth is around 1.4 percent annually. All of the Maghreb countries struggle with high unemployment rates, especially for young men. The United Nations Development Program estimates the regional rate of unemployment at 16 percent and urban youth unemployment at almost 30 percent (Rachami 2008). The International Labor Organization's 2007 Global Employment Trends show that the Maghreb has the lowest labor-force participation rate in the world.[6] According to UN reports, most Maghreb countries except Tunisia have low levels of human development, in large part due to the low quality of education systems. Enterprising young men and women seeking better prospects often flee to Europe.[7]

The economies of Libya and Algeria are highly dependent on petroleum and natural gas, which are great sources of foreign exchange but poor sources of employment. Agriculture remains an important source of employment for Maghreb countries, particularly for Morocco (45 percent of the workforce), despite its low share of GDP (World Bank 2007). However, global warming is likely to impact significantly the agricultural output of Maghreb countries. Morocco can expect a decrease in its agricultural capacity of around 31 to 40 percent by 2080—an effect that would be exacerbated by other consequences of a rise in temperature, such as insect pests, severe droughts, and water scarcity (Cline 2007).

---

6. Available at the International Labor Organization's website, www.ilo.org (accessed July 3, 2008).

7. Moreover, large numbers of sub-Saharan citizens transit through the Maghreb to Europe, often illegally.

Regional integration and stronger ties with the European Union and the United States could significantly boost growth prospects for the region, but so far the international economic agenda has been the subject of much talk and little action—as the next chapter details.

References

Cline, William R. 2007. *Global Warming and Agriculture: Impact Estimates by Country*. Washington: Peterson Institute for International Economics.

Rachami, Jawad. 2008. *Maghreb Integration and the Four-Sided Development Squeeze*. Washington: Center for International Private Enterprise.

World Bank. 2007. *World Development Report 2008: Agriculture for Development*. Washington.

3

Maghreb Regional Integration

CLAIRE BRUNEL

Many attempts have been made at regional integration in the Maghreb, but unfortunately, most have stalled. Table 3.1 gives a timeline of trade agreements and commitments for the five Maghreb nations. Figure 3.1 shows the regional agreements that the five Maghreb nations have signed: the Arab Maghreb Union (AMU), Greater Arab Free Trade Area (GAFTA), Euro-Mediterranean (Euro-Med) Partnership, Agadir Agreement, Community of Sahel-Saharan States (CEN-SAD), and Common Market for Eastern and Southern Africa (COMESA).

Arab Maghreb Union

Established in 1989, the AMU is the only regional initiative that includes all five Maghreb countries. It originally aimed to strengthen economic cooperation and achieve regional economic integration while respecting each country's political, economic, and social interests. Member countries also aspired to reach a common stance in foreign affairs and national defense. A customs union was planned for 1995, and eventually an economic common market in 2000. Neither goal was accomplished, even in part. As AMU decisions are reserved for the annual meetings of its heads of state, two obstacles explain the AMU's failure to achieve meaningful progress. First, all decisions must be unanimously agreed upon and implemented. Second, political tensions among members halted the meetings in 1994.

Claire Brunel is a research assistant at the Peterson Institute for International Economics.

Table 3.1 Trade agreements and commitments of the five Maghreb nations

Agreement/commitment	Algeria	Libya	Mauritania	Morocco	Tunisia
World Trade Organization membership	Applied in June 1987; in final phase of negotiations	Applied in June 2004; working group created in July 2004	Member since May 1995	Member since January 1995	Member since March 1995
Arab Maghreb Union[a]	Member since 1989	Member since 1989	Member since 1989	Member since 1989	Member since 1989
GAFTA[b]		Member since 1997		Member since 1997	Member since 1997
Agadir Agreement[c]				Signed in 2004	Signed in 2004
CEN-SAD[d]		Member since 1998		Member since 2001	Member since 2001
COMESA[e]		Member since 2005			
Euro-Med Partnership[f]	Association Agreement signed in April 2002 and entered into effect in September 2005; free trade area planned for 2017	Has observer status in the Euro-Med process since 1999	"Special guest" at foreign ministers' meetings	Association Agreement signed in February 1996 and entered into effect in March 2000; free trade area planned for 2012	Member of the Euro-Med Free Trade Area for manufactured goods since January 1, 2008
Free trade agreement with the United States				Signed in March 2004 and entered into effect in January 2006	

a. The Arab Maghreb Union was signed in February 1989 between Algeria, Libya, Mauritania, Morocco, and Tunisia.
b. The Greater Arab Free Trade Area (GAFTA) was signed in 1997, and the area launched in 2005; current members are Jordan, Bahrain, United Arab Emirates, Tunisia, Saudi Arabia, Syria, Iraq, Oman, Qatar, Kuwait, Lebanon, Libya, Egypt, Morocco, Sudan, Yemen, and Palestine.
c. Signed in February 2004 between Morocco, Tunisia, Egypt, and Jordan, the agreement is considered a first step toward a Euro-Mediterranean Free Trade Area.
d. The Community of Sahel-Saharan States (CEN-SAD) was established in 1998; current members are Benin, Burkina Faso, Central African Republic, Chad, Ivory Coast, Djibouti, Egypt, Eritrea, Gambia, Ghana, Guinea Bissau, Liberia, Libya, Mali, Morocco, Niger, Nigeria, Senegal, Sierra Leone, Somalia, Sudan, Togo, and Tunisia.
e. The Common Market of Eastern and Southern Africa (COMESA) was established in December 1994; current members are Burundi, Comoros, Democratic Republic of the Congo, Djibouti, Egypt, Eritrea, Ethiopia, Kenya, Libya, Madagascar, Malawi, Mauritius, Rwanda, Seychelles, Sudan, Swaziland, Uganda, Zambia, and Zimbabwe.
f. Partnership between the European Union and 10 Mediterranean countries: Algeria, Egypt, Israel, Jordan, Lebanon, Morocco, Palestine, Syria, Tunisia, and Turkey. The partnership consists of association agreements at the bilateral level and of cooperation in the political, economic, and cultural fields at the regional level. Ultimately, the goal is to achieve a free trade area.

Figure 3.1 Regional trading agreements of Maghreb countries

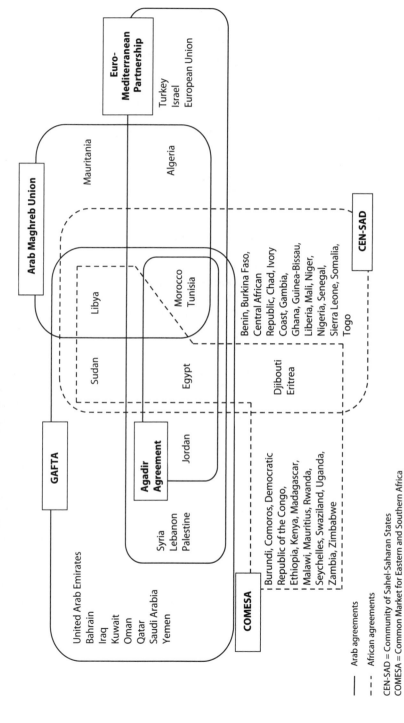

CEN-SAD = Community of Sahel-Saharan States
COMESA = Common Market for Eastern and Southern Africa
GAFTA = Greater Arab Free Trade Area

——— Arab agreements
- - - African agreements

The Western Sahara dispute between Algeria and Morocco is a key stumbling block. Since Spain withdrew its forces from the resource-rich region in 1975, control of the area has been claimed both by Morocco, on the basis of historic and cultural ties, and by the Polisario Front, a local independence movement supported by Algeria. Algeria's interest in Western Sahara is sparked by aspirations of a land route to the Atlantic and developing oil or gas reserves that might lie under the Saharan sands or offshore. Morocco simply wants to cement its historic claim to the area. The parties' failure to reach an agreement at UN-brokered talks led to the closing of the Algeria-Morocco border in 1994.[1] The border closing is particularly harmful for the region, as the combined population of the two countries represents 77 percent of the AMU total and the countries' combined GDP covers 66 percent of the AMU total. Morocco proposed a compromise on the territory in April 2007, calling for broad autonomy under Moroccan sovereignty, and encouraged the United Nations to launch a new round of negotiations to settle the conflict politically. After four rounds of talks resulted in a stalemate, the most recent UN Security Council report called for "realism" in reaching a solution.[2]

Political tensions hamper commercial relations between other AMU members as well. In 1992, the UN Security Council imposed an air and arms embargo on Libya to pressure Tripoli into delivering two suspects in the bombing of Pan Am Flight 103 in 1988. The other four AMU members decided to implement the Security Council resolution, leading Libya to boycott the AMU. Mauritania and Libya face additional troubles as Mauritania has accused the Libyan secret service of involvement in an attempted coup against President Maaouiya Ould Sid Ahmed Taya in June 2003. More recent attempts to revive the AMU also have failed. In May 1999 Algeria reconvened the meeting of AMU foreign ministers with no tangible results. In December 2003 Algeria attempted to hand over the AMU presidency to Libya to renew Libyan interest in the union, but Libya refused the office.

Opinions diverge as to how the AMU could be revitalized. Most Maghreb countries are torn between bonds to the rest of the Arab world, links to their continental African neighbors, and colonial ties to the European Union. Morocco and Algeria want to turn north to integrate the AMU into the Euro-Med Partnership (see below). Libya, however, is looking south; it would prefer to anchor the AMU initiative in the African Union. Tunisia and Morocco, the two best performing countries in the region, have shifted their focus toward bilateral relations with the European Union and the United States. This shift both arises from and contributes to the AMU's lack of progress.

---

1. Nearly all shipments between Algeria and Morocco take place by sea.

2. Claudia Parsons, "UN Council Urges Realism in Western Sahara Dispute," Reuters, May 1, 2008.

Limited progress can be observed in the past few years. Since 2005 the five Maghreb countries have organized three ministerial conferences to foster regional integration. The first two conferences focused on financial integration and trade facilitation: harmonization of regulations, tariff and custom reforms, and transport infrastructure. The most recent conference put the spotlight on strengthening the business environment and fostering private investment. In March 2007 foreign ministers announced the establishment of a Maghreb Investment and Foreign Trade Bank (BMICE) owned by the central banks of the member countries, with initial capital of $1 billion and a mandate to promote investment, trade, and cross-border economic cooperation. This step represents the long-delayed implementation of agreements made when the AMU began.

Table 3.2 compares the economic performance of AMU members and the region as a whole in 2007 and 1989, the year of the AMU's inception. Other than Libya, all countries reduced their rates of inflation. Expressed in US dollars at market exchange rates, GDP per capita doubled in nominal terms for the region as a whole. However, between 1989 and 2007, the US GDP price deflator increased from 79 to 120. Thus, in real terms, Maghreb GDP per capita has increased by only 30 percent, or about 1.6 percent a year. That said, as noted earlier, the past five years have been much better than the average over the entire 18 years, with per capita income growth of around 4.1 percent annually.

Intraregional trade as a share of total trade has remained very low at 1.3 percent. Total merchandise trade as a share of GDP in 2007 was 72.5 percent for the entire region, up from 41.7 percent in 1989. Inward FDI stock as a share of GDP for the Maghreb more than doubled between 1990 and 2006. However, the numbers vary widely across the region. In 2006 the figure for Libya stood at 7.4 percent, compared with 70.6 percent for Tunisia.

Greater Arab Free Trade Area

Adopted in 1997, GAFTA was agreed upon by 17 of the 22 members of the Arab League, including Libya, Morocco, and Tunisia.[3] The largest regional initiative in the Middle East and North Africa region, its ultimate goal was to establish a free trade area by 2008. At the Arab Summit in 2001, countries advanced the deadline to 2005. Since then all industrial and agricultural goods have traveled through the region duty free (Abedini and Peridy 2007). The agreement covers merchandise trade only; services and investment are excluded.

---

3. The League of Arab States, or Arab League, was started in 1945 and now counts 22 countries as members: Algeria, Bahrain, Comoros, Djibouti, Egypt, Iraq, Jordan, Kuwait, Lebanon, Libya, Mauritania, Morocco, Oman, Palestine, Qatar, Saudi Arabia, Somalia, Sudan, Syria, Tunisia, United Arab Emirates, and Yemen. All but Algeria, Comoros, Djibouti, Mauritania, and Somalia participate in GAFTA.

Table 3.2 Performance of the Arab Maghreb Union, 1989 and 2007

Country	Population (millions)		GDP Billions of US dollars		GDP Per capita (US dollars)		Inflation (percent)		Bilateral merchandise trade (percent of total trade) With Arab Maghreb Union		With European Union		With United States		Total merchandise trade (percent of GDP)		Inward FDI stock (percent of GDP)	
	1989	2007[a]	1989	2007[a]	1989	2007[a]	1989	2007[a]	1989	2007[b]	1989	2007[b]	1989	2007[b]	1989	2007	1990	2006
Maghreb	63.1	84.1	114.4	301.5	1,813	3,586	6.7[d]	6.4[d]	1.3	1.3	69.7	59.4	7.8	11.3	41.8	72.6	10.6	25.5
Algeria	24.7	34.0	52.6	125.9	2,128	3,702	9.2	4.5	1.6	1.3	65.3	47.6	15.5	22.2	34.6	67.7	3.3	8.9
Libya[c]	4.6	6.1	25.1	66.0	5,457	10,840	4.5	16.2	2.2	3.1	81.5	71.0	0.5	6.6	51.8	20.9	2.3	7.4
Mauritania	1.9	3.0	1.1	2.7	574	928	9.0	7.6	1.2	6.0	56.1	33.9	3.7	5.1	72.0	118.3	4.9	60.6
Morocco	24.0	30.7	25.5	72.8	1,066	2,368	3.1	2.5	2.6	2.1	62.5	59.6	6.5	3.9	34.5	64.8	8.7	45.6
Tunisia	7.9	10.3	10.1	34.1	1,277	3,313	7.7	3.0	5.4	6.6	70.1	73.8	3.8	2.4	74.8	98.4	61.8	70.6

FDI = foreign direct investment

a. Estimates of the International Monetary Fund staff.
b. Estimates calculated based on figures for the first eight months of 2007.
c. Libya was under UN and US sanctions for a large portion of the time period studied.
d. Average inflation rate for the region weighted by GDP.

Sources: International Monetary Fund, *Direction of Trade Statistics,* January 2008, and *World Economic Outlook,* October 2007; United Nations Conference on Trade and Development (UNCTAD) foreign direct investment (FDISTAT) database, available at www.unctad.org.

Strict rules of origin are a major obstacle to the smooth working of GAFTA with respect to covered products. Member countries follow an origination rule requiring that over 40 percent of value added be contributed in another GAFTA member country if the imported product is to qualify for tariff relief. Moreover, the approval process for certificates of origin in the importing country's embassy has proven cumbersome, acting as its own nontariff barrier (NTB) (Afifi 2005).

Sanitary and phytosanitary standards (SPSs) and technical barriers to trade (TBTs) are not covered by GAFTA, and several disputes have emerged under these headings. Combined with the absence of dispute settlement mechanisms, SPS and TBT issues constitute a serious hurdle to GAFTA's effective implementation. Likewise, a working group on NTBs has achieved only limited progress and these barriers remain high. Attempts to harmonize rules or adopt a mutual recognition approach quickly stalled. Consultations in issue areas such as competition policy, intellectual property rights, and government procurement were planned but never materialized. For trade remedies involving countervailing and antidumping duties as well as safeguards, the original GAFTA text sought to apply international rules. However, at the time of signing in 1997, only seven GAFTA members were also members of the World Trade Organization (WTO). Most countries did not have the institutional capacity to implement trade remedy rules in a reasonable way (Lawrence 2006).

Euro-Med Partnership

The Euro-Med Partnership, or Barcelona Process, establishes a framework for economic, political, and social relations between the European Union and ten Mediterranean partners. The process has two complementary dimensions: a bilateral dimension, whereby each country has an association agreement (AA) with the European Union; and a regional dimension to promote strategic cooperation while emphasizing national complementarities. The partnership was launched in 1995 between the European Union and nine Mediterranean countries with a view to establishing a free trade area by 2010.[4] In this context, Algeria, Morocco, and Tunisia have all signed AAs with the European Union.[5]

Libya has enjoyed observer status in the Barcelona Process since the UN sanctions over Pan Am Flight 103 were lifted in 1999. Brussels is aiming toward Libyan accession, but Libya has not yet undertaken the necessary

---

4. Syria, Lebanon, Palestine, Jordan, Egypt, Morocco, Tunisia, Israel, and Algeria.

5. The AA between the European Union and Algeria is in the process of being reviewed, possibly to include an energy deal. See "Benita Ferrero-Waldner visits Algeria to prepare for rehaul of Association Agreement," Agence Europe, March 4, 2008.

political and economic reforms. The release in July 2007 of Bulgarian medics accused of infecting Libyan children with human immunodeficiency virus (HIV) opened the door for further cooperation. In February 2007 the European Union proposed launching talks on closer collaboration, notably in the areas of energy and illegal immigration, eventually leading to a free trade agreement.[6] Mauritania attends foreign minister meetings as a special guest.

Since the launch of the Barcelona Process, there has been some progress in liberalizing merchandise trade. Mediterranean countries now enjoy duty-free access to the EU market for manufactured goods. The AAs also provide for a gradual dismantling of tariffs on EU exports to the Mediterranean. On the other hand, liberalization in the agricultural sector has been limited. Morocco, however, has a special agricultural agreement with the European Union to supplement its AA by further liberalizing agricultural trade between the parties. Finally, although the liberalization of services and investment is among the key objectives for the AAs, negotiations have not taken place.

The Euro-Med partners also agreed on a series of measures to facilitate trade, including the convergence of legislation on standards and conformity assessment.[7] For rules of origin, Algeria, Morocco, and Tunisia apply full cumulation[8] among themselves and diagonal cumulation[9] with other pan-European countries.

The European Union provides financial and technical assistance to its Euro-Med partners through various means. Its MEDA program is the main financial instrument of the Euro-Med process. It supports the implementation process of the AAs and the adoption of key social and eco-

---

6. "Brussels Proposes First Ever Framework for EU-Libya Ties," Agence France Presse, February 27, 2008.

7. "Conformity assessment" covers self-testing or independent testing to ensure that the prescribed product and process standards are met.

8. Full cumulation allows the parties to an agreement to carry out the working or processing on nonoriginating products in the geographic area formed by the member countries. Full cumulation means that all operations carried out in the participating countries are given credit. Other forms of cumulation require that the goods originate in one party before being exported to another party to obtain credit for working or processing, but this is not the case with full cumulation. Full cumulation simply demands that all the working or processing on nonoriginating material be carried out within the geographic area for the final product to qualify under the rules of origin.

9. Diagonal cumulation operates between more than two countries, provided they have free trade agreements containing identical origin rules and provision for cumulation between them. As with bilateral cumulation, only originating products or materials can benefit from diagonal cumulation. Although more than two countries can be involved in the manufacture of a product, it will have the origin of the country where the last working or processing operation took place, provided that the activity was more than a minimal operation.

nomic reforms in the Mediterranean countries. The European Neighbor-hood and Partnership Instrument (ENPI) and European Investment Bank (EIB) are other important funding sources of the Euro-Med Partnership. In March 2002 the EIB's existing activities in the Mediterranean were en-hanced through the creation of the Facility for Euro-Mediterranean Investment and Partnership (FEMIP), which focuses on the financial needs of the private sector.

Agadir Agreement

The Agadir Agreement was signed in 2004 between Morocco, Tunisia, Egypt, and Jordan; implementation began in March 2007. The agreement remains open to other countries in the region, particularly those that enjoy AAs with the European Union and have implemented GAFTA. These tests exclude the AMU members that are not already in the Agadir Agreement: Algeria, Libya, and Mauritania.

The Agadir Agreement has been reasonably successful, as it builds heavily on existing regional and bilateral initiatives. Some of the temporary exceptions are taken from the liberalization schedules of the AAs that countries have with the European Union. The liberalization of agriculture follows GAFTA, although progress in this part of the GAFTA agenda has been limited. Service liberalization draws from WTO commitments (Lawrence 2006). Countries abide by pan-European rules of origin, even though this measure is potentially incompatible with GAFTA rules (Wippel 2005). The countries benefit from technical assistance from the European Union.

CEN-SAD

CEN-SAD was established in February 1998; Libya, Morocco, and Tunisia are members along with 20 other African countries.[10] The organization covers investment in the agricultural, industrial, social, cultural, and energy fields. Some accomplishments include the creation of the African Bank for Development and Trade in 1999 and the Special Program for Food Security (SPFS) in 1995.[11] However, progress in CEN-SAD, as in the initiatives above, has been limited, as the community essentially focuses on resolving large-scale political conflicts in Darfur and instability in Somalia.

---

10. The others are Benin, Burkina Faso, Central African Republic, Chad, Djibouti, Egypt, Eritrea, Ivory Coast, Gambia, Ghana, Guinea Bissau, Liberia, Mali, Niger, Nigeria, Senegal, Sierra Leone, Somalia, Sudan, and Togo.

11. The SPFS operates in all countries but Libya, Tunisia, and Somalia.

COMESA

Libya is the only Maghreb country to participate in COMESA. Established in 1994, COMESA has 19 members.[12] On October 31, 2000, free trade was achieved between a subset of nine countries in agricultural and animal products, mineral and nonmineral ores, and manufactured goods—but Libya is not one of the nine.

Conclusion

All these regional integration initiatives involving Maghreb countries have made limited progress, with the exception of the GAFTA, which achieved its goal of tariff liberalization, at least on paper. Despite failed attempts, the Maghreb countries understand that regional cooperation is essential for them to acquire more weight in global affairs, both in commercial and political terms. Obstacles springing from past political differences are not insurmountable. The next chapter relates the experiences of other regions in the world that were able to successfully integrate while facing similar hurdles as the Maghreb.

References

Abedini, Jawad, and Nicolas Peridy. 2007. The Greater Arab Free Trade Area (GAFTA): An Estimation of the Trade Effects. Preliminary version available online at www.gate.cnrs.fr (accessed July 2, 2008).

Afifi, Tamer. 2005. Egypt in an Arab-African Sandwich: Are GAFTA and COMESA to be implemented? Paper presented at a conference on Middle East and North African Economics: Past Perspectives and Future Challenges, sponsored by the Free University of Brussels, June, Brussels.

Lawrence, Robert Z. 2006. *A US–Middle East Trade Agreement: A Circle of Opportunity?* Policy Analyses in International Economics 81. Washington: Peterson Institute for International Economics.

Wippel, Steffen. 2005. *The Agadir Agreement and Open Regionalism.* Paper 45 (September). Lisbon: EuroMeSCo.

---

12. Members are Burundi, Comoros, Democratic Republic of the Congo, Djibouti, Egypt, Ethiopia, Eritrea, Kenya, Libya, Madagascar, Malawi, Mauritius, Rwanda, Seychelles, Sudan, Swaziland, Uganda, Zambia, and Zimbabwe.

4

The Maghreb and Other Regional Initiatives: A Comparison

CLAIRE BRUNEL

Regions are growing in size and power, starting with the Maghreb's close neighbors in the European Union and extending to regional alliances in Asia. The wave of regional integration over the past two decades is making it more difficult for a single country of moderate size to thrive in the global economy. Certain regional groups, such as the Association of Southeast Asian Nations (ASEAN) and the various organizations of Central American countries, are considered successful today, but they faced major obstacles in the past. This section reviews the integration processes in ASEAN and Central America and compares their experiences with that of the Maghreb.

Association of Southeast Asian Nations

Established in 1967, ASEAN initially comprised Indonesia, Malaysia, Philippines, Singapore, and Thailand; over time, these countries were joined by Brunei Darussalam (1984), Vietnam (1995), Laos (1997), Myanmar/Burma (1997), and Cambodia (1999). ASEAN started as a political organization in response to intraregional conflict. The communist threat throughout the

Claire Brunel is a research assistant at the Peterson Institute for International Economics.

region furnished its rallying force, as sponsored guerilla wars, notably in the Philippines and Malaysia, contributed to the region's instability. In addition, all member states coordinated their efforts to deal with large refugee flows.

The Zone of Peace, Freedom, and Neutrality (1971) was the first major step toward political cooperation under ASEAN, but it was the Treaty of Amity and Cooperation, signed at the First ASEAN Summit in Bali in 1976, that set the organization's basic principles. Most prominent among these were the peaceful settlement of disputes, judicial cooperation, coordination of political positions, and, at first, noninterference in the affairs of other members. As the Cambodia conflict developed and threatened the region, however, the need for ASEAN was evident; ASEAN dropped its noninterference commitment and was instrumental in peacefully resolving the conflict.

After 25 years of political cooperation under ASEAN, the ASEAN Free Trade Area (AFTA) was launched in 1992, with a single market planned for 2020. Progress during AFTA's first decade was slow because of political suspicions. Moreover, AFTA member states were competing against each other in third-country markets, as several countries exported similar tropical products and manufactured goods. As often happens in regional groups, AFTA members were reluctant to open their markets for sensitive products, such as rice and automobiles. Other obstacles to AFTA included fears of dominance, politically by Indonesia and economically by Singapore.

The 1997 Asian crisis gave new impetus to strengthening the free trade area, as one means of coping with the deep recession was to accelerate and broaden the integration process. Market integration in Europe and North America and the emergence of low-cost competition from China and Latin America contributed to the push for stronger economic ties within AFTA. On the political side, the financial crisis paved the way for the fall of authoritarian regimes in Thailand, Indonesia, and Malaysia, and the new leaders proved more willing to cooperate with their AFTA neighbors.

The simple average preferential tariff for products of the ASEAN-6—Brunei Darussalam and the five originating states—was reduced from 12 percent in 1992 to less than 2 percent in 2008. The remaining four countries reduced their tariffs to the target range of 0 to 5 percent for 81 percent of the products in their inclusion lists. Countries aim to remove tariffs completely on all products by 2015 for the ASEAN-6 and by 2018 for the other members. Intraregional merchandise trade as a share of total trade increased from 9.7 percent in 1992 to 19.2 percent in 2007. In real terms, GDP per capita increased 54 percent between 1992 and 2007, an average annual increase of 3.8 percent. This period encompasses the Asian financial crisis, which hit Indonesia particularly hard. Real GDP per capita growth for ASEAN countries between 1997 and 2007, excluding Indonesia, reached 7.3 percent (table 4.1).

Table 4.1   Regional comparisons between the Maghreb, ASEAN, and CAFTA-DR, 2007

Agreement	Population[a] (millions)	GDP[a] Billions of US dollars	GDP[a] Per capita (US dollars)	Annual real GDP per capita growth, 1997–2007 (percent)	Merchandise trade within the region[b] (percent of total trade)	Total merchandise trade[b] (percent of GDP)	FDI stock in the region, 2006 (percent of GDP)
Maghreb	84	302	3,585	4.4	1.3	72.5	25.5
ASEAN							
Total	576	1,201	2,086	2.7	19.2	119.5	39.5
Excluding Indonesia	350	793	2,266	7.3	11.7	158.6	57.3
CAFTA-DR[c]	47	128	2,697	6.8	6.8	74.2	23.5

ASEAN = Association of Southeast Asian Nations
CAFTA-DR = Central American Free Trade Agreement–Dominican Republic
FDI = foreign direct investment

a. International Monetary Fund staff estimates.
b. Estimates based on figures for the first eight months of 2007.
c. Excludes the United States.

Sources: International Monetary Fund, *Direction of Trade Statistics,* January 2008, and *World Economic Outlook,* October 2007; United Nations Conference on Trade and Development (UNCTAD) foreign direct investment (FDISTAT) database, available at www.unctad.org.

AFTA included measures on trade facilitation and technical barriers to accompany tariff liberalization. Regionwide projects have also materialized in finance, transportation, and energy. Adopted in 2003, the Roadmap for Financial and Monetary Integration of ASEAN planned for the market infrastructure and legal and regulatory frameworks necessary to develop capital markets. Another specific aspect of the project targets collaboration between countries in training networks, product development, market linkages, and harmonization of capital market standards.

The trans-ASEAN transportation network and the Roadmap for Integration of Air Travel Sector (2007) promote the building of major networks of roads, railways, and inland waterway transport. Regional cooperation is also apparent in the trans-ASEAN energy networks, namely the ASEAN Power Grid and Trans-ASEAN Gas Pipeline projects (1997). Finally, in other areas, such as customs procedures and electrical and telecommunications standards, ASEAN countries are working on harmonizing national standards to international ones.

Adopted in October 1998, the Framework Agreement on the ASEAN Investment Area aims to establish an ASEAN Investment Area (AIA) to promote external foreign direct investment (FDI) into the region as well as intra-ASEAN investment. Although the agreement contemplates cooperation among the ASEAN countries in attracting FDI, it excludes services and portfolio investments, except services related to manufacturing, agriculture, forestry, fisheries, and mining. The heart of the initiative lies in increased transparency of investment regulations through joint publications and information sharing as well as the simplification of procedures. The AIA provided for the immediate liberalization of investment barriers and rules in all industries for ASEAN investors and the application of national treatment to all ASEAN investors. Temporary exemptions were granted for opening up particular industries with a maximum horizon of 2015.

Central America

The first step toward economic integration in Central America was the Central American Common Market (CACM) founded in 1960 between Guatemala, El Salvador, Honduras, and Nicaragua. Costa Rica joined in 1963. The Permanent Secretariat for Economic Integration (SIECA) and the Central American Bank for Economic Integration (BCIE), both created in 1961, are the main regional institutions for economic integration.

During the first two decades of its existence, the CACM made limited progress in liberalizing markets, primarily because import substitution was then the reigning economic philosophy throughout Latin America; also, the less developed countries—Honduras and Nicaragua—feared that they would not get a fair share of the gains from integration. Economic relations between members sharply deteriorated in 1969 when the Football War between El Salvador and Honduras erupted in response to large flows of Salvadoran immigrants to Honduras. The border was closed for ten years and trade between the two countries was seriously disrupted. In the 1980s the Latin American debt crisis led to economic collapse and civil wars broke out in El Salvador and Nicaragua.

As political relations between member countries improved in the 1990s, summit meetings between CACM leaders resumed. The Central American Integration System (SICA), established in 1991, was intended to revitalize the market by focusing on export promotion. A common external tariff ranging from 0 to 15 percent was implemented in January 1993. Panama participates in SICA and Belize attends as an observer. Honduras, which had withdrawn from CACM after the Football War, was readmitted in 1992. Also part of SICA are political organizations, such as the Parliament of Central America (Parlacen), the Central American Court of Justice, and the Consultative Committee.

The Central American Free Trade Agreement–Dominican Republic (CAFTA-DR) freshly spurred integration. Because of its recent implementation,[1] the effects of the agreement are difficult to evaluate. However, be-

---

1. Delayed by national political opposition, implementation began in March 2006 in El Salvador. It has yet to enter into force in Costa Rica.

tween March 2006 and October 2007, intraregional trade grew by 17 percent, as opposed to 7 percent growth of trade between member countries and the rest of the world. The Inter-American Development Bank (IDB) observes some diversification away from traditional exports.

At the heart of the CAFTA-DR agreement are provisions designed to increase commercial ties between members. The chapter on trade facilitation and reform of customs is an essential tool, as it achieved considerable progress in eliminating barriers to investment and modernizing the legal framework for business transactions throughout the region (Hufbauer and Kotschwar 2008). Also, the investment chapter of CAFTA-DR provides for an open and transparent investor-state dispute settlement mechanism, among other provisions. However, CACM countries are currently negotiating an Agreement on Investment and Trade in Services, which is compatible with the CAFTA-DR chapter but goes further. The treaty was signed in March 2002 and modified in February 2007, but has not yet come into effect, as the national annexes—which, for transparency, detail each country's commitments—have not been finalized yet (IDB 2007).

In addition, large-scale regional projects have been initiated in Central America, notably to link electricity grids and infrastructure in the region. The flexibility of the various rules under CAFTA-DR was a crucial element of these policies' sound implementation and political backing; the rules allowed more time for implementation by Honduras and Nicaragua, the poorest member countries.

Comparison with the Maghreb

In both the ASEAN region and Central America, the need for stability was key to promoting integration. A similar threat—terrorism—infects the Maghreb. As of now, security collaboration between Maghreb countries is limited to information sharing. Serious economic integration measures would be a major step forward.

For CAFTA-DR, the need to build bargaining power in talks with major trading partners, notably the United States, was instrumental. In a similar spirit, a strong Maghreb would not only provide the region with more weight in its trade negotiations with the European Union; it would also solidify the region's position as a leader in Africa.

In the 1990s, ASEAN was handicapped by weak supranational institutions. The Asia Pacific Economic Cooperation forum helped restructure and strengthen ASEAN institutions. Similarly, Central American countries benefit from US technical aid provided in conjunction with CAFTA-DR chapters on customs administration and reform, trade facilitation, and sanitary and phytosanitary measures. The European Union is playing the same role in the Maghreb through the Euro-Med partnership and the European Neighborhood Policy.

Both ASEAN and CAFTA-DR dealt with different economic development levels and resistance to dismantling tariffs because of production similarities among members. Both groups coped with extensive power disparities between their members and different political regimes as well. As Anós Casero and Seshan (2006) show, the Maghreb faces identical challenges.

Table 4.1 summarizes the economic situation of the Maghreb, CAFTA-DR, and ASEAN in 2007.[2] Intraregional merchandise trade in the Maghreb stands at only 1.3 percent of total merchandise trade, compared with 6.3 percent for CAFTA-DR and 19.2 percent for ASEAN. Total merchandise trade as a percent of GDP is similar for the Maghreb and CAFTA-DR, but significantly lower than it is for ASEAN. The FDI stock in the region as a percent of GDP in 2006 is roughly equal for the Maghreb and CAFTA-DR, but much lower than it is for ASEAN. Over the past decade (1997–2007), on a per capita basis, real GDP has grown more slowly in the Maghreb than in ASEAN (excluding Indonesia) or in CAFTA-DR. On the other hand, in 2007 GDP per capita in the Maghreb was 1.7 times higher than it was in ASEAN and 1.3 times higher than in CAFTA-DR. As the following chapters argue, the Maghreb has a great deal of untapped economic potential, which economic integration—regionally and with the world economy generally—could help to realize.

References

Anós Casero, Paloma, and Ganesh Kumar Seshan. 2006. *Is There A New Vision For Maghreb Economic Integration?* World Bank Report 38359. Washington: World Bank.

Hufbauer, Gary Clyde, and Barbara Kotschwar. 2008. CAFTA-DR Pact: Opening Up New Frontiers. *Americas Quarterly* 2, no. 2 (Spring): 103–104.

IDB (Inter-American Development Bank). 2007. *Central American Report 3*. Washington.

---

2. The CAFTA-DR data exclude the United States.

5

Maghreb Trade and Investment

DEAN A. DeROSA

Economically speaking, the Maghreb countries compare favorably to the countries of the Middle East and other developing regions (table 5.1). With a total population of 83 million (in 2005), the region is nearly equal in size to the Mashreq countries (108 million), but on an individual basis the Maghreb nations are dwarfed in the Middle East by Iran and Turkey (about 70 million each). Sustained by their energy wealth, Algeria and Libya lead the Maghreb countries in per capita income (over $3,000) and are in the same league as higher-income developing countries in Latin America, Europe, and Central Asia (about $4,500). However, Maghreb income levels are skewed—especially for Libya—and unreliable as indicators of general well being. They certainly do not reflect the circumstances of the lower-income Maghreb countries, which are less well endowed with energy resources. Recent growth in the Maghreb (about 2.5 percent over 2001–05) has been modest compared with the robust growth of the developing countries of East Asia (7.4 percent), South Asia (4.8 percent), and Europe and Central Asia (5.2 percent). This lackluster growth likely contributes to the smoldering terrorist insurgency in parts of the Maghreb and has motivated national leaders to consider measures to promote Maghreb regional integration, with other economic reforms, to stimulate their economies.

Dean DeRosa is principal economist at ADR International Ltd. and a visiting fellow at the Peterson Institute for International Economics.

Table 5.1 Economic indicators for the Maghreb, Middle East, and other country groups and regions, 2005

Country/region	Population (millions)	National output (GDP)						Trade and foreign investment			
		GDP (billions of US dollars)	Per capita (US dollars)	Per capita growth, 2001–05 (percent)	Structure (percent of GDP)			Goods and services trade, 2004			Inward FDI stock (percent of GDP)
					Agri-culture	Industry	Services	Exports (billions of US dollars)	Imports (billions of US dollars)	Total trade (percent of GDP)	
Maghreb	83.1	225.6	3,078	2.5	16	36	48	64.4	57.1	86.6	28.9
Algeria	33.3	101.8	3,098	3.4	10	56	34	34.1	21.8	65.7	8.1
Libya	6.0	41.7	7,118	1.3	n.a.	n.a.	n.a.	n.a.	n.a.	n.a.	1.4
Mauritania	3.2	1.8	598	1.1	26	28	46	0.5	1.2	110.6	35.3
Morocco	30.5	51.6	1,713	3.0	16	30	54	16.6	20.0	73.2	43.9
Tunisia	10.1	28.7	2,860	3.5	13	28	59	13.2	14.0	96.8	56.1
Middle East											
Mashreq countries	108.3	156.4	2,305	0.9	12	30	57	41.2	52.9	81.5	33.0
GCC countries	35.1	575.6	28,777	2.8	3	56	42	303.0	186.4	111.8	20.7
Israel	7.0	123.4	17,828	0.0	n.a.	n.a.	n.a.	51.5	57.6	93.3	29.4
Iran	69.2	189.8	2,781	4.2	11	43	46	47.4	42.3	55.0	1.9
Turkey	72.9	363.4	5,042	3.2	13	22	65	87.4	105.0	63.6	11.6
Other developing regions											
East Asia and Pacific	1,899.6	3,049.5	1,618	7.4	13	45	42	1,140.8	1,053.6	82.7	35.1
South Asia	1,492.5	1,016.9	692	4.8	20	27	53	161.4	182.6	38.9	6.2
Latin America and Caribbean	555.9	2,538.8	4,625	1.2	7	31	62	526.6	468.5	47.8	36.7
Europe and Central Asia	460.0	2,073.6	4,509	5.2	9	31	61	663.0	660.2	78.5	21.2
Sub-Saharan Africa	770.3	630.8	838	2.1	15	32	53	174.5	179.5	66.3	30.2
Major OECD countries	740.9	26,934.6	36,394	1	2	26	72	5,306.9	5,630.4	40.3	16.2
European Union	314.3	9,984.1	31,807	0.8	2	27	71	3,520.4	3,309.0	70.7	33.5
Japan	127.6	4,534.0	35,484	1.3	2	30	68	612.7	523.7	24.8	2.2
United States	299.0	12,416.5	41,890	1.5	1	22	77	1,173.8	1,797.8	25.4	13.0
World	6,517.8	44,795.4	6,949	1.5	3	28	69	10,803.4	10,831.1	52.1	22.7

n.a. = not available
FDI = foreign direct investment
GCC = Gulf Cooperation Council
OECD = Organization for Economic Cooperation and Development

Sources: UNCTAD (2006); World Bank (2007).

As background for subsequent chapters on the macroeconomic and sectoral prospects of regional and global integration schemes for the Maghreb countries, this chapter examines the basic dimensions of the trade and investment relations of the Arab Maghreb Union (AMU) countries today, including trade in services. Our discussion is purposefully descriptive. However, we also consider the comparative advantages of the AMU countries revealed in their recent trade statistics, the height of current import tariffs, and other barriers to trade and investment in the major Maghreb countries.

Overview

Trade and investment in the Maghreb countries are conditioned by the natural and human resources of the AMU countries, individually and regionally (table 5.2). Geographically, Algeria and Libya are clearly the largest countries, and Tunisia the smallest country, in the Maghreb. However, the interior regions of all five countries are mostly desert, in which little agriculture is commercially viable. The natural resource base of the region is predominantly petroleum and natural gas (especially in Algeria and Libya), metallic and nonmetallic minerals, and Atlantic fisheries (Mauritania and Morocco). Only Morocco and Tunisia have significant arable and cultivated lands relative to their total area, by virtue of their location predominantly in the Maghreb's relatively temperate Mediterranean climate zone.

With 33 million to 34 million persons each, Morocco and Algeria have the largest populations among Maghreb countries. Mauritania is the least populous, with 3 million persons. Relative to land area, Morocco and Tunisia are the most labor-abundant countries in the region, with 76 and 63 persons per square kilometer, respectively.[1] Mauritania has the lowest level of human capital in the region, with a literacy level of only 60 percent of the male population and 46 percent of the population under the age of 15 years. Overall, Mauritania is the least developed Maghreb country, which probably contributes to its high rate of population growth (2.9 percent).

Merchandise Trade

From 2004 to 2006, Maghreb merchandise trade (exports plus imports) with the world amounted to about $145 billion per year, or just 1.5 percent of world trade (table 5.3). Trade within the Maghreb amounted to only

---

1. By comparison, the population density is 14 persons per square kilometer in Algeria and just 3 persons per square kilometer in Libya and Mauritania.

Table 5.2 Geography and population indicators for the Maghreb countries, 2007

Indicator	Algeria	Libya	Mauritania	Morocco	Tunisia
Geography					
Land area (square meters)	Total: 2,381,740 Land: 2,381,740 Water: 0	Total: 1,759,540 Land: 1,759,540 Water: 0	Total: 1,030,700 Land: 1,030,400 Water: 300	Total: 446,550 Land: 446,300 Water: 250	Total: 163,610 Land: 155,360 Water: 8,250
Climate	Arid to semiarid; mild, wet winters with hot, dry summers along coast; drier with cold winters and hot summers on high plateau	Mediterranean along coast; dry, extreme desert interior	Desert; constantly hot, dry, dusty	Mediterranean, becoming more extreme in the interior	Temperate in north with mild, rainy winters and hot, dry summers; desert in south
Land use (percent of total land use)	Arable land: 3.2 Crops: 0.3 Other: 96.6 (2005)	Arable land: 1.0 Crops: 0.2 Other: 98.8 (2005)	Arable land: 0.2 Crops: 0.0 Other: 99.8 (2005)	Arable land: 19.0 Crops: 2.0 Other: 79.0 (2005)	Arable land: 17.1 Crops: 13.1 Other: 69.9 (2005)
Natural resources	Petroleum, natural gas, iron ore, phosphates, uranium, lead, zinc	Petroleum, natural gas, gypsum	Iron ore, gypsum, copper, phosphate, diamonds, gold, oil, fish	Phosphates, iron ore, manganese, lead, zinc, fish, salt	Petroleum, phosphates, iron ore, lead, zinc, salt
Population					
In millions	33.3 (2007 est.)	6.0 (2007 est.)	3.3 (2007 est.)	33.8 (2007 est.)	10.3 (2007 est.)
Age structure (percent)	0–14 years: 27.2 15–64 years: 67.9 65 years and over: 4.8 (2007 est.)	0–14 years: 33.4 15–64 years: 62.4 65 years and over: 4.2 (2007 est.)	0–14 years: 45.5 15–64 years: 52.4 65 years and over: 2.2 (2007 est.)	0–14 years: 31 15–64 years: 63.9 65 years and over: 5.1 (2007 est.)	0–14 years: 24 15–64 years: 69.2 65 years and over: 6.9 (2007 est.)
Growth rate (percent)	1.22 (2007 est.)	2.26 (2007 est.)	2.87 (2007 est.)	1.53 (2007 est.)	0.99 (2007 est.)
Literacy (percent)	Total population: 69.9 Male: 79.6 Female: 60.1 (2002 est.)	Total population: 82.6 Male: 92.4 Female: 72 (2003 est.)	Total population: 51.2 Male: 59.5 Female: 43.4 (2000 census)	Total population: 52.3 Male: 65.7 Female: 39.6 (2004 census)	Total population: 74.3 Male: 83.4 Female: 65.3 (2004 census)

est. = estimate

Source: Central Intelligence Agency (CIA) *World Factbook,* 2008.

$2.4 billion per annum during the same period, under 2 percent of world trade with the region (table 5.4).

Maghreb Trade with the World

The resource base of the Maghreb countries is strongly reflected in the composition of Maghreb trade with the world (table 5.3). Algeria's and Libya's exports are heavily concentrated in petroleum, natural gas, and related products, while the exports of Mauritania, Morocco, and Tunisia are appreciably devoted to other primary products, including fisheries and fruits and vegetables. Reflecting the relative abundance of labor, more than half of Morocco's and Tunisia's exports are intermediate and finished manufactures, principally apparel and machinery products. The principal destinations of these exports are the European Union and other European countries, though Mauritania ships about 25 percent of its exports to China.[2]

Greater diversity of imports than exports is a common feature among Maghreb countries as can be seen in merchandise imports (table 5.3). Firms and households in the Maghreb—as elsewhere—demand a wide variety of world-class industrial and consumer goods, and the region does not make most of these products. Thus producers and consumers in the AMU countries extensively import high-income cereals and cereal products, road vehicles, iron and steel products, general and electrical machinery, telecommunications equipment, and pharmaceuticals. The three major Maghreb countries—Algeria, Morocco, and Tunisia—clearly account for the bulk of these imports, in keeping with their economic size and the concentration of labor-intensive manufacturing in Morocco and Tunisia. The principal trading partners for Maghreb imports are mainly EU countries. However, China, the United States, and other emerging-market countries, such as Turkey, South Korea, and Brazil, also account for appreciable imports by the AMU countries.

Maghreb Regional Trade

The natural and human endowments of the Maghreb are reflected in the composition of intra-Maghreb trade, but somewhat less sharply. Mineral fuels dominate Algerian and Libyan exports to the region and account for more than half of regional imports by Morocco and Tunisia. Manufactures dominate Tunisian regional exports and account for more than half of Algerian and Mauritanian regional imports. Beyond petroleum and natural

---

2. The information presented here and further below in this section about the country partners in Maghreb trade is compiled from the *CIA World Factbook*, 2008.

Table 5.3 International trade of Maghreb countries, European Union, United States, and world by SITC category, 2004–06 (average values in millions of US dollars)

Code	Category description	Arab Maghreb Union						Percent	EU-25	United States	World
		Algeria	Libya	Mauritania	Morocco	Tunisia	Total				
Exports											
Aggregates											
0–9	All goods	39,270	29,573	1,152	12,545	10,516	93,056	100.0	3,541,096	890,683	10,013,882
0–2,4	Primary products, excluding fuels	355	55	946	3,852	1,159	6,367	6.8	379,292	102,238	1,018,433
3	Mineral fuels	38,221	28,564	192	416	1,156	68,550	73.7	191,257	29,981	1,374,996
5–8	Manufactures	690	923	13	8,271	8,199	18,096	19.4	2,964,028	755,622	7,573,073
SITC groups											
0	Food and animals	63	13	453	2,570	373	3,471	3.7	218,668	49,921	524,176
1	Beverages and tobacco	7	1	0	26	29	61	0.1	53,039	7,004	82,817
2	Crude materials	277	39	493	1,137	212	2,158	2.3	95,058	43,574	373,854
3	Mineral fuels	38,221	28,564	192	416	1,156	68,550	73.7	191,257	29,981	1,374,996
4	Fats and oils	8	3	0	120	546	676	0.7	12,527	1,739	37,586
5	Chemicals	323	612	0	1,204	766	2,905	3.1	594,097	137,670	1,102,202
6	Material manufactures	181	283	3	618	990	2,075	2.2	576,949	89,049	1,405,578
7	Machinery, transport equipment	178	23	6	2,469	2,095	4,771	5.1	1,419,539	425,346	3,862,423
8	Miscellaneous manufactures	8	5	4	3,981	4,348	8,346	9.0	373,443	103,556	1,202,870
Top Maghreb exports											
33	Petroleum, petroleum products	28,432	28,052	192	414	1,156	58,246	62.6	146,667	18,408	1,108,233
34	Gas, natural and manufactured	9,788	506	0	0	0	10,294	11.1	25,479	6,519	181,700
84	Articles of apparel, clothing	0	1	3	3,475	3,568	7,047	7.6	56,945	3,121	285,100
77	Electrical machinery	4	3	2	2,208	1,502	3,719	4.0	215,833	102,308	928,933
03	Fish, crustaceans, molluscs	22	12	436	1,048	161	1,679	1.8	15,798	3,761	76,415
05	Vegetables and fruit	27	0	0	1,367	151	1,545	1.7	46,457	10,321	117,400
52	Inorganic chemicals	221	43	0	632	254	1,151	1.2	22,468	7,809	62,710
56	Fertilizers, manufactured	44	120	0	492	437	1,094	1.2	7,047	2,898	28,923
28	Metal ores, metal scrap	233	32	491	239	78	1,072	1.2	30,236	11,220	150,933
27	Crude fertilizers	40	0	0	710	89	839	0.9	8,069	1,928	25,721

Imports

Aggregates

0–9	All goods	20,040	2,106	805	20,642	8,633	52,225	100.0	3,884,235	1,650,243	10,013,882
0–2,4	Primary products, excluding fuels	4,512	370	140	3,019	1,092	9,132	17.5	440,129	101,263	1,018,433
3	Mineral fuels	207	15	141	4,168	1,040	5,572	10.7	466,042	282,737	1,374,996
5–8	Manufactures	15,320	1,721	524	13,423	6,487	37,475	71.8	2,970,383	1,260,126	7,573,073

SITC groups

0	Food and animals	3,567	296	103	1,578	557	6,100	11.7	252,801	53,894	524,176
1	Beverages and tobacco	64	4	19	107	47	240	0.5	40,332	14,690	82,817
2	Crude materials	520	30	5	1,086	362	2,003	3.8	131,965	30,091	373,854
3	Mineral fuels	207	15	141	4,168	1,040	5,572	10.7	466,042	282,737	1,374,996
4	Fats and oils	361	40	14	248	126	789	1.5	15,031	2,588	37,586
5	Chemicals	2,370	81	26	1,948	849	5,273	10.1	505,323	129,212	1,102,202
6	Material manufactures	3,672	443	85	4,474	2,199	10,873	20.8	577,171	202,242	1,405,578
7	Machinery, transport equipment	8,314	1,004	388	5,658	2,545	17,909	34.3	1,417,644	661,366	3,862,423
8	Miscellaneous manufactures	965	192	25	1,342	894	3,419	6.5	470,245	267,305	1,202,870

Top Maghreb imports

33	Petroleum, petroleum products	101	12	132	3,177	899	4,321	8.3	350,233	245,100	1,108,233
78	Road vehicles	2,151	212	38	1,176	586	4,164	8.0	409,333	200,800	870,500
67	Iron and steel	1,698	232	15	1,049	385	3,378	6.5	131,067	31,714	315,233
77	Electrical machinery	1,010	185	11	1,284	679	3,168	6.1	237,733	103,358	928,933
65	Textile yarn, fabrics	154	13	11	1,839	1,093	3,110	6.0	66,555	21,856	185,267
74	General industrial machinery	1,436	229	20	728	363	2,777	5.3	144,267	51,849	366,000
04	Cereals, cereal preparations	1,421	209	32	786	247	2,695	5.2	26,466	4,186	76,194
72	Specialized machinery	1,377	72	62	805	323	2,640	5.1	81,535	32,329	259,733
76	Telecommunications equipment	904	44	9	670	211	1,837	3.5	167,933	103,547	480,033
54	Medicinal products	1,107	22	4	289	191	1,613	3.1	161,800	40,204	282,233

SITC = Standard International Trade Classification

Source: World Bank and UNCTAD, World Integrated Trade Solution, 2007.

Table 5.4   Regional trade of Maghreb countries by SITC category, 2004–06 (average values in millions of US dollars)

		Arab Maghreb Union									
Code	Category description	Algeria	Libya	Mauritania	Morocco	Tunisia	Total	Percent	EU-25	United States	World
Exports											
Aggregates											
0–9	All goods	398.2	383.9	20.4	102.6	308.7	1,213.7	100.0	29,121.0	2,453.9	52,224.8
0–2,4	Primary products, excluding fuels	6.2	2.6	20.2	32.1	65.1	126.1	10.4	3,611.2	766.4	9,132.1
3	Mineral fuels	294.9	294.8	0.0	6.7	0.5	596.8	49.2	1,650.5	109.2	5,571.8
5–8	Manufactures	97.1	86.5	0.2	63.9	243.1	490.9	40.4	23,853.0	1,578.1	37,475.0
SITC groups											
0	Food and animals	2.9	1.8	2.2	18.7	42.6	68.3	5.6	2,319.8	584.4	6,099.9
1	Beverages and tobacco	0.0	0.1	0.0	0.4	2.7	3.2	0.3	101.8	21.8	240.1
2	Crude materials	1.0	0.5	17.9	11.4	1.6	32.4	2.7	1,021.6	102.1	2,002.8
3	Mineral fuels	294.9	294.8	0.0	6.7	0.5	596.8	49.2	1,650.5	109.2	5,571.8
4	Fats and oils	2.3	0.1	0.0	1.6	18.2	22.2	1.8	167.9	58.1	789.3
5	Chemicals	43.3	59.3	0.0	22.5	51.0	176.0	14.5	3,608.4	165.2	5,273.5
6	Material manufactures	52.3	26.1	0.0	30.1	130.8	239.3	19.7	6,785.3	164.6	10,873.2
7	Machinery, transport equipment	0.6	0.7	0.1	6.6	41.7	49.8	4.1	11,062.8	1,112.2	17,909.5
8	Miscellaneous manufactures	1.1	0.4	0.0	4.7	19.5	25.7	2.1	2,396.6	136.1	3,418.8
Top intra-Maghreb exports											
34	Gas, natural and manufactured	283.8	24.6	0.0	0.0	0.0	308.4	25.4	425.8	0.4	803.0
32	Coal, coke and briquettes	11.0	270.2	0.0	6.7	0.5	288.4	23.8	43.8	61.0	447.5
67	Iron and steel	33.2	25.2	0.0	11.8	21.3	91.5	7.5	1,442.0	36.3	3,378.5
52	Inorganic chemicals	33.2	12.2	0.0	2.8	30.5	78.7	6.5	196.8	4.1	445.9
66	Nonmetallic mineral manufactures, nes	0.0	0.0	0.0	2.2	34.0	36.2	3.0	358.8	4.0	611.4
56	Fertilizers, manufactured	6.1	18.4	0.0	1.3	1.9	27.7	2.3	86.6	0.3	196.3
68	Nonferrous metals	14.6	0.1	0.0	8.6	2.8	26.0	2.1	461.9	1.6	672.9
05	Vegetables and fruit	1.6	0.1	0.0	2.7	20.9	25.2	2.1	179.0	7.1	479.9
58	Artificial resins, plastic materials, cellulose	3.5	14.2	0.0	1.7	5.0	24.5	2.0	732.9	59.7	1,320.4
64	Paper, paperboard, and paper products	2.3	0.0	0.0	3.3	18.1	23.8	2.0	581.6	16.8	765.7

Imports

Aggregates

SITC		1	2	3	4	5	6	7	8	9	10
0–9	All goods	207.8	62.9	11.9	508.3	422.9	1,213.7	100.0	61,170.2	13,816.8	93,056.5
0–2,4	Primary products, excluding fuels	42.1	38.1	2.4	24.7	18.8	126.1	10.4	4,347.5	247.8	6,367.4
3	Mineral fuels	0.5	0.3	2.4	265.9	327.7	596.8	49.2	42,473.9	13,189.4	68,549.7
5–8	Manufactures	165.2	24.5	7.1	217.6	76.5	490.9	40.4	14,337.2	379.4	18,096.1

SITC groups

SITC		1	2	3	4	5	6	7	8	9	10
0	Food and animals	16.9	20.9	1.7	20.2	8.5	68.3	5.6	2,416.7	74.5	3,471.4
1	Beverages and tobacco	0.1	0.9	0.4	1.7	0.1	3.2	0.3	45.6	0.3	61.4
2	Crude materials	21.1	0.9	0.0	0.4	10.0	32.4	2.7	1,312.8	117.1	2,158.0
3	Mineral fuels	0.5	0.3	2.4	265.9	327.7	596.8	49.2	42,473.9	13,189.4	68,549.7
4	Fats and oils	4.0	15.4	0.3	2.4	0.1	22.2	1.8	572.4	56.0	676.5
5	Chemicals	43.2	5.5	0.6	104.3	22.4	176.0	14.5	1,282.3	48.1	2,904.6
6	Material manufactures	85.1	9.9	3.2	92.5	48.6	239.3	19.7	1,590.5	25.1	2,075.0
7	Machinery, transport equipment	25.8	7.0	2.1	13.1	1.8	49.8	4.1	3,710.7	128.0	4,770.6
8	Miscellaneous manufactures	11.0	2.1	1.2	7.8	3.7	25.7	2.1	7,753.7	178.2	8,346.0

Top intra-Maghreb imports

SITC		1	2	3	4	5	6	7	8	9	10
34	Gas, natural and manufactured	0.0	0.0	0.0	242.1	66.3	308.4	25.4	7,074.9	1,311.6	10,294.3
33	Petroleum, petroleum products	0.5	0.3	2.4	23.9	261.4	288.4	23.8	35,396.3	11,871.6	58,246.0
67	Iron and steel	10.3	0.9	0.6	41.2	38.6	91.5	7.5	420.6	4.7	606.1
52	Inorganic chemicals	14.4	0.6	0.1	60.6	3.0	78.7	6.5	441.4	6.9	1,150.9
66	Nonmetallic mineral manufactures, nes	30.6	1.9	0.9	1.9	0.9	36.2	3.0	93.8	5.2	151.1
56	Fertilizers, manufactured	2.8	1.3	0.2	19.4	4.0	27.7	2.3	420.9	29.0	1,093.6
68	Nonferrous metals	7.7	0.4	0.2	16.0	1.7	26.0	2.1	115.8	6.2	175.7
05	Vegetables and fruit	2.1	4.1	0.5	17.6	0.9	25.2	2.1	1,229.1	44.5	1,545.3
58	Artificial resins, plastic materials, cellulose	4.7	0.3	0.1	7.4	12.0	24.5	2.0	61.9	0.1	141.0
64	Paper, paperboard, and paper products	11.8	2.7	0.7	6.1	2.5	23.8	2.0	23.1	0.0	67.3

nes = not elsewhere specified
SITC = Standard International Trade Classification

Source: World Bank and UNCTAD, World Integrated Trade Solution, 2007.

31

gas products, the top categories of intrabloc merchandise trade are basic and intermediate manufactures that are closely related to minerals found in selected locations across the Maghreb: iron and steel products (from iron ores); inorganic chemicals, fertilizers, and other mineral manufactures (from phosphates, gypsum, and salt); and nonferrous metals (from copper, lead, and zinc ores). However, intrabloc trade in these items is dwarfed by the Maghreb's trade in the same items with Europe, the United States, and the world at large. Thus, while there are sensible, resource-based channels of intrabloc trade in the region, the volume of trade among the Maghreb countries seems constrained, especially compared with the volume of the region's trade with the world in the same product categories. Restrictions that hinder greater commerce among the Maghreb countries are evidently at play.

Revealed Comparative Advantage

We now consider the comparative advantage of the Maghreb countries in global and regional trade more formally. Using the trade statistics underlying tables 5.3 and 5.4, in table 5.5 we calculate indicators of revealed comparative advantage (RCA), a concept originally formulated by Balassa (1965). A country's advantages and disadvantages relative to competing countries in international trade are calculated by computing the shares of different commodities in the total exports of the given country versus the shares of the same commodities in total world trade (or, alternatively, total regional trade). If the computed RCA ratio for a traded good is appreciably greater than unity, then the country is judged to have a comparative advantage in the production and export of that good. If the computed RCA ratio is appreciably less than unity, then the country is judged to have a comparative disadvantage in producing the good, and accordingly should import most of its consumption.[3] The RCA calculations for the Maghreb countries support, and even amplify, many of the previous observations regarding the strengths and weaknesses of the AMU countries in world and regional trade.

For world trade, the computed RCA values indicate the exceptionally strong comparative advantage of Algeria and Libya in gas and petroleum; Morocco and Tunisia in fertilizers, inorganic chemicals, and apparel; Mauritania and Morocco in fish products; Mauritania in crude materials; Morocco in fruits and vegetables; and Tunisia in vegetable fats and oils. At the same time, the Maghreb countries exhibit comparative disadvantage in a wide variety of manufactures and food items. According to the RCA val-

---

3. Following the basic principles of Ricardian comparative advantage theory, the country is better off importing low-RCA goods and devoting domestic resources to producing and exporting products with high RCA indexes.

ues, these goods are best supplied by Europe, the United States, or other countries worldwide.

The RCA indexes pertaining to Maghreb regional trade are also illuminating. Beyond the acknowledged competitiveness of Algeria and Libya in gas and petroleum, Morocco appears to enjoy substantial comparative advantage in producing and exporting inorganic chemicals and fertilizers to other AMU countries. Libya is strong in fertilizers and fish products; Mauritania in metal ores, other crude materials, and fish; Morocco in pulp and waste paper, charcoal, fish, beverages, inorganic chemicals, and fertilizers; and Tunisia in inorganic chemicals, nonmetallic mineral manufactures, beverages, fats and oils, and vegetables and fruit.

Notwithstanding the revealed regional advantages of individual Maghreb countries in certain products, the European Union and the United States enjoy important advantages in trade with the Maghreb in a number of broad categories. Reflecting again the Maghreb's particular natural and human resources, these categories are principally foods, beverages and tobacco, and crude materials (the United States); materials and miscellaneous manufactures (the European Union); and machinery and transport equipment (both the European Union and the United States).

In sum, we again find that Maghreb trade is conditioned to a large degree by the particular natural resources and population densities across the vast but mainly desert lands of the region. Ample scope exists to enjoy significant gains from larger trade within the region itself, and with the European Union, the United States, and other countries with complementary resource bases. However, as we argue below, significant political barriers prevent Maghreb regional and global trade from expanding further.

Services Trade

Commercial business services, plus the provision of local and central government services and utilities, are integral to the functioning of a modern market economy. These services account for 70 percent or more of economic activity in the advanced Organization for Economic Cooperation and Development economies and for much more than 50 percent of the emerging-market economies in Europe, Latin America, and East and Southeast Asia (table 5.1).[4] Presently, only the service sectors of Morocco and Tunisia—respectively, 54 and 59 percent of GDP in 2005—begin to meet the minimum standard service-sector size in emerging-market countries.

International trade in services has flourished with recent advances in transportation and communications, accommodated by liberalization

---

4. The statistics in table 5.1 do not adequately represent the importance of the services sector in East and Southeast Asia, where arguably the earliest and most dynamic emerging-market countries, such as Korea, Hong Kong, Singapore, and Taiwan, are located.

Table 5.5 Revealed comparative advantage (RCA) of the Maghreb countries, European Union, and United States in world trade and Maghreb trade by major SITC categories, 2004–06

Code	Category description	Arab Maghreb Union						EU-25	United States	World
		Algeria	Libya	Mauritania	Morocco	Tunisia	Total			
World trade										
Aggregates										
0–9	All goods	1.00	1.00	1.00	1.00	1.00	1.00	1.00	1.00	1.00
0–2,4	Primary products, excluding fuels	0.09	0.02	8.08	3.02	1.08	0.67	1.05	1.13	1.00
3	Mineral fuels	7.09	7.03	1.22	0.24	0.80	5.36	0.39	0.25	1.00
5–8	Manufactures	0.02	0.04	0.02	0.87	1.03	0.26	1.11	1.12	1.00
SITC Groups										
0	Food and animals	0.03	0.01	7.51	3.91	0.68	0.71	1.18	1.07	1.00
1	Beverages and tobacco	0.02	0.00	0.00	0.25	0.33	0.08	1.81	0.95	1.00
2	Crude materials	0.19	0.04	11.47	2.43	0.54	0.62	0.72	1.31	1.00
3	Mineral fuels	7.09	7.03	1.22	0.24	0.80	5.36	0.39	0.25	1.00
4	Fats and oils	0.05	0.02	0.05	2.54	13.84	1.94	0.94	0.52	1.00
5	Chemicals	0.07	0.19	0.00	0.87	0.66	0.28	1.52	1.40	1.00
6	Material manufactures	0.03	0.07	0.02	0.35	0.67	0.16	1.16	0.71	1.00
7	Machinery, transport equipment	0.01	0.00	0.01	0.51	0.52	0.13	1.04	1.24	1.00
8	Miscellaneous manufactures	0.00	0.00	0.03	2.64	3.44	0.75	0.88	0.97	1.00
Top RCA categories for Maghreb trade										
34	Gas, natural and manufactured	13.74	0.94	0.00	0.00	0.00	6.10	0.40	0.40	1.00
33	Petroleum, petroleum products	6.54	8.57	1.50	0.30	0.99	5.66	0.37	0.19	1.00
56	Fertilizers, manufactured	0.39	1.40	0.00	13.58	14.40	4.07	0.69	1.13	1.00
27	Crude fertilizers	0.39	0.00	0.12	22.02	3.29	3.51	0.89	0.84	1.00
84	Articles of apparel and clothing	0.00	0.00	0.09	9.73	11.92	2.66	0.56	0.12	1.00
03	Fish, crustaceans, molluscs, preparations	0.07	0.05	49.60	10.94	2.01	2.36	0.58	0.55	1.00
42	Fixed vegetable oils and fats	0.04	0.03	0.02	2.57	16.94	2.29	0.88	0.33	1.00
52	Inorganic chemicals	0.90	0.23	0.01	8.04	3.86	1.97	1.01	1.40	1.00
05	Vegetables and fruit	0.06	0.00	0.03	9.29	1.22	1.42	1.12	0.99	1.00
61	Leather, leather manufacturers, nes	0.11	0.03	0.10	2.10	5.90	1.01	1.00	0.68	1.00

Regional trade

Aggregates

0–9	All goods	1.00	1.00	1.00	1.00	1.00	1.00	1.00	1.00	1.00
0–2,4	Primary products, excluding fuels	0.09	0.04	5.67	1.79	1.21	0.59	0.71	1.79	1.00
3	Mineral fuels	6.94	7.20	0.00	0.61	0.01	4.61	0.53	0.42	1.00
5–8	Manufactures	0.34	0.31	0.01	0.87	1.10	0.56	1.14	0.90	1.00

SITC groups

0	Food and animals	0.06	0.04	0.94	1.56	1.18	0.48	0.68	2.04	1.00
1	Beverages and tobacco	0.02	0.07	0.00	0.83	1.88	0.58	0.76	1.94	1.00
2	Crude materials	0.06	0.04	22.97	2.89	0.14	0.70	0.91	1.08	1.00
3	Mineral fuels	6.94	7.20	0.00	0.61	0.01	4.61	0.53	0.42	1.00
4	Fats and oils	0.38	0.01	0.00	1.02	3.90	1.21	0.38	1.57	1.00
5	Chemicals	1.08	1.53	0.00	2.17	1.64	1.44	1.23	0.67	1.00
6	Material manufactures	0.63	0.33	0.00	1.41	2.04	0.95	1.12	0.32	1.00
7	Machinery, transport equipment	0.00	0.01	0.02	0.19	0.39	0.12	1.11	1.32	1.00
8	Miscellaneous manufactures	0.04	0.02	0.01	0.70	0.97	0.32	1.26	0.85	1.00

Top RCA categories for intra-Maghreb trade

32	Coal, coke and briquettes	3.24	82.16	0.00	7.62	0.17	27.73	0.18	2.90	1.00
34	Gas, natural and manufactured	46.36	4.16	0.00	0.00	0.00	16.52	0.95	0.01	1.00
28	Metalliferous ores and metal scrap	0.11	0.27	481.84	0.00	0.02	8.20	0.55	1.48	1.00
52	Inorganic chemicals	9.77	3.72	0.00	3.25	11.57	7.60	0.79	0.20	1.00
56	Fertilizers, manufactured	4.08	12.75	0.00	3.26	1.67	6.07	0.79	0.03	1.00
25	Pulp and waste paper	0.11	0.32	0.00	53.75	0.02	4.69	0.95	5.42	1.00
11	Beverages	0.08	0.35	0.00	4.19	8.25	2.59	1.54	0.11	1.00
66	Nonmetallic mineral manufactures, nes	0.01	0.00	0.01	1.80	9.39	2.54	1.05	0.14	1.00
03	Fish, crustaceans, molluscs, preparations	0.06	2.35	56.90	6.05	0.38	2.32	0.71	0.06	1.00
05	Vegetables and fruit	0.44	0.01	0.00	2.83	7.35	2.26	0.67	0.31	1.00

nes = not elsewhere specified
SITC = Standard International Trade Classification

Source: Author's calculations based on tables 5.3 and 5.4.

under the General Agreement on Trade in Services, adopted in 1996 under the auspices of the World Trade Organization (WTO). Many EU, US, and other bilateral free trade agreements (FTAs) include WTO-plus provisions for liberalizing trade in services and ensuring national treatment of foreign investments by multinational service firms. As a result, beyond the growth in transport and travel services, the increases in trade of financial, engineering, legal, and other professional services have been pronounced. Foreign direct investment (FDI) has also spurred trade in professional services, as multinational firms have sought familiar and modern suppliers to support their activities in host countries. In turn, the increased provision of foreign traded services has integrated the local service economies of host countries more closely with the global service economy. An important side effect is the transfer of modern service technologies and managerial knowhow to host-country firms.

Detailed information about the services trade of the Maghreb countries is not widely reported. However, a new UN database on world trade in services (UNSD 2008) offers a glimpse of the dimensions of Maghreb services trade with its principal partners in 2005, reporting aggregate transport, travel, professional, and other traded services (table 5.6). The UN services trade data suggest that, on a combined basis, the Maghreb countries enjoyed a net surplus position on trade in services in 2005, exporting about $9.4 billion and importing about $7.8 billion. Morocco and Tunisia are the principal Maghreb exporters of services to the world ($3.6 billion each). Algeria is the principal Maghreb importer of services ($3.6 billion). For each Maghreb country, such trade appears to be centered on professional and other services, amounting in total for the five AMU countries to about $6.8 billion for service imports and roughly the same for service exports.

The European Union is the primary partner of the Maghreb countries in services trade. The other prominent reporting-partner countries in table 5.6 are Russia and selected southeast European countries: Croatia, Romania, and Ukraine.[5] The service trade relations of the Maghreb countries with these countries are likely driven by Maghreb trade in petroleum and other mineral products, whereas Maghreb commerce with the European Union reflects more general determinants of bilateral trade in services.

Among the Maghreb countries, only Tunisia reports trade in services with its Maghreb neighbors. In 2005 Tunisia imported services totaling $63 million, supplied by Libya ($43 million) and Algeria ($19 million), and exported services totaling $332 million, also sold to Libya ($223 million) and Algeria ($109 million). Tunisia's imports of services from Libya were about equally divided among transport, travel, and professional and

---

5. The services trade data of the United States, including those reported to the United Nations by the US Department of Commerce, do not show US trade in services with the individual Maghreb countries. US trade in services with these countries is included in the aggregate of US services trade with Africa.

Table 5.6 Trade in services by Maghreb countries, 2005 (millions of US dollars)

Reporting partner country	Services exports						Services imports					
	Algeria	Libya	Mauritania	Morocco	Tunisia	Total	Algeria	Libya	Mauritania	Morocco	Tunisia	Total
All traded services												
European Union	1,318.0	721.3	137.0	3,549.6	3,434.5	9,160.5	3,431.7	1,193.5	103.4	1,658.5	1,055.1	7,442.2
Croatia	1.2	1.2	0.0	0.7	1.2	4.4	1.2	5.0	0.0	0.2	1.2	7.6
Romania	1.2	3.7	0.0	1.2	19.9	26.2	1.2	6.2	0.0	3.7	7.5	18.7
Russia	1.4	0.2	0.0	2.9	131.0	135.5	4.2	4.3	0.8	2.4	5.1	16.7
Ukraine	1.4	0.6	0.3	0.6	1.2	4.0	5.7	3.3	0.1	2.0	2.7	13.8
Tunisia	19.2	43.8	0.0	0.0		63.1	108.8	222.9	0.0	0.0		331.7
World	1,342.5	770.9	137.3	3,555.0	3,587.8	9,393.6	3,552.8	1,435.1	104.3	1,666.9	1,071.7	7,830.8
Transport												
European Union	0.0	0.0	0.0	725.5	0.0	725.5	0.0	0.0	0.0	456.7	0.0	456.7
Croatia	n.a.	n.a.	n.a.	n.a.	n.a.	n.a.	n.a.	n.a.	n.a.	n.a.	n.a.	n.a.
Romania	n.a.	n.a.	n.a.	n.a.	n.a.	n.a.	0.0	0.0	0.0	0.0	0.0	0.0
Russia	0.7	0.0	0.0	2.3	4.2	7.2	2.4	0.4	0.6	1.5	3.4	8.3
Ukraine	0.1	0.1	0.0	0.0	0.0	0.2	3.2	1.8	0.1	0.6	1.6	7.3
Tunisia	12.0	15.1	0.0	0.0		27.0	12.5	24.0	0.0	0.0		36.5
World	n.a.	n.a.	n.a.	n.a.	n.a.	n.a.	n.a.	n.a.	n.a.	n.a.	n.a.	n.a.
Travel												
European Union	0.0	0.0	0.0	1,636.1	0.0	1,636.1	0.0	0.0	0.0	185.3	0.0	185.3
Croatia	n.a.	n.a.	n.a.	n.a.	n.a.	n.a.	n.a.	n.a.	n.a.	n.a.	n.a.	n.a.
Romania	n.a.	n.a.	n.a.	n.a.	n.a.	n.a.	0.0	0.0	0.0	2.5	0.0	2.5
Russia	0.0	0.0	0.0	0.0	122.1	122.1	0.0	0.0	0.0	0.0	1.3	1.3
Ukraine	0.0	0.0	0.0	0.2	1.0	1.2	0.0	0.8	0.0	1.3	1.0	3.2
Tunisia	3.6	15.7	0.0	0.0		19.3	79.6	174.4	0.0	0.0		254.0
World	n.a.	n.a.	n.a.	n.a.	n.a.	n.a.	n.a.	n.a.	n.a.	n.a.	n.a.	n.a.
Professional and other services												
European Union	1,318.0	721.3	137.0	1,188.0	3,434.5	6,798.9	3,431.7	1,193.5	103.4	1,016.5	1,055.1	6,800.2
Croatia	n.a.	n.a.	n.a.	n.a.	n.a.	n.a.	n.a.	n.a.	n.a.	n.a.	n.a.	n.a.
Romania	n.a.	n.a.	n.a.	n.a.	n.a.	n.a.	1.2	6.2	0.0	1.2	7.5	16.2
Russia	0.7	0.1	0.0	0.6	4.7	6.2	1.8	3.9	0.2	1.0	0.4	7.2
Ukraine	1.3	0.5	0.3	0.5	0.2	2.6	2.4	0.6	0.0	0.1	0.1	3.2
Tunisia	3.6	13.1	0.0	0.0		16.7	16.7	24.5	0.0	0.0		41.2
World	n.a.	n.a.	n.a.	n.a.	n.a.	n.a.	n.a.	n.a.	n.a.	n.a.	n.a.	n.a.

n.a. = not available

Source: United Nations Statistics Division, 2008, www.unstats.un.org.

other services. However, its imports of services from Algeria were predominantly transport services. On the export side, Tunisia's exports of services to both Libya and Algeria were predominantly travel services.

For want of better data for the Maghreb countries, the above sketch of Maghreb trade in services may well be incomplete. But it illustrates both the level of development among AMU countries and their limited economic integration with one another and the world economy at large.

Foreign Investment

In 2005 total inward stocks of FDI in the Maghreb countries amounted to $49.2 billion, or about 30 percent of the combined GDP of the five AMU countries (tables 5.1 and 5.7). Accumulated FDI in relation to aggregate output appears to be particularly low in Algeria (8 percent) and Libya (less than 2 percent), but comparable to that found in other developing counties in the two relatively labor-abundant Maghreb countries, Morocco (44 percent) and Tunisia (over 50 percent).

Table 5.7 summarizes Maghreb inward stocks of FDI by source country. The data are compiled from the database underlying the United Nations Conference on Trade and Development *2006 World Investment Report* (UNCTAD 2006), but the figures are seriously incomplete because the inward FDI stocks held by all source countries combined fall well below the UNCTAD estimates for total inward FDI stocks held by the world in the Maghreb.

Inward stocks of FDI in the Maghreb countries held by reporting source countries amount to only $9.1 billion, or just 18 percent of the UNCTAD estimate of total FDI holdings of the world in the Maghreb ($49.2 billion). Foreign investment in petroleum and natural gas production likely dominate the FDI picture. Interestingly, US and Norwegian investment in Algeria—$4.1 billion and $1.5 billion, respectively—account for over 92 percent of total inward FDI stocks in Algeria and nearly 62 percent of total FDI stocks in the five Maghreb countries held by the limited number of individual source countries identified in table 5.7.

Including US long-term investment in Morocco and Tunisia—about $300 million in each country—total US investment in the Maghreb is $4.7 billion. By comparison, total EU long-term investment appears to total just $2.0 billion, of which the largest part is reported to be Swedish investment in Morocco ($1.3 billion). These statistics suggest that US oil and gas interests in the Maghreb are greater than those of the European Union. Given the large discrepancy in aggregate totals (noted above), the FDI data by source country shown in table 5.7 may miss some important EU investments in the Maghreb. Among the other source countries with appreciable reported foreign investment in the Maghreb, the most prominent are China ($229 million, principally in Algeria), Switzerland ($244

Table 5.7 Inward stocks of foreign direct investment in Maghreb countries by source country, 2005 (millions of US dollars at historical cost)

Source country	Algeria	Libya	Mauritania	Morocco	Tunisia	Total
	\<center\>**Maghreb host country**\</center\>					
European Union	0.7	0.0	0.0	1,715.1	295.1	2,010.9
Czech Republic[a]	0.2	—	—	—	—	0.2
Germany[a]	—	—	—	203.0	115.8	318.8
Netherlands	—	—	—	132.1	—	132.1
Portugal[b]	0.5	—	—	123.1	179.3	302.9
Slovenia[a]	—	—	—	0.4	—	0.4
Sweden	—	—	—	1,256.5	—	1,256.5
Other Europe	1,522.5	0.0	0.0	217.0	27.2	1,766.7
Norway[a]	1,522.5	—	—	—	—	1,522.5
Switzerland	—	—	—	217.0	27.2	244.2
North America	4,308.4	0.0	5.0	285.0	286.0	4,884.4
United States	4,092.0	—	5.0	285.0	286.0	4,668.0
Canada	216.4	—	—	—	—	216.4
Asia	279.1	91.6	2.4	48.4	2.2	423.7
China	171.2	33.1	2.4	20.6	2.2	229.4
Korea	107.9	—	—	25.4	0.1	133.4
Malaysia	—	—	—	2.4	—	2.4
Pakistan[a]	—	58.5	—	—	—	58.5
Arab Maghreb Union	1.2	0.0	49.1		1.0	51.3
Morocco[a]	1.2	—	49.1		1.0	51.3
Memorandum items: Total inward stocks						
Source countries	6,112	92	57	2,266	612	9,137
World	8,272	533	684	22,818	16,924	49,231

— = value is not reported by source

a. 2004 value.
b. 2003 value.

Sources: Source-country figures are those reported by either the source country or the host country in UNCTAD, *Trade and Development Report*, 2006 and 2007. World figures are estimates from UNCTAD, *World Investment Report*, 2006.

million, principally in Morocco), Canada ($216 million in Algeria), and Korea ($139 million, principally in Algeria). All these figures are likely to be understated in light of the discrepancy in aggregate totals. Finally, the UNCTAD data indicate that, within the AMU, only Morocco-based multinational firms have invested substantially in the region: $49 million in Mauritania and just $1 million in Algeria. Even if these figures are understated, they suggest that there is little integration of economic activity within the AMU based on cross-border investments.

Barriers to Trade and Investment

As in many developing countries, central planning and import substitution policies dominated economic policies in the Maghreb until global pressures led to economic reforms in the 1990s. These reforms are anchored in multiple international accords: the lending programs of bilateral and multilateral donors with several AMU countries, EU association agreements and the Barcelona Process, US trade and investment framework agreements (TIFAs) and the US-Morocco FTA, and the process of WTO accession presently being pursued by Algeria (since 1987) and Libya (since 2004).[6] Because of these accords, regional trade and investment barriers are coming under pressure to be substantially reduced if not eradicated. Actual progress can sometimes be detected in liberalizing restrictive border measures and sometimes behind-the-border measures.

A detailed examination of the trade and investment reforms either underway or proposed in the Maghreb is beyond the present study. To conclude this introduction, however, we present a thumbnail sketch of trade and investment protection in the region.

Tariffs

The readiest indicator of protection enforced in the Maghreb countries is the level and structure of most favored nation (MFN) tariffs (table 5.8).[7] Surprisingly, given that it is the least-developed country in the AMU, Mauritania posts the most liberal tariff regime in the Maghreb, with an average tariff rate of just 12 percent on both agricultural and nonagricultural goods and a maximum tariff of just 20 percent across the board. The three major Maghreb countries—Algeria, Morocco, and Tunisia—enforce

---

6. Mauritania, Morocco, and Tunisia are among the founding members of the WTO.

7. Tariff data for Libya are not yet reported by the WTO. Also, our discussion of protection in the Maghreb countries abstracts from duty-free entry of merchandise imports from the European Union under the EU association agreements with Algeria, Morocco, and Tunisia, and from the United States under the US-Morocco FTA. It also abstracts from the uncertain progress of trade liberalization under the various bilateral and regional trading agreements with other MENA countries to which several of the Maghreb countries are party, including particularly the Arab Maghreb Union (AMU; all five Maghreb countries) and the Greater Arab Free Trade Area established under the auspices of the League of Arab States (GAFTA; Libya, Morocco, and Tunisia with 14 other Arab League members). By most reports (e.g., Dennis 2006), the AMU free trade area has yet to be fully established owing, inter alia, to territorial disputes and sharp political differences between countries in the Maghreb. Moreover, although import tariffs on merchandise trade among the GAFTA countries were reportedly eliminated in 2005, the GAFTA rules of origin stipulate a somewhat steep domestic content requirement of 40 percent for goods to qualify for duty-free treatment. Most importantly, it is uncertain whether the GAFTA has also completely eliminated nontariff barriers restricting trade between the signatory Arab League members.

Table 5.8 Most favored nation (MFN) applied duties in the world versus Maghreb countries by product group, 2006
(percent)

Product group	World average	OECD average	LDC average	Maghreb average	Algeria Average	Algeria Free	Algeria Maximum	Mauritania Average	Mauritania Free	Mauritania Maximum	Morocco Average	Morocco Free	Morocco Maximum	Tunisia Average	Tunisia Free	Tunisia Maximum
Agricultural	14.3	11.5	15.2	33.3	21.9	—	30	11.6	—	20	43.7	—	329	55.8	—	150
Animal products	16.6	8.4	18.4	60.6	27.9	0	30	16.6	4	20	112.4	0	329	85.6	0	150
Dairy products	18.1	21.4	18.2	51.4	22.4	0	30	13.5	10	20	78.2	0	109	91.3	0	154
Fruit, vegetables, plants	12.2	8.6	13.2	43.9	24.8	0	30	16.1	6	20	43.4	0	52	91.1	3	150
Coffee, tea	15.0	9.8	16.7	31.4	26.5	0	30	15.1	0	20	37.8	0	50	46.1	5	73
Cereals and preparations	12.2	23.1	12.1	39.3	24.7	1	30	11.8	15	20	45.4	0	172	75.1	3	150
Oilseeds, fats and oils	9.9	7.6	10.6	22.4	19.4	0	30	4.9	34	20	25.8	0	152	39.6	0	150
Sugars and confectionery	14.0	5.8	15.5	24.8	25.0	0	30	6.6	6	20	33.1	0	60	34.3	13	100
Beverages and tobacco	24.4	16.1	25.5	36.5	26.6	0	30	17.9	0	20	37.2	0	52	64.2	0	150
Cotton[a]	—	—	—	3.3	5.0	0	5	5.0	0	5	3.0	0	3	0.0	100	0
Other agricultural products	6.4	2.7	6.9	19.4	17.1	0	30	8.4	3	20	21.0	0	52	31.0	16	150
Nonagricultural	9.4	2.9	10.3	20.1	19.3	—	30	11.8	—	20	26.3	—	50	23.1	—	43
Fish and fish products	14.0	2.9	15.8	33.9	29.2	0	30	19.9	0	20	46.6	0	50	39.7	0	43
Minerals and metals	8.0	1.9	8.8	16.7	16.6	1	30	10.4	4	20	20.0	0	50	19.7	12	43
Petroleum	8.0	1.5	9.0	16.1	19.4	29	30	9.0	11	20	30.3	16	50	5.5	70	43
Chemicals	6.0	2.1	6.4	13.0	14.7	0	30	5.6	22	20	17.3	0	50	14.3	8	43
Wood, paper	9.3	1.5	10.5	24.7	19.4	0	30	8.8	20	20	38.2	0	50	32.3	4	43
Textiles	13.5	7.4	14.7	21.2	24.3	0	30	13.6	3	20	22.0	0	50	24.8	6	43
Clothing[b]	—	—	—	35.3	30.0	0	30	20.0	0	20	48.4	0	50	42.7	0	43
Leather, footwear	11.1	5.0	12.1	25.0	19.3	1	30	12.4	1	20	39.3	0	50	28.8	0	43
Nonelectrical machinery	5.3	2.0	5.5	8.5	9.0	0	30	6.4	15	20	8.9	0	50	9.6	58	43
Electrical machinery	8.6	2.3	9.3	15.1	17.1	0	30	10.0	0	20	13.4	0	50	19.8	13	43
Transport equipment	9.3	3.1	10.0	15.2	11.0	21	30	12.1	16	20	18.7	0	50	19.1	29	43
Manufactures, nes	10.3	2.4	11.5	17.2	22.0	6	30	13.6	9	20	12.3	0	50	20.7	20	43

— = value is not computed or reported by source
OECD = Organization for Economic Cooperation and Development
LDC = less developed country
nes = not elsewhere specified

a. World, OECD, and LDC averages for other agricultural products include cotton.
b. World, OECD, and LDC averages for textiles include apparel.

Notes: Duty rates are simple averages. World denotes all reporting countries, OECD all high-income OECD countries, and LDC all low- and middle-income developing countries in the Trade Analysis and Information System (TRAINS) database, 2008.

Sources: World Trade Organization statistics database, 2008, for Maghreb duty rates, available at www.stat.wto.org; UN Conference on Trade and Development, Trade Analysis and Information System (TRAINS) database, 2008, for world, OECD, and LDC duty rates.

much more restrictive tariff regimes. Applied MFN tariffs average 20 percent in Algeria and are even higher in Morocco and Tunisia. Also, both Morocco and Tunisia maintain higher tariff rates on animal and food products than on most other imports. This pattern presumably reflects concerns about food security and may well be accompanied by direct controls on domestic food prices. At the same time, the bias against agriculture (except food) enforced through industrial protection in the Maghreb appears to have been reduced during the last decade through some liberalization of erstwhile import substitution tariff policies that favored urban-based manufacturing.[8]

Except Mauritania, the average height of applied tariffs in the Maghreb is, nearly everywhere, at least double the height of applied tariffs found in the world at large or in the aggregate of low- and middle-income countries worldwide (table 5.8). Protection is thus significantly higher in the Maghreb than in competing countries in the global economy, hindering the Maghreb countries from enjoying greater gains from enlarged trade and making them generally less attractive to outward-oriented foreign investment by multinational firms.

Nontariff Barriers

NTBs to protect domestic producers from import competition can take many forms and they have long been recognized as generally more distortionary than tariffs—and hence more costly in economic terms. They are seldom entirely transparent to consumers, making them resistant to effective political opposition. They are favored, of course, by protected domestic firms and the numerous public officials who benefit from bribes collected in the course of administration.

Current information about NTBs applied in the five Maghreb countries is difficult to acquire. The most recent information, available from the UNCTAD Trade Analysis and Information System (TRAINS),[9] covers only Morocco for 2001 and Algeria and Tunisia for 2002. The figures indicate that the three countries augment their import tariff regimes using a variety of restrictive measures. Algeria appears to apply NTBs less frequently than either Morocco or Tunisia do. The TRAINS data indicate that Algeria applies nontariff measures to 417 products that are predominantly nonagricultural goods (65 percent), whereas Tunisia applies non-

---

8. On the structure of protection in North African countries during the early 1990s, see DeRosa (2000). See Bautista and Valdes (1993) for discussion of the issue of the bias against agriculture in developing countries.

9. The Trade Analysis and Information System (TRAINS) is available at www.unctad.org (accessed July 7, 2008).

tariff measures to 746 products that are also predominantly nonagricultural goods (75 percent). Morocco applies NTBs to 1,204 products that are more or less evenly divided between agricultural and nonagricultural goods. However, Algeria employs the greatest variety of NTBs, including administered pricing schemes, restrictive licensing of imports, outright prohibitions, single channels for imports (involving state or monopoly trading firms), and assorted technical barriers. Tunisia's NTBs, on the other hand, are limited mainly to import licensing arrangements and various technical barriers that discriminate against foreign goods. Finally, Morocco's arsenal of direct import controls and other nontariff measures include quantitative restrictions, state trading organizations, and a number of technical barriers, as well as requirements for the preshipment inspection of some imported goods.

Barriers to Investment and Trade in Services

Many public and private economic policymakers recognize severe barriers as a problem in the Maghreb. With renewed regional integration efforts in the greater Middle East and North Africa (MENA) area, the Maghreb countries have become engaged more actively in bilateral and regional discussions. New or renewed economic cooperation arrangements—covering not only merchandise trade, but also foreign investment and trade in services—are contemplated within the region and with other prominent MENA countries. In addition, ratification of the US-Morocco FTA in 2004 and the increasing number of Maghreb countries that have signed or will sign US TIFAs both attest to considerable regional interest in taking more determined steps toward economic growth through closer economic relations with the United States, if not also with the European Union through the Barcelona Process and European Neighborhood Policy (ENP) dialogues.

If Morocco's experience in its FTA negotiations with the United States holds true for the other Maghreb countries, a number of barriers to foreign investment and trade in services in the region will be identified and discussed in the near future in both the TIFA talks and the ENP dialogues with Algeria, Libya, and Tunisia. Primary areas for discussion are likely to be the transparency of national laws and regulations, national treatment of foreign manufacturing and services firms, establishment rights and nondiscriminatory entry to local markets for foreign firms producing goods and services,[10] protection of private contracts and intellectual property rights, and freedom to repatriate profits (see, for example, USTR 2008).

---

10. Including finance and banking, telecommunications, computer services, distribution services, mining and construction, and engineering.

References

Balassa, Bela. 1965. Trade Liberalization and Revealed Comparative Advantage. *Manchester School* 33, no. 2: 99–123.

Bautista, Romeo M., and Alberto Valdes. 1993. *The Bias against Agriculture: Trade and Macroeconomic Policies in Developing Countries*. San Francisco: ICS Press.

Dennis, Allen. 2006. *The Impact of Regional Trade Agreements and Trade Facilitation in the Middle East and North Africa Region*. World Bank Policy Research Working Paper 3837. Washington: World Bank.

DeRosa, Dean A. 2000. Agricultural Trade and Rural Development in the Middle East and North Africa: Recent Developments and Prospects. In *Catching Up with the Competition: Trade Policy Challenges and Options for the Middle East and North Africa,* eds., Bernard Hoekman and Jamel Zarrouk. Ann Arbor: University of Michigan Press.

UNCTAD (United Nations Conference on Trade and Development). 2006. FDI from Developing and Transition Economies: Implications for Development. *World Investment Report*. Geneva.

UNSD (United Nations Statistics Division). 2008. Service Trade Statistics Database. Available at http://unstats.un.org (accessed March 30, 2008).

USTR (United States Trade Representative). 2008. *2008 National Trade Estimate Report on Foreign Trade Barriers*. Available at www.ustr.gov (accessed on June 10, 2008).

6

Gravity Model Analysis

DEAN A. DeROSA

In recent years the gravity model has become a workhorse for quantitative studies of international trade and investment policy (Eichengreen and Irwin 1998). Essentially the model uses econometric techniques to evaluate thousands of individual observations on trade and investment between countries over time against the "gravitational mass" of explanatory variables that describe the characteristics of bilateral trade and investment partners. Two familiar explanatory variables are the joint real GDP levels of partners and the distance between them. But numerous other explanatory variables are frequently specified as well, including geographic, political, and institutional factors that either augment or diminish the gravitational forces giving rise to commerce between countries. Most important, recent gravity models incorporate indicators for bilateral and regional free trade agreements (FTAs), enabling the models to assess the FTAs' contribution to international commerce.

The Gravity Model and Dataset

The Peterson Institute gravity model (DeRosa 2007) is based on bilateral merchandise trade flows and inward stocks of foreign direct investment (FDI) among approximately 170 countries from 1976 to 2005 (with numerous gaps, mainly in the observations of bilateral FDI stocks), as compiled

---

Dean DeRosa is principal economist at ADR International Ltd. and a visiting fellow at the Peterson Institute for International Economics.

from the UN COMTRADE database, using the World Integrated Trade Solution software of the World Bank[1] and the United Nations Conference on Trade and Development (UNCTAD) FDISTAT database.[2] The explanatory variables of the model, identified in table 6.1, are taken mainly from an extensive dataset for gravity models compiled by Rose (2004). The model also incorporates indicator variables for over 500 FTAs based on historical notifications of the dates on which the agreements entered into force and their contemporary participants. These indicators are dichotomous (0, 1) variables, often called dummy variables; they take a value of 1 if trade or investment partner countries are FTA members and their mutual trade agreement is in force and a value of 0 otherwise.[3] The FTA indicators are grouped into nine prominent individual FTAs and groups of FTAs worldwide, including the North American Free Trade Agreement (NAFTA) and those of the European Union.[4] Related indicator variables are included in the gravity model to assess the effect of the FTAs on the trade and investment of members with nonmember countries.[5]

Notwithstanding the large number of explanatory variables already specified in most gravity models (including our own), it is common practice to consider any explanatory variables that might be missing or unobservable. This is done in two ways. To account for systemic global influences on trade, we specify year-effect variables that are essentially indicator variables representing episodic global effects on international

---

1. The World Trade International Statistics database is available at www.worldbank.org (accessed July 7, 2008).

2. The FDISTAT database is available at www.unctad.org (accessed July 7, 2008). The UNCTAD FDI data stock figures are inward FDI stocks, not outward FDI stocks. However, for convenience in our descriptive text and tables, we refer to inward FDI stocks in country B from country A as outward FDI stocks from country A.

3. To illustrate, the NAFTA indicator variable for US-Mexico trade would not take on a value of 1 until 1994.

4. The FTAs and preferential trade agreements are grouped as follows: European Union (EU); European Free Trade Area (EFTA); EU bilateral free trade agreements (EU FTAs); North American Free Trade Agreement (NAFTA); Southern Common Market (Mercosur); Chile, Mexico, Australia, and Singapore (CMAS) FTAs, separately distinguished because these are truly free trade countries; ASEAN Free Trade Area (AFTA); South Asia Free Trade Agreement (SAFTA); and all other customs unions and FTAs.

5. The change in trade or investment between FTA members is most often measured in percentage terms. Given the log-linear specification of the gravity model, the impact of an FTA on bilateral trade or inward FDI stocks can be computed in percentage terms as $100^*[\exp(b_{fta}) - 1.00]$. In this expression, b_{fta} is the estimated coefficient for the dummy variable representing the presence of an FTA and $\exp(b_{fta})$ is the value of the natural number e raised to the exponent b_{fta}. If the coefficient b_{fta} is 0.50, then the value of $\exp(b_{fta})$ is 1.65 and the percentage expansion in bilateral commerce is estimated as $100^*[1.65 - 1.00]$, or 65 percent.

Table 6.1 Gravity model estimates for trade and inward foreign direct investment stocks specifying major customs unions and free trade agreements, 1976–2005

Variable	Merchandise trade	Inward FDI stocks
Distance	−0.91***	−0.50***
Joint GDP	0.03***	−0.10***
Joint GDP per capita	0.04***	0.22***
Common language	−0.03***	0.98***
Common border	0.40***	0.62***
Landlocked	−0.82***	−0.35***
Island	0.48***	0.59***
Land area	0.26***	0.16***
Common colonizer	−0.64***	−0.34***
Current colony	0.42***	−0.37
Ever a colony	1.06***	1.74***
Common country	1.11***	2.09***
GSP	0.37***	0.19***
Joint FDI stocks	0.11***	—
Joint trade with all partners	—	0.54***
EU	0.25***	0.62***
EU FTAs	0.15***	0.17***
NAFTA	0.80***	−0.37***
Mercosur	0.69***	1.25***
CMAS FTAs	0.08***	0.52***
AFTA	0.69***	0.80***
Other FTAs	0.34***	0.07**
Constant	7.67***	−7.94***
R-squared	0.96	0.92
Observations (thousands)	36	36
Clusters (thousands)	4	4

FDI = foreign direct investment; GSP = generalized system of preferences

Notes: Fixed-effects estimates obtained by a multistep method developed by Plumper and Troeger (2007). Dependent variables are bilateral trade and bilateral inward FDI stocks, both measured in log real terms. Distance, joint real GDP, joint real GDP per capita, joint land area, joint real FDI stocks, and joint real trade with all partners are measured in log terms. Estimates for year-effects and indicators of FTA members' trade and investment with nonmember countries are not reported. ** and *** denote statistical significance at the 5 and 1 percent levels, respectively. Trade agreements represented by indicator variables are: European Union (EU), European Free Trade Area (EFTA, not reported), EU bilateral free trade agreements (EU FTAs), North American Free Trade Agreement (NAFTA), Southern Common Market (Mercosur), Chile, Mexico, Australia, and Singapore bilateral free trade agreements (CMAS FTAs), ASEAN Free Trade Area (AFTA), South Asia Free Trade Agreement (SAFTA, not reported), and all other customs unions and free trade agreements (Other FTAs). Clusters are the number of ordered country pairs in the panel dataset.

trade and investment such as oil shocks, fluctuations in the value of the dollar, and the extent of globalization. More important, we specify indicator variables for each ordered country pair in the dataset. This technique minimizes the possible bias in the estimated coefficients of the gravity model that arises from missing or unobservable explanatory variables. Finally we estimate the parameters of our gravity model separately for bilateral trade and inward FDI stocks, using a multistep, fixed-effects method for panel datasets developed recently by Plumper and Troeger (2007). This approach yields reliable coefficient estimates for both time-invariant and time-varying explanatory variables.

Estimation Results

Table 6.1 presents the estimation results for our gravity model, for both bilateral trade flows and inward FDI stocks. A number of regularities are discernible in the results that, broadly speaking, match the findings of other gravity models. Above all, the specified explanatory variables contribute significantly to explaining variations in bilateral trade flows and inward FDI stocks, as indicated by the high R-squared statistics for the two gravity model equations.[6]

As expected, distance between partners reduces bilateral trade and investment, while the joint GDP of partners, expressed in either level or per capita form, expands bilateral commerce in the model, holding other factors constant.[7] The individual influences of the other core explanatory variables are also sensible and generally conform to the results of other gravity model analyses. A common border between countries tends to expand bilateral commerce, as does being an island economy, having had a colonial relationship with a trading partner, or being a beneficiary of the Generalized System of Preferences (GSP).[8] In addition to distance, the

---

6. Although the R-squared statistic is greater than 0.90 for both equations, the reported value of the statistic may be somewhat inflated by the Plumper and Troeger (2007) multi-stage estimation, which measures the statistic only in the last stage of the procedure.

7. The economic theory underlying the gravity model suggests that the estimated coefficient of the joint GDP-level variable should approximate unity when the dependent variable of the estimating equation is bilateral trade. The expected sign of the joint GDP per capita variable is uncertain, but in our estimation results it appears to vie with the joint GDP-level variable for statistical significance in explaining both bilateral trade flows and FDI stocks.

8. Under the GSP, a number of advanced countries extend trade preferences to less developed countries on a nonreciprocal basis. The GSP programs of major industrial and other countries are monitored by UNCTAD, including through a series of manuals describing the individual programs (UNCTAD 2005).

principal resistance factors to trade, according to the gravity model, are being a landlocked country or a member of a country pair with a common colonizer (e.g., India and Kenya, both former UK colonies).

There are also significant interrelationships between trade and foreign investment in the estimation results. The greater is the joint stock of foreign investment in partner countries, the greater is their mutual trade. Analogously, the greater is the joint trade of partner countries with the world, the greater is the level of investment of the two countries in each other's economy, presumably because of both their mutual trade and their general openness to the global economy.

Finally, as a stylistic device in table 6.1, the coefficient estimates for the FTA indicator variables are framed for emphasis. Like the estimates for the other explanatory variables, they are statistically significant in most instances and predominantly bear the anticipated positive sign. The significant negative coefficient estimated for the NAFTA indicator variable in the inward FDI stocks equation is the most important anomaly. It could reflect appreciable tariff-jumping investment between the United States and Canada before NAFTA was established in 1994 as well as some natural unwinding of investment positions between the two NAFTA partners after 1994.[9]

Table 6.2 summarizes the bilateral trade-and-investment impact percentages implied by the FTA coefficients estimates in table 6.1. In some cases, the implied medium- to long-term trade and investment impacts are substantially greater than 100 percent. In general, however, the positive impact effects, measured by an elasticity percentage, range between 15 percent and 100 percent.

The gravity model can simulate the prospective impacts on trade and foreign investment resulting from greater economic integration once we choose appropriate FTA coefficients to apply to the Maghreb scenarios. Reflecting the nature of their underlying trade agreements, the various FTA coefficient estimates in tables 6.1 and 6.2 differ in important ways. The EU and NAFTA coefficients should be regarded as representing the potential impacts of the deepest, most thoroughgoing economic integration schemes, followed by the coefficients for the EU FTAs and Chile,

---

9. Not reported individually in table 6.1 are estimated year effects representing global influences on trade and investment over the estimation period 1976–2005 and cross-FTA indicators that indicate the influence of the FTAs on trade and investment by member countries with nonmember countries. However, estimated coefficients for cross-FTA indicators in the gravity model equation for bilateral trade are widely positive and significant. In other words, the FTAs appear to stimulate not only intrabloc trade, but also trade with countries outside the trading blocs—an unexpected form of trade diversion. For further discussion, see DeRosa and Hufbauer (2007).

Table 6.2   Gravity model estimates for free trade agreement (FTA) indicator variables and implied impact elasticities

Agreement	Merchandise trade		Inward FDI stocks	
	Coefficient estimate	Impact elasticity (percent)	Coefficient estimate	Impact elasticity (percent)
European Union	0.25	29	0.62	85
EU FTAs	0.15	16	0.17	18
North American Free Trade Agreement	0.80	123	−0.37	−31
Mercosur	0.69	98	1.25	247
Chile, Mexico, Australia, and Singapore FTAs	0.08	9	0.52	68
ASEAN Free Trade Agreement	0.69	99	0.80	123
Other FTAs	0.34	41	0.07	7

ASEAN = Association of Southeast Asian Nations
FDI = foreign direct investment

Source: Table 6.1 and author's calculations.

Mexico, Australia, and Singapore (CMAS) FTAs, which represent the recent burgeoning crop of high-standard FTAs established with emerging market countries. At the other end of the FTA spectrum are a large number of early and frequently unsuccessful bilateral and regional FTAs among less developed countries, a description that includes the Arab Maghreb Union (AMU). Notably, however, two prominent developing-country FTAs shown in table 6.2—the Southern Common Market (Mercosur) in Latin America and the Association of Southeast Asian Nations (ASEAN) Free Trade Area (AFTA) in Southeast Asia—post some of the largest trade and investment impact coefficients estimated for the several groups of FTAs identified in the model. These considerations are prominent in our selection of FTA coefficients for application to the Maghreb economic integration scenarios.

Maghreb Integration Scenarios

Established in 1989 by Algeria, Libya, Mauritania, Morocco, and Tunisia, the AMU began with the principal objective of creating a free trade area in goods, services, and factors of production by 1992 and a common market by 2000. To date, however, the free trade area has yet to be fully established and economic integration among the Maghreb countries remains weak at best (see chapter 3).[10]

Efforts to advance and strengthen the AMU have been attempted in recent years, including by the World Bank and the International Monetary Fund.[11] Beyond simply reinvigorating the original AMU plan, these proposals have emphasized initiatives to build greater private-sector support in the Maghreb; accelerate and deepen EU plans for widely establishing bilateral FTAs with Maghreb countries, culminating in the envisioned Euro-Mediterranean free trade area; and, more generally, increase integration of the Maghreb countries with the world economy. To this mix of recommendations, we add consideration of the US plan announced by US President George W. Bush in 2003 to establish high-standard US bilateral FTAs with the countries of the Middle East and North Africa (MENA) and eventually to establish a US-MENA free trade area.[12]

Using the Peterson Institute gravity model, we carry out three basic sets of scenarios for achieving greater economic integration of the Maghreb countries that yield estimates of the impacts of the integration schemes on aggregate merchandise trade and inward FDI stocks for the individual Maghreb countries, the European Union, and the United States. The first scenario set covers an AMU free trade area. The second set covers EU and US bilateral FTAs with Algeria, Morocco, and Tunisia.[13] The third scenario involves EU and US regional FTAs with the Maghreb countries.[14]

The first scenario represents a meaningful free trade and investment area among the five AMU countries, largely as envisioned by the current

---

10. Also see Dennis (2006) and Brenton, Baroncelli, and Malouche (2006). Additionally, it should be noted that as signatories to the Greater Arab Free Trade Area established under the auspices of the League of Arab States (GAFTA), Libya, Morocco, and Tunisia may have eliminated the import tariffs on their mutual trade in 2005. Accordingly, to the extent that their mutual trade meets the 40 percent domestic content requirement of the GAFTA rules of origin and, most importantly, that it is not restricted by nontariff barriers, these three Maghreb countries may already enjoy some of the trade gains from regional integration simulated by the gravity model and presented in the next section.

11. See, e.g., World Bank (2006), Allain and Loko (2007), and Tahiri et al. (2007).

12. To date, the United States has signed FTAs with Israel, Jordan, Morocco, and Bahrain in the MENA region. Additionally, it has begun FTA negotiations with Oman and the United Arab Emirates. See www.ustr.gov for details (accessed July 7, 2008).

13. Specifically, this includes the EU-Algeria FTA, EU-Morocco FTA, EU-Tunisia FTA, EU-Algeria+ FTA, EU-Morocco+ FTA, EU-Tunisia+ FTA, US-Algeria FTA, US-Morocco FTA, US-Tunisia FTA, US-Algeria+ FTA, US-Morocco+ FTA, and US-Tunisia+ FTA. See below for explanation of "plus" scenarios.

14. Specifically, this includes an EU-Maghreb free trade area, a US-Maghreb free trade area, and an EU-US-Maghreb free trade area.

AMU plan for regional economic integration. In the second set, the integration scenarios depict perhaps less ambitious but potentially more outward-oriented bilateral FTAs by the European Union and United States with the three major Maghreb countries—Algeria, Morocco, and Tunisia—individually. These scenarios are regarded as the most politically feasible approaches to establishing and deepening Maghreb integration in the near future. They are also regarded as potential instruments for encouraging the Maghreb countries to reach out gradually to one another and liberalize intraregional economic relations, in part to offset the distortions in foreign trade, especially in investment, that can emerge from the hub-and-spoke structure of a network of EU and US bilateral FTAs (Wonnacott 1996). The implications of such regional outreach are illustrated by our hypothesized "plus" scenarios for EU and US bilateral FTAs with the three major Maghreb countries. In these scenarios, the European Union and United States strike bilateral FTAs with the three individual Maghreb countries as before, but the three countries also simultaneously eliminate barriers to trade and investment with their AMU partners, widening the liberalization of their markets within the Maghreb.

The third set of scenarios depicts the establishment of full-fledged EU and US regional free trade areas with the Maghreb countries, both individually by the European Union and the United States and on a combined basis. These scenarios envision the widest possible liberalization of the Maghreb countries with one another and the global economy, through their integration with either the European Union or the United States.

The final element of the scenarios is to select the appropriate gravity model FTA coefficients for the simulation analysis. Our choice of coefficient estimates for the AMU scenario and EU-Maghreb FTA scenarios is straightforward. We assume that the trade and investment impacts of the hypothesized AMU free trade area will be governed by the gravity model coefficient estimates for the group of other FTAs (tables 6.1 and 6.2), whereas those of the hypothesized EU bilateral and regional FTAs will be governed by the coefficient estimates for the group of EU FTAs. Choosing estimates for the US bilateral and regional FTA scenarios is more difficult, as we hesitate to specify the NAFTA coefficients estimated by our gravity model because of the aforementioned anomaly of the negative coefficient estimated for NAFTA in the gravity model for inward FDI stocks. Additionally, the estimated coefficient for NAFTA in the gravity model for merchandise trade is the largest estimated FTA coefficient in our gravity model, implying a trade impact elasticity of 123 percent in table 6.2. To avoid these extremes and the uncertainties that underlie them, we represent the trade and investment impacts of the bilateral and regional FTAs between the United States and Maghreb countries by the average of the estimated coefficients for the CMAS FTAs and AFTA. The assumption essentially balances the experience of recent high-standard FTAs between the United States and advanced countries, such as Australia and Singapore, against the experience of the relatively dynamic ASEAN developing countries with regional free trade. This implies an average impact of US-Maghreb FTAs of about 55 percent on bilateral trade and about 85 percent on bilateral inward FDI stocks.

In the enhanced EU and US FTA scenarios, we assume that by extending some preferences to Libya and Mauritania and among themselves, the three major Maghreb countries of Algeria, Morocco, and Tunisia will achieve only half the percentage gains in trade and investment that the European Union and United States achieve in expanding their economic relations with the three major Maghreb countries. This assumption recognizes the reality of current intra-Maghreb relations, which, since the adoption of the AMU, have been slow in opening Maghreb borders to greater regional trade and investment.

Simulation Results

The gravity model simulation results for merchandise trade and inward stocks of FDI for the Maghreb countries, the European Union, and the United States under the three sets of Maghreb integration scenarios are reported in tables 6.3 and 6.4, respectively. To facilitate comparison, the two tables also report the base levels of Maghreb, EU, and US trade and FDI stocks in the gravity model as well as the simulated trade and investment impacts of the integration scenarios, expressed as percentages of the base level of trade and investment with the world for each of the countries.

The impacts of the integration scenarios were obtained by first predicting trade and investment outcomes in the gravity model over the period 2001–05, assuming that the relevant FTA indicator—for example, the EU FTA variable in the case of the EU bilateral and regional FTAs—was zero. Then we replaced the FTA variable with an FTA indicator tailored specifically to the individual scenario and re-solved the model to predict the new trade and investment outcomes over the same period. We then averaged the difference between the second and the first values predicted by the gravity model over the five-year period (at 2005 prices) to determine the average annual impacts for trade and investment under each scenario reported in tables 6.3 and 6.4.

Through this methodology, the gravity model provides estimates of the bilateral impacts of the different Maghreb integration scenarios even when no underlying trade or investment is reported. In other words, impacts are computed on the basis of the predictions of the gravity model assuming that the trade or investment levels of the partner countries conform to the norms that the model estimates for other country pairs with similar characteristics. When no trade or investment is reported, the estimated impacts are underestimated substantially, as they ascribe base

Table 6.3 Average impacts on merchandise trade of Maghreb economic integration scenarios, 2001–05
(millions of US dollars at 2005 prices; percent in parentheses)

Country	Base: Trade with the world	Arab Maghreb Union	EU and US bilateral FTAs				EU and US regional FTAs		
			EU-Alg EU-Mor EU-Tun	EU-Alg+ EU-Mor+ EU-Tun+	US-Alg US-Mor US-Tun	US-Alg+ US-Mor+ US-Tun+	EU-Maghreb	US-Maghreb	EU-US-Maghreb
Total trade									
Maghreb	115,130	893 (0.8)	2,654 (2.3)	2,793 (2.4)	3,110 (2.7)	3,534 (3.1)	3,604 (3.1)	5,216 (4.5)	8,820 (7.7)
Algeria	42,410	254 (0.6)	469 (1.1)	518 (1.2)	1,734 (4.1)	1,885 (4.4)	620 (1.5)	2,258 (5.3)	2,878 (6.8)
Libya	24,073	242 (1.0)	0 (0.0)	32 (0.1)	0 (0.0)	95 (0.4)	429 (1.8)	703 (2.9)	1,133 (4.7)
Mauritania	1,406	122 (8.7)	0 (0.0)	9 (0.6)	0 (0.0)	26 (1.9)	217 (15.5)	340 (24.2)	558 (39.7)
Morocco	26,738	138 (0.5)	1,770 (6.6)	1,792 (6.7)	793 (3.0)	862 (3.2)	1,846 (6.9)	1,061 (4.0)	2,907 (10.9)
Tunisia	20,504	136 (0.7)	415 (2.0)	442 (2.2)	583 (2.8)	665 (3.2)	492 (2.4)	853 (4.2)	1,345 (6.6)
European Union	6,182,919	0 (0.0)	2,654 (0.0)	2,654 (0.0)	0 (0.0)	0 (0.0)	3,086 (0.0)	0 (0.0)	3,086 (0.0)
United States	2,285,789	0 (0.0)	0 (0.0)	0 (0.0)	3,110 (0.1)	3,110 (0.1)	0 (0.0)	3,411 (0.1)	3,411 (0.1)
World	16,407,561	893 (0.0)	5,308 (0.0)	5,447 (0.0)	6,219 (0.0)	6,643 (0.0)	6,691 (0.0)	8,627 (0.1)	15,318 (0.1)
Exports									
Maghreb	66,296	446 (0.7)	461 (0.7)	531 (0.8)	198 (0.3)	410 (0.6)	934 (1.4)	1,194 (1.8)	2,128 (3.2)
Algeria	26,952	136 (0.5)	170 (0.6)	186 (0.7)	32 (0.1)	81 (0.3)	251 (0.9)	313 (1.2)	564 (2.1)
Libya	18,506	120 (0.6)	0 (0.0)	32 (0.2)	0 (0.0)	95 (0.5)	213 (1.2)	271 (1.5)	485 (2.6)

Imports

(Exports)

Reporter	Total	Maghreb	Algeria	Libya	Mauritania	Morocco	Tunisia	European Union	United States
Mauritania	755	46 (6.1)	0 (0.0)	9 (1.2)	0 (0.0)	26 (3.5)	100 (13.2)	166 (21.9)	265 (35.2)
Morocco	11,031	73 (0.7)	172 (1.6)	177 (1.6)	105 (1.0)	121 (1.1)	211 (1.9)	245 (2.2)	456 (4.1)
Tunisia	9,053	70 (0.8)	119 (1.3)	128 (1.4)	61 (0.7)	88 (1.0)	158 (1.7)	199 (2.2)	357 (3.9)
European Union	3,025,399	0 (0.0)	2,192 (0.1)	2,192 (0.1)	0 (0.0)	0 (0.0)	2,412 (0.1)	0 (0.0)	2,412 (0.1)
United States	842,357	0 (0.0)	0 (0.0)	0 (0.0)	2,911 (0.3)	2,911 (0.3)	0 (0.0)	3,120 (0.4)	3,120 (0.4)
World	8,203,780	446 (0.0)	2,654 (0.0)	2,724 (0.0)	3,110 (0.0)	3,322 (0.0)	3,345 (0.0)	4,313 (0.1)	7,659 (0.1)

Imports

Reporter	Total	Maghreb	Algeria	Libya	Mauritania	Morocco	Tunisia	European Union	United States
Maghreb	48,834	446 (0.9)	2,192 (4.5)	2,262 (4.6)	2,911 (6.0)	3,123 (6.4)	2,671 (5.5)	4,022 (8.2)	6,692 (13.7)
Algeria	15,458	118 (0.8)	298 (1.9)	332 (2.1)	1,701 (11.0)	1,804 (11.7)	368 (2.4)	1,945 (12.6)	2,314 (15.0)
Libya	5,567	122 (2.2)	0 (0.0)	0 (0.0)	0 (0.0)	0 (0.0)	216 (3.9)	432 (7.8)	648 (11.6)
Mauritania	651	75 (11.6)	0 (0.0)	0 (0.0)	0 (0.0)	0 (0.0)	118 (18.1)	175 (26.8)	292 (44.9)
Morocco	15,707	65 (0.4)	1,598 (10.2)	1,616 (10.3)	688 (4.4)	742 (4.7)	1,635 (10.4)	816 (5.2)	2,451 (15.6)
Tunisia	11,451	66 (0.6)	296 (2.6)	314 (2.7)	522 (4.6)	577 (5.0)	334 (2.9)	654 (5.7)	988 (8.6)
European Union	3,157,520	0 (0.0)	461 (0.0)	461 (0.0)	0 (0.0)	0 (0.0)	675 (0.0)	0 (0.0)	675 (0.0)
United States	1,443,433	0 (0.0)	0 (0.0)	0 (0.0)	198 (0.0)	198 (0.0)	0 (0.0)	292 (0.0)	292 (0.0)
World	8,203,780	446 (0.0)	2,654 (0.0)	2,724 (0.0)	3,110 (0.0)	3,322 (0.0)	3,345 (0.0)	4,313 (0.1)	7,659 (0.1)

Source: Peterson Institute gravity model.

Table 6.4 Average impacts on inward foreign direct investment stocks of Maghreb economic integration scenarios, 2001–05 (millions of US dollars at 2005 prices; percent in parentheses)

Country	Base: Inward FDI stocks	Arab Maghreb Union	EU and US bilateral FTAs				EU and US regional FTAs		
			EU-Alg EU-Mor EU-Tun	EU-Alg+ EU-Mor+ EU-Tun+	US-Alg US-Mor US-Tun	US-Alg+ US-Mor+ US-Tun+	EU-Maghreb	US-Maghreb	EU-US-Maghreb
Total inward FDI stocks									
Maghreb	8,096	156 (1.9)	3,719 (45.9)	3,859 (47.7)	1,366 (16.9)	1,996 (24.6)	5,376 (66.4)	4,356 (53.8)	9,732 (120.2)
Algeria	4,827	54 (1.1)	1,370 (28.4)	1,423 (29.5)	779 (16.1)	1,013 (21.0)	1,524 (31.6)	1,563 (32.4)	3,087 (64.0)
Libya	458	50 (11.0)	0 (0.0)	33 (7.2)	0 (0.0)	155 (33.8)	1,197 (261.2)	1,436 (313.6)	2,633 (574.7)
Mauritania	35	2 (6.3)	0 (0.0)	1 (3.2)	0 (0.0)	5 (15.2)	161 (455.8)	50 (142.1)	212 (597.9)
Morocco	2,286	20 (0.9)	1,506 (65.9)	1,528 (66.8)	268 (11.7)	367 (16.0)	1,563 (68.4)	555 (24.3)	2,118 (92.6)
Tunisia	489	30 (6.1)	842 (172.2)	874 (178.6)	318 (65.1)	455 (93.1)	931 (190.2)	751 (153.6)	1,682 (343.8)
European Union	7,478,118	0 (0.0)	3,719 (0.0)	3,719 (0.0)	0 (0.0)	0 (0.0)	4,926 (0.1)	0 (0.0)	4,926 (0.1)
United States	3,286,223	0 (0.0)	0 (0.0)	0 (0.0)	1,366 (0.0)	1,366 (0.0)	0 (0.0)	2,081 (0.1)	2,081 (0.1)
World	14,881,710	156 (0.0)	7,437 (0.0)	7,578 (0.0)	2,731 (0.0)	3,361 (0.0)	10,301 (0.1)	6,437 (0.0)	16,738 (0.1)
Inward FDI stocks "exported"									
Maghreb	397	78 (19.7)	1,393 (351.2)	1,463 (368.9)	254 (64.0)	569 (143.4)	2,190 (552.0)	1,736 (437.5)	3,926 (989.5)
Algeria	0	30 (6,584.4)	643 (>999.9)	662 (>999.9)	169 (>999.9)	255 (>999.9)	726 (>999.9)	595 (>999.9)	1,321 (>999.9)
Libya	71	27 (37.9)	0 (0.0)	33 (46.4)	0 (0.0)	155 (218.9)	566 (801.2)	709 (>999.9)	1,275 (>999.9)

Inward FDI stocks "imported"

Mauritania	2	1 (72.3)	0 (0.0)	1 (70.6)	0 (0.0)	5 (331.9)	78 (>999.9)	32 (>999.9)	110 (>999.9)
Morocco	323	7 (2.1)	388 (120.1)	394 (121.8)	23 (7.0)	44 (13.7)	410 (127.0)	123 (38.0)	533 (164.9)
Tunisia	1	14 (1,801.8)	362 (>999.9)	374 (>999.9)	62 (>999.9)	109 (>999.9)	410 (>999.9)	278 (>999.9)	687 (>999.9)
European Union	3,875,859	0 (0.0)	2,325 (0.1)	2,325 (0.1)	0 (0.0)	0 (0.0)	2,961 (0.1)	0 (0.0)	2,961 (0.1)
United States	1,781,483	0 (0.0)	0 (0.0)	1,112 (0.1)	1,112 (0.1)	0 (0.0)	1,483 (0.1)	1,483 (0.1)	
World	7,440,855	78 (0.0)	3,719 (0.0)	3,789 (0.1)	1,366 (0.0)	1,681 (0.0)	5,151 (0.1)	3,219 (0.0)	8,369 (0.1)
Maghreb	7,699	78 (1.0)	2,325 (30.2)	2,396 (31.1)	1,112 (14.4)	1,427 (18.5)	3,186 (41.4)	2,621 (34.0)	5,806 (75.4)
Algeria	4,826	24 (0.5)	727 (15.1)	761 (15.8)	610 (12.6)	758 (15.7)	798 (16.5)	968 (20.1)	1,766 (36.6)
Libya	387	23 (6.0)	0 (0.0)	0 (0.0)	0 (0.0)	0 (0.0)	630 (162.7)	728 (187.9)	1,358 (350.5)
Mauritania	34	1 (3.2)	0 (0.0)	0 (0.0)	0 (0.0)	0 (0.0)	83 (247.1)	19 (55.2)	102 (302.3)
Morocco	1,963	14 (0.7)	1,118 (56.9)	1,135 (57.8)	246 (12.5)	323 (16.4)	1,153 (58.7)	432 (22.0)	1,585 (80.7)
Tunisia	488	16 (3.3)	481 (98.4)	500 (102.4)	256 (52.5)	346 (70.9)	521 (106.7)	474 (97.0)	995 (203.7)
European Union	3,602,259	0 (0.0)	1,393 (0.0)	1,393 (0.0)	0 (0.0)	0 (0.0)	1,965 (0.1)	0 (0.0)	1,965 (0.1)
United States	1,504,740	0 (0.0)	0 (0.0)	0 (0.0)	254 (0.0)	254 (0.0)	0 (0.0)	598 (0.0)	598 (0.0)
World	7,440,855	78 (0.0)	3,719 (0.0)	3,789 (0.1)	1,366 (0.0)	1,681 (0.0)	5,151 (0.1)	3,219 (0.0)	8,369 (0.1)

Source: Peterson Institute gravity model.

levels of trade or investment as predicted by the gravity model when in fact no trade or investment may have actually occurred.[15]

Trade Impacts

We first consider the trade impacts of the three sets of Maghreb integration scenarios summarized in table 6.3. All the calculations refer to merchandise trade; at this time, the gravity model data set does not cover service trade flows.

Given the small economic size of the AMU and the limited diversity of endowments among its members, a full-fledged free trade area among the Maghreb countries yields a gain in total trade (merchandise exports plus imports) of only about $1 billion, or about 1 percent of base total trade. Notwithstanding this modest impact for the AMU bloc as a whole, the impacts on the total trade of Mauritania ($122 million, or 8.7 percent) and the total imports of Libya ($122 million, or 2.2 percent) are significant and would improve general welfare substantially in both countries.

As emphasized previously, fully establishing the AMU has not proven politically feasible owing to deep-seated rivalries. More feasible may be the establishment of FTAs between the European Union or the United States on one hand and the major Maghreb countries (Algeria, Morocco, and Tunisia) on the other. The simulation results in table 6.3 support this view, although the economic benefits are clearly concentrated in the combined imports of the three Maghreb partner countries, at $2 billion to $3 billion or about 5 to 6 percent of the combined base imports of those countries. Although the European Union trades more extensively than the United States with the Maghreb countries, the US FTA impacts on AMU trade are somewhat greater than the impacts of the EU FTA because the assumed gravity model coefficients for US FTAs are larger in value.

The "plus" integration scenarios—in which Algeria, Morocco, and Tunisia extend the trade and investment preferences under the EU and US FTAs to one another and to Libya and Mauritania—yield only modest trade gains to the latter two countries, Libya and Mauritania. Yet such an approach to leveraging wider liberalization in the Maghreb might still be the most feasible path to spread globalization more widely and quickly in the region.[16]

While the bilateral EU and US FTAs with the three major Maghreb countries are probably the most politically feasible route in the near term and

---

15. These instances arise in the simulation results mainly for inward FDI stocks (table 6.4), where the percentage impacts are reported to be greater than 999 percent.

16. The macroeconomic benefits to EU and US economies are clearly not appreciable in percentage terms from the simulation results presented in table 6.3. EU and US trade with the Maghreb countries does expand, however, and to the individual EU and US exporters and importers involved in the expansion of trade, the gains from trade may well be substantial and significant.

would yield substantial economic benefits to the Maghreb partners, still of interest are the potential economic gains from true globalization of the AMU countries. That scenario is represented by the hypothesized EU and US regional FTAs in the third set of Maghreb integration calculations in table 6.3. As expected, the simulated trade gains under the regional FTA scenarios are the largest of all, for the Maghreb countries considered individually and as a bloc. Total Maghreb trade expands by $4 billion to $5 billion, or 3 to 4.5 percent, when the European Union and the United States separately establish free trade areas with the Maghreb countries. The same trade expands by nearly $9 billion, nearly 8 percent, when both the European Union and the United States establish regional FTAs with the AMU countries (table 6.3).

The estimated impacts on Maghreb imports are especially strong. Under a combined EU-US-Maghreb FTA, total Maghreb imports expand by $6.7 billion or nearly 14 percent. Moreover, the stimulus to the imports of the individual Maghreb countries ranges between about 10 percent (Tunisia) and 45 percent (Mauritania). Total Maghreb exports expand substantially less, by $2.1 billion or 3.2 percent. Yet the export gains are significant in percentage terms for Mauritania (35 percent) and for Morocco and Tunisia (4 percent). Also, if Maghreb imports expanded as much as the simulation results suggest, it seems likely that greater efficiencies would stimulate exports in ways not covered, such as by larger service exports. Furthermore, the potential trade gains could create considerable incentives for the Maghreb countries to build on the foundations of either EU or US FTAs, through a process of competitive liberalization to embrace a wide range of economic reforms.[17]

FDI Impacts

In recent years it has become widely accepted that trade and FDI are closely linked (see box 6.1), with worldwide investment by multinational firms motivating trade flows and guiding their directions in important ways. The limited inward stocks of FDI in the Maghreb, which are especially small outside its energy sector, reflects the region's failure to keep pace with the world economy.

The FDI impacts of the three sets of Maghreb integration scenarios represented in table 6.4 indicate the extent to which greater openness might boost foreign investment in the Maghreb. Broadly speaking, the FDI impacts are similar to the trade impacts, suggesting that inward FDI stocks increase substantially more when closer economic ties are pursued with either the European Union or the United States, rather than simply on an AMU basis.[18] Closer Maghreb economic ties with the European Union and

---

17. On the notion of competitive liberalization, see Bergsten (1996).

18. EU and US bilateral and regional FTAs with the Maghreb imply very little change in inward FDI for either the European Union or the United States.

Box 6.1 Trade and FDI linkages in the gravity model

The impacts on Maghreb trade and investment of the proposed EU and US bilateral and regional FTAs with the countries of the region should be determined simultaneously in the Peterson Institute gravity model. This is because the separate gravity model equations for bilateral trade and inward FDI stocks are interrelated by including the joint FDI variable and the joint trade variable, respectively, as explanatory variables in the two equations. Thus, an initial expansion of either bilateral trade or FDI under an EU or US FTA with one or more Maghreb countries should lead to additional rounds of increases in bilateral trade and stocks of FDI for the FTA partners until a final equilibrium is reached at levels greater than those reported in tables 6.3 and 6.4.

Algebraically determining the appropriate adjustment of the two right-hand side variables—joint trade with the world and joint total inward FDI stocks—to changes in the two left-hand side (or predicted) variables in the gravity model— bilateral trade and bilateral FDI stocks—reveals that the relationships involve calculations of changes in two-way trade and FDI stock holdings weighted by baseline shares of both FTA partners and non-FTA partners that are too extensive to be computed readily in successive simulations of the Peterson gravity model.

Nonetheless, the initial bilateral impacts of FTAs on bilateral trade and inward FDI stocks in the gravity model are highly symmetric when measured in proportional changes. This allows us to approximate the adjustment in the two right-hand side variables with a simple linear relationship. Based on baseline shares of country pairs in their joint trade with the world and their joint inward FDI stocks in the gravity model, we assume that the proportional change in the joint trade variable equals 0.10 times the corresponding proportional change in the predicted level of bilateral exports. We also assume that the proportional change in the joint inward FDI stocks variable equals 0.15 times the corresponding proportional change in the predicted bilateral level of outward FDI stocks.

Table 6.5 presents the results of incorporating these linkages in the gravity model and then applying the model to the case—chosen for illustration—of the enhanced ("plus") EU FTAs with Algeria, Morocco, and Tunisia. These results are placed alongside the results for the same Maghreb integration scenario without linking the trade and FDI first reported in tables 6.3 and 6.4. In the simultaneous gravity model, general equilibrium is effectively reached after five successive iterations of the model after the establishment of the enhanced EU FTAs with the three major Maghreb countries.

In table 6.5, the results of incorporating the trade-FDI linkages are fairly straightforward. The simulated trade impacts of the enhanced EU FTAs are greater than

(box continues next page)

those found without the trade-FDI linkages, but only marginally so (about 2 percent across the board). Thus, total Maghreb trade expands by nearly $2.9 billion
when the trade-FDI linkages are built into the model, compared with $2.8 billion
without the linkages.

The general equilibrium impacts on FDI stocks, however, are substantially
greater than those found without the trade-FDI linkages: They are over 5 percent
greater across the board. Total outward and inward Maghreb FDI stocks expand by
nearly $4.1 billion, compared with $3.9 billion without accounting for the linkages.
The impacts on FDI stocks when the trade-FDI linkages are included in the model
are substantially greater because of the relatively large estimated coefficient (0.54)
in table 6.1 for the joint trade explanatory variable in the gravity model equation
for FDI stocks.

the United States tend to result in greater impacts on inward FDI stocks
than outward FDI stocks. The FDI impacts for EU bilateral and regional
FTAs are larger than those for US FTAs because the gravity model predicts
substantially greater base-period investment between the Maghreb and
the European Union than between the Maghreb and the United States.

In the most ambitious hypothesized EU-US-Maghreb free trade area,
total Maghreb inward FDI stocks increase by $5.8 billion (75 percent) com-
pared with the simulated increase in total Maghreb outward FDI stocks
amounting to $3.9 billion. These potential impacts of Maghreb integration
scenarios on FDI reinforce the conclusions of the previous discussion of
trade flows. In their own right, the FDI calculations add significantly to
the potential gains that the Maghreb countries might enjoy by forging
closer economic relations with the European Union and the United States,
through competitive liberalization and other strategies to engage the Maghreb with the world economy.

Impacts on Output, Employment, and Growth

The gravity model's predicted impacts of Maghreb economic integration
on merchandise trade and FDI for the AMU countries are expected to
materialize over a horizon of two to five years. However, as Maghreb consumers and producers adapt during this period to the opportunities provided by greater openness—and the likely accompanying domestic economic reforms to facilitate the bilateral or regional FTAs—adjustments in
other economic variables may take place with additional impacts on trade
and investment. Greater openness, particularly added domestic and for-

eign investment in the Maghreb, should be expected to result in greater employment and higher growth in the region in the long run.

The apparent imbalance between the impacts of greater economic integration on Maghreb exports and imports in table 6.3 point to the most immediate adjustment of other economic variables in the aftermath of the several Maghreb integration scenarios involving the European Union and the United States. The greater expansion of imports than exports for the Maghreb countries implies a deterioration in the balance of payments positions of these countries, requiring exchange rate depreciation and further adjustments in Maghreb trade to maintain the countries' external payments positions.[19] This deterioration is accounted for in the final estimates of the impacts of greater economic integration on Maghreb trade (table 6.5). The final trade impacts assume that exchange rate adjustments in the five Maghreb countries moderate the initial expansion of Maghreb imports by 25 percent and expand Maghreb exports until each country's balance of payments returns to equilibrium.[20] Comparing the initial trade impacts to the final impacts for the Maghreb countries in tables 6.3 and 6.5, respectively, one observes a modest reduction in final imports and the very remarkable increase in final exports of the Maghreb countries under each of the several integration scenarios except the scenario depicting the AMU plan. The combined exports of the Maghreb countries more than double in the scenarios depicting the prospective EU and US FTAs with the AMU countries when the gravity model simulations account for balance of payment constraints.

Table 6.5 also provides estimates of the medium- to long-term impacts of the final levels of trade under the Maghreb integration scenarios on the Maghreb countries' levels of aggregate output (GDP). The GDP impacts are based on the findings of Cline (2004), whose survey of empirical studies on the relationship between openness and per capita output in mainly developing countries finds an average elasticity of 0.5 when the changes in the two variables are measured over periods of 5 to 10 years. When translated into the dimensions of the present analysis, this average elasticity implies that for every percentage point that total trade expands in a

---

19. The initial decline in the balance of payments positions of the Maghreb countries might be ameliorated in part by the changes in long-term net foreign asset holdings of the AMU countries implied by the FDI impacts reported in table 6.4. However, the changes in net foreign asset holdings are one-time adjustments in FDI stocks, whereas the trade impacts reported in table 6.3 represent perpetual changes in international payment flows that must be factored into the balance of payments constraint of the individual Maghreb countries. For expository ease, we do not consider here the possible secondary impacts of the integration scenarios on EU and US trade to maintain equilibrium in the international payments positions of the European Union and the United States, though the secondary impacts should be expected to be small relative to overall levels of EU and US trade.

20. In effect, this methodology assumes that, not unlike in most other small trading countries, the demand for imports in the Maghreb countries is less price elastic than is the supply of exports.

Maghreb country, the aggregate output of the country should be expected to increase by 0.33 percentage points in the long run.[21]

In table 6.5, the GDP impacts for the three major Maghreb countries under the combined EU and US free trade areas with the AMU countries range between about 2.5 percent (Algeria and Tunisia) and 4.5 percent (Morocco). For Libya and Mauritania, the GDP impacts are below and above this range, at 1.3 percent and 10.3 percent, respectively. In comparison, the average GDP impact for the three major Maghreb countries under the EU and US bilateral FTAs ranges between about 1.0 percent and 1.5 percent. The average for all the Maghreb countries under the AMU plan is only 0.3 percent. These results suggest that the prospective EU and US FTAs with the Maghreb countries would add appreciably to output in the region if they were to be pursued to the widest possible extent, namely, as a unified free trade area with the two external trading partners.

The gravity model can also derive the long-term employment and growth effects of the prospective EU and US FTAs on the Maghreb countries. These effects are best and most fundamentally related to the FDI impacts in table 6.4. This is because increased FDI in the Maghreb countries from EU and US multinational firms implies the addition to the Maghreb economies of particularly productive, world-class resources, accompanied often by the considerable technological and managerial knowhow of these generally internationally competitive, outward-oriented firms.

The long-term employment gains presented in table 6.6 assume that increased foreign investment in the Maghreb economies employs surplus (or underemployed) labor. The magnitudes of the estimated employment gains in table 6.6 are based on the recent level of employment supported by US FDI in a representative Central American economy, Nicaragua (Hufbauer and Adler 2008). These data indicate that each full-time job in US foreign-affiliate firms in the representative economy is supported by $90,000 in US FDI.[22] Applying this rule of thumb to the FDI impacts in the gravity model's Maghreb integration scenarios reveals that, while the

---

21. Cline's (2004) average elasticity estimate of 0.5 for per capita output levels (GDP/N) in relation to trade openness (X + M/GDP) may be expressed as (GDP/N)* = 0.5 ([X + M]/GDP)*, where asterisks (*) denote percentage change. Solving for the change in aggregate output in terms of changes in total trade (X + M) and population (N) yields GDP* = 0.33 (X + M)* + 0.5 N*, which is the relation used to derive the GDP impacts for unchanged population levels in the Maghreb countries reported in table 6.5.

22. US Department of Commerce, Bureau of Economic Analysis, interactive tables, available at www.bea.gov (accessed July 7, 2008). The data for US foreign investment in the Maghreb countries in this dataset were viewed as too sparse for some countries and too heavily concentrated in the capital-intensive oil sector for other countries to be relied on for the present analysis. By contrast, the data for Nicaragua were viewed as a more appropriate and conservative norm for representing the proximate employment impacts in the Maghreb of greater FDI from the European Union, United States, and other countries under fully liberalized trade and investment regimes in the region.

Table 6.5   Average impacts on merchandise trade and gross domestic output of Maghreb economic integration scenarios assuming trade flows adjust to maintain balance-of-payments equilibrium, 2001–05

(millions of US dollars at 2005 prices; percent in parentheses)

Country	Base: Trade with the world; 2005 GDP	Arab Maghreb Union	EU and US bilateral FTAs				EU and US regional FTAs		
			EU-Alg EU-Mor EU-Tun	EU-Alg+ EU-Mor+ EU-Tun+	US-Alg US-Mor US-Tun	US-Alg+ US-Mor+ US-Tun+	EU-Maghreb	US-Maghreb	EU-US-Maghreb
Total trade									
Maghreb	115,130	918 (0.8)	3,289 (2.9)	3,393 (2.9)	4,367 (3.8)	4,685 (4.1)	4,006 (3.5)	6,033 (5.2)	10,038 (8.7)
Algeria	42,410	296 (0.7)	448 (1.1)	498 (1.2)	2,552 (6.0)	2,706 (6.4)	553 (1.3)	2,918 (6.9)	3,470 (8.2)
Libya	24,073	183 (0.8)	0 (0.0)	0 (0.0)	0 (0.0)	0 (0.0)	324 (1.3)	648 (2.7)	972 (4.0)
Mauritania	1,406	113 (8.1)	0 (0.0)	0 (0.0)	0 (0.0)	0 (0.0)	176 (12.5)	262 (18.6)	438 (31.2)
Morocco	26,738	162 (0.6)	2,397 (9.0)	2,424 (9.1)	1,032 (3.9)	1,113 (4.2)	2,452 (9.2)	1,224 (4.6)	3,676 (13.7)
Tunisia	20,504	164 (0.8)	444 (2.2)	471 (2.3)	783 (3.8)	866 (4.2)	501 (2.4)	981 (4.8)	1,481 (7.2)
Exports									
Maghreb	66,296	459 (0.7)	1,644 (2.5)	1,697 (2.6)	2,183 (3.3)	2,342 (3.5)	2,003 (3.0)	3,016 (4.5)	5,019 (7.6)
Algeria	26,952	148 (0.5)	224 (0.8)	249 (0.9)	1,276 (4.7)	1,353 (5.0)	276 (1.0)	1,459 (5.4)	1,735 (6.4)
Libya	18,506	91 (0.5)	0 (0.0)	0 (0.0)	0 (0.0)	0 (0.0)	162 (0.9)	324 (1.8)	486 (2.6)
Mauritania	755	57 (7.5)	0 (0.0)	0 (0.0)	0 (0.0)	0 (0.0)	88 (11.7)	131 (17.4)	219 (29.0)
Morocco	11,031	81 (0.7)	1,199 (10.9)	1,212 (11.0)	516 (4.7)	556 (5.0)	1,226 (11.1)	612 (5.5)	1,838 (16.7)
Tunisia	9,053	82 (0.9)	222 (2.5)	236 (2.6)	391 (4.3)	433 (4.8)	250 (2.8)	490 (5.4)	741 (8.2)

Imports

Maghreb	48,834	459	(0.9)	1,644	(3.4)	1,697	(3.5)	2,183	(4.5)	2,342	(4.8)	2,003	(4.1)	3,016	(6.2)	5,019	(10.3)
Algeria	15,458	148	(1.0)	224	(1.4)	249	(1.6)	1,276	(8.3)	1,353	(8.8)	276	(1.8)	1,459	(9.4)	1,735	(11.2)
Libya	5,567	91	(1.6)	0	(0.0)	0	(0.0)	0	(0.0)	0	(0.0)	162	(2.9)	324	(5.8)	486	(8.7)
Mauritania	651	57	(8.7)	0	(0.0)	0	(0.0)	0	(0.0)	0	(0.0)	88	(13.5)	131	(20.1)	219	(33.7)
Morocco	15,707	81	(0.5)	1,199	(7.6)	1,212	(7.7)	516	(3.3)	556	(3.5)	1,226	(7.8)	612	(3.9)	1,838	(11.7)
Tunisia	11,451	82	(0.7)	222	(1.9)	236	(2.1)	391	(3.4)	433	(3.8)	250	(2.2)	490	(4.3)	741	(6.5)

GDP

Maghreb	225,593	567	(0.3)	2,087	(0.9)	2,156	(1.0)	3,040	(1.3)	3,252	(1.4)	2,492	(1.1)	4,027	(1.8)	6,519	(2.9)
Algeria	101,786	234	(0.2)	354	(0.3)	395	(0.4)	2,021	(2.0)	2,143	(2.1)	438	(0.4)	2,311	(2.3)	2,749	(2.7)
Libya	41,667	104	(0.3)	0	(0.0)	0	(0.0)	0	(0.0)	0	(0.0)	185	(0.4)	370	(0.9)	555	(1.3)
Mauritania	1,837	49	(2.7)	0	(0.0)	0	(0.0)	0	(0.0)	0	(0.0)	76	(4.1)	113	(6.2)	189	(10.3)
Morocco	51,621	103	(0.2)	1,527	(3.0)	1,544	(3.0)	657	(1.3)	709	(1.4)	1,562	(3.0)	780	(1.5)	2,342	(4.5)
Tunisia	28,683	76	(0.3)	205	(0.7)	218	(0.8)	361	(1.3)	400	(1.4)	231	(0.8)	453	(1.6)	684	(2.4)

Source: Author's calculations based on the initial impacts on merchandise trade of Maghreb integration scenarios in table 6.3 and Cline's (2004) finding that the long-term elasticity of output per head with respect to openness, as measured by total trade relative to GDP, tends to equal 0.5 across a wide variety of empirical studies.

Table 6.6 Employment and growth impacts of increased foreign direct investment under Maghreb economic integration scenarios

Country	Arab Maghreb Union	EU and US bilateral FTAs				EU and US regional FTAs		
		EU-Alg EU-Mor EU-Tun	EU-Alg+ EU-Mor+ EU-Tun+	US-Alg US-Mor US-Tun	US-Alg+ US-Mor+ US-Tun+	EU-Maghreb	US-Maghreb	EU-US-Maghreb
Average increase in foreign direct investment, 2001–05 (millions of US dollars at 2005 prices)								
Maghreb	78	2,325	2,396	1,112	1,427	3,186	2,621	5,806
Algeria	24	727	761	610	758	798	968	1,766
Libya	23	0	0	0	0	630	728	1,358
Mauritania	1	0	0	0	0	83	19	102
Morocco	14	1,118	1,135	246	323	1,153	432	1,585
Tunisia	16	481	500	256	346	521	474	995
Average increase in foreign direct investment, 2001–05 (percent of GDP)								
Maghreb	0.0	1.0	1.1	0.5	0.6	1.4	1.2	2.6
Algeria	0.0	0.7	0.7	0.6	0.7	0.8	1.0	1.7
Libya	0.1	0.0	0.0	0.0	0.0	1.5	1.7	3.3
Mauritania	0.1	0.0	0.0	0.0	0.0	4.5	1.0	5.6
Morocco	0.0	2.2	2.2	0.5	0.6	2.2	0.8	3.1
Tunisia	0.1	1.7	1.7	0.9	1.2	1.8	1.7	3.5
Employment gain (number of workers)								
Maghreb	869	25,837	26,618	12,354	15,854	35,397	29,117	64,513
Algeria	270	8,075	8,454	6,779	8,423	8,866	10,757	19,623
Libya	260	0	0	0	0	7,003	8,087	15,091
Mauritania	12	0	0	0	0	928	207	1,135
Morocco	151	12,420	12,608	2,728	3,584	12,811	4,800	17,612
Tunisia	177	5,342	5,556	2,847	3,846	5,788	5,265	11,053
GDP growth (percentage points)								
Maghreb	0.0	0.5	0.5	0.2	0.3	0.7	0.6	1.3
Algeria	0.0	0.4	0.4	0.3	0.4	0.4	0.5	0.9
Libya	0.0	0.0	0.0	0.0	0.0	0.8	0.9	1.6
Mauritania	0.0	0.0	0.0	0.0	0.0	2.3	0.5	2.8
Morocco	0.0	1.1	1.1	0.2	0.3	1.1	0.4	1.5
Tunisia	0.0	0.8	0.9	0.4	0.6	0.9	0.8	1.7

Source: Tables 6.4 and 6.5 and author's calculations assuming that $90,000 in new foreign direct investment (FDI) supports each additional job and that increasing the inflow rate of FDI by 2 percent of GDP will increase the growth rate by 1 percentage point.

AMU plan results in total increased Maghreb employment of just under 875 workers, the EU and US FTAs result in vastly higher employment growth in the Maghreb. Bilateral EU and US FTAs with the major Maghreb countries could create total gains of 12,000 to 27,000 jobs, while the EU and US regional FTAs involving all five AMU countries result in total employment gains more than two times greater: 29,000 to 65,000 workers added to the Maghreb's formal employment rolls.

Finally, table 6.6 considers the impacts on growth in the Maghreb economies resulting from the increases in inward FDI stocks under the Maghreb integration scenarios. The growth impacts are based on recent review by Hufbauer and Adler (2008) of an extensive body of empirical studies on the benefits of inward FDI, especially for host developing countries. These studies suggest that increasing FDI inflows by 2 percent of aggregate output (GDP) tends to increase the growth rate of the economy by 1 percentage point. In table 6.6 it is apparent on applying this norm that the AMU plan does not contribute appreciably to growth in the region because it does not increase foreign investment perceptibly among the member countries. However, the story is different when the major Maghreb countries pursue bilateral FTAs with the United States and especially the European Union: Average growth rates in the region increase by between 0.2 percentage points (US bilateral FTAs) and 0.5 percentage points (EU bilateral FTAs). When the AMU purses regional FTAs with the two external trading partners, average growth in the Maghreb increases by between 0.7 percentage points (EU or US) and 1.3 percentage points (EU and US combined).

References

Allain, Laurence, and Boileau Loko. 2007. Fresh Impetus toward Maghreb Integration. *IMF Survey* 36, no. 12: 188–89.

Bergsten, C. Fred. 1996. *Competitive Liberalization and Global Free Trade: A Vision for the Early 21st Century*. Working Paper 96-15. Washington: Institute for International Economics.

Brenton, Paul, Eugenia Baroncelli, and Mariem Malouche. 2006. *Trade and Investment Integration of the Maghreb*. Middle East and North Africa Working Paper Series 44. Washington: World Bank.

Cline, William A. 2004. *Trade Policy and Global Poverty*. Washington: Center for Global Development and Peterson Institute for International Economics.

Dennis, Allen. 2006. *The Impact of Regional Trade Agreements and Trade Facilitation in the Middle East and North Africa Region*. Policy Research Working Paper WPS 3837. Washington: World Bank.

DeRosa, Dean A. 2007. *International Trade and Investment Data Set by 1-Digit SITC, 1976–2005*. Washington: Peterson Institute for International Economics.

DeRosa, Dean A., and Gary Clyde Hufbauer. 2007. "What Do Gravity Models Tell Us about PTAs' Impacts on Trade Flows: More Creation or More Diversion?" Available at voxeu.org (accessed July 8, 2008).

Eichengreen, Barry, and Douglas A. Irwin. 1998. The Role of History in Bilateral Trade Flows. In *The Regionalization of the World Economy*, ed. Jeffrey A. Frankel. Chicago: University of Chicago Press.

Hufbauer, Gary C., and Matthew Adler. 2008. FDI Promotion in Nicaragua. Peterson Institute for International Economics, Washington. Photocopy (May 23, 2008).

Plumper, Thomas, and Vera E. Troeger. 2007. Efficient Estimation of Time-Invariant and Rarely Changing Variables in Finite Sample Panel Analyses with Unit Fixed Effects. *Political Analysis* 15, no. 2: 124–39.

Rose, Andrew K. 2004. Do We Really Know That the WTO Increases Trade? *American Economic Review* 94, no. 1: 98–114.

Tahiri, Amor, Patricia Brenner, Erik DeVrijer, Marina Moretti, Abdelhak Senhadji Semlali, Gabrial Sensenbrenner, and Juan Sole. 2007. *Financial-Sector Reforms and Prospects for Financial Integration in Maghreb Countries.* Working Paper 07/125. Washington: International Monetary Fund.

UNCTAD (UN Conference on Trade and Development). 2005. Generalized System of Preferences. Available at www.unctad.org (accessed July 4, 2008).

Wonnacott, Richard J. 1996. Trade and Investment in a Hub-and-Spoke System vs. a Free Trade Area. *The World Economy* 19, no. 3: 237–52.

World Bank. 2006. *Is There a New Vision for Maghreb Economic Integration?* World Bank Report 38359. Washington.

7

Evaluation of Trade Integration Using the Mirage Model

MARCELLE THOMAS, MOHAMED HEDI BCHIR, ANTOINE BOUËT, and BETINA DIMARANAN

The Maghreb countries share more than geographical proximity and similarities in culture, language, and religion. Notwithstanding the differences in their sizes and income levels, the five North African countries face similar economic and political challenges arising from long-standing records of poor economic growth, high unemployment (as formally measured), and limited integration, both in the global economy and across the southern Mediterranean region (International Food Policy Research Institute and International Fund for Agricultural Development 2007).

Our study focuses on the challenge of forging greater integration among the Maghreb economies and with the outside world. Using a computable general equilibrium model, we explore the prospective impacts of bilateral and regional free trade agreements (FTAs) for the Maghreb countries in two steps. The first step consists of examining the benefits of greater south-south integration under the auspices of the Arab Maghreb Union (AMU) compared with the benefits of greater north-south integration of the Maghreb countries with the European Union and the United States. The second step extends the analysis to consider the long-run impacts of

Marcelle Thomas is a research analyst in the Markets, Trade, and Institutions Division of the International Food Policy Research Institute (IFPRI). Mohamed Hedi Bchir is principal country economist at the African Development Bank in Egypt. Antoine Bouët has been a senior research fellow in the Markets, Trade, and Institutions Division of IFPRI since February 2005. Betina Dimaranan has been a research fellow in the Markets, Trade, and Institutions Division of IFPRI since July 2007.

more intense market competition within Maghreb economies by liberalizing trade and adopting complementary economic policies: liberalization of trade in services, trade facilitation initiatives, and increased domestic investment.

After World War II, trade regimes in the Maghreb were founded on the twin models of import substitution and large public sector involvement to promote industry and modernize more rapidly. Since the 1990s globalization and international competition have sparked greater interest in trade liberalization within the Maghreb and contributed to some reduction in tariff levels and dismantling of nontariff barriers. Nonetheless, the Maghreb today maintains high levels of protection and a rigid and unfavorable business environment. Despite the region's potential, the free flow of goods and productive resources in the Maghreb remains elusive, mainly for political reasons. Thus the structure and orientation of Maghreb trade are still dominated by the traditional profile of agricultural and mineral exports and trade relations with Europe (table 7.1).[1]

To quantify the impacts on the Maghreb countries of prospective FTAs and complementary economic policies, this study uses Mirage, a global general equilibrium model. Mirage is a multisector model that captures intraregional and interregional linkages among trading partners in the global economy based on the extensive Global Trade Analysis Project (GTAP 6.2) database of social accounting matrices and the MAcMapHS6-v2 database of applied tariffs.[2]

This chapter is organized into three sections. The first section introduces the model, lays out the decomposition of regions and sectors selected for the study, and describes the basic dimensions of protection in the Maghreb countries. The second section briefly introduces the Maghreb FTA scenarios that we consider and presents the simulation results carried out in the static and dynamic steps of the analysis. The final section highlights the major findings and conclusions.

Model and Database

The multisector and multiregion Mirage model was developed by the Centre d'Etudes Prospectives et d'Informations Internationales (CEPII). The dynamic version of the model incorporates a sequential recursive framework that accounts for worldwide projections of GDP and population growth through 2020 and modifies national stocks of physical capital

---

1. In addition to the discussion in other chapters of this volume, see International Food Policy Research Institute and International Fund for Agricultural Development (2007).

2. For a full description of the model see Bchir et al. (2002) and Decreux and Valin (2007). For a discussion of the GTAP 6.2, see Dimaranan (2006). For a discussion of the MAcMapHS6-v2 dataset, see Bouët et al. (2006).

Table 7.1   Maghreb trade relations and exports, 2006 (percent)

Category	Algeria	Libya	Mauritania[b]	Morocco	Tunisia
WTO status	Observer	Observer	Member	Member	Member
Trade openness (2004–06)[a]	35.4	50.8	59.7	38.3	50.6
Composition of merchandise exports					
Agricultural products	0.2	0.0	41.5	20.7	12.7
Fuels and mining products	98.8	98.0	58.5	12.9	15.9
Manufactures	1.0	2.0	Negligible	64.9	71.3
Destination of merchandise exports					
European Union	52.5	75.8	75.9	73.1	80.1
United States	27.2	6.1	n.a.	1.9	n.a.
Japan	n.a.	n.a.	13.8	n.a	n.a.
Canada	6.6	n.a.	n.a.	n.a	n.a.
Algeria	n.a.	n.a.	2.5	n.a	1.7
Libya	n.a.	n.a.	n.a.	n.a	4.5
Morocco	n.a.	n.a.	n.a.	n.a	1.0
Tunisia	n.a.	1.5	n.a.	n.a	n.a.
Brazil	3.5	n.a.	n.a.	2.3	n.a.
China	n.a.	3.9	1.5	n.a	n.a.
India	n.a.	n.a.	n.a.	4.3	n.a.
Nigeria	n.a.	n.a.	1.7	n.a	n.a.
Turkey	3.4	5.3	n.a.	n.a	n.a.
Switzerland	n.a.	n.a.	n.a.	1.3	n.a.

n.a. = not available
WTO = World Trade Organization

a. Average trade relative to GDP.
b. Mauritania's main exports are fisheries products and iron ore. Figures are for 1999.

Sources: WTO Country Profiles, 2008; WTO Trade Policy Review for Mauritania, 2002; and International Monetary Fund, *Direction of Trade Statistics*, 2007 for Libya.

each year to account for depreciation and investment growth. The dynamic version also assumes that monopolistic competition holds for some sectors, including most service sectors. Agriculture, primary commodities, and transport services, however, are assumed to be perfectly competitive with constant returns to scale. Our study obtains macroeconomic closure of the model by assuming that the balance of payments on goods and services plus foreign direct investment (FDI) is constant for each country and region.

The Mirage model uses the GTAP 6.2 database for baseline national accounts and international trade data and the MAcMap-HS6 database for bilateral data on applied protection of goods. The GTAP 6.2 database combines national and regional input-output (I-O) tables adjusted to match international datasets on macroeconomic aggregates, bilateral merchandise and services trade, protection, and energy. The data contain detailed economic information for 96 countries and regions as well as 57 sectors representing global economic activity for 2001, the reference year. Because the GTAP 6.2 dataset includes data for only two Maghreb countries—Morocco and Tunisia—we have augmented it with social accounting matrices for Algeria, Libya, and Mauritania.[3]

The MAcMapHS6-v2 (2004) database on protection provides equivalent measures of applied protection at the six-digit level of the Harmonized System (HS) for 5,111 products, 166 reporting countries, and 208 trading partners. The equivalent protection measure combines ad valorem tariffs and ad valorem equivalent measures of specific tariffs, tariff quotas, prohibitions, and antidumping duties. All these are measured at the bilateral level, accounting for the large number of preferential trade agreements that have been implemented through 2004. The Mirage model aggregates the MAcMap bilateral measures of protection across regions and products using a weighting methodology created by CEPII and based on reference groups of countries instead of the standard import-weighted average of protection.[4] The database is supported by reconciled data on bilateral trade averaged over 2002–04.

Regional Decomposition

Our study's geographical decomposition divides the global economy into 15 regions, including the five Maghreb countries and their main trading partners (table 7.2). Among developed countries the European Union and United States are the richest markets and the sources of the largest trade preferences for the developing world. Japan maintains extremely high protection in agriculture. In the developing world China, India, and Brazil are the largest exporters, highly protected in the case of India (table 7.2).

Table 7.3 presents the rates of protection that limit bilateral trade in agricultural products and industrial goods among the Maghreb countries, the European Union, and the United States. In our study these protection rates indicate the magnitude of applied tariffs governing intra-Maghreb

---

3. The I-O data for the three missing Maghreb countries were constructed from I-O data of GTAP countries with a similar economic structure. The data for Algeria and Libya were based on I-O data for Iran. Data for Mauritania were based on I-O data for Senegal. The I-O tables were adjusted to match external data on macroeconomic aggregates, bilateral trade data, and energy data specific to the three Maghreb countries.

4. This reference-group weighting scheme reduces the endogeneity bias in measuring protection and usually provides better assessments of average protection. See Bouët et al. (2006).

Table 7.2 Geographical protection and market access, 2004
(equivalent applied tariffs, percent)

Country/region	Tariffs on imports			Tariffs facing exports		
	Total	Agriculture	Industry	Total	Agriculture	Industry
EU-25	1.9	10.3	1.3	3.3	10.6	2.6
United States	2.1	3.6	2.0	5.3	18.7	3.9
Japan	3.5	28.7	1.3	5.6	15.0	5.5
Other developed countries	6.0	30.3	3.9	4.9	20.4	3.6
Algeria	13.3	16.0	13.0	1.5	12.6	1.5
Libya	21.0	13.1	21.7	1.6	6.5	1.5
Mauritania	8.7	9.2	8.7	5.6	9.0	1.6
Morocco	19.3	41.3	17.3	4.8	9.6	3.6
Tunisia	19.7	50.7	16.9	5.0	20.2	3.8
Egypt	14.4	60.0	10.3	5.3	16.6	3.7
Other Africa	13.1	21.9	11.9	4.9	12.8	3.4
China	5.4	14.6	4.6	5.4	18.3	4.9
India	18.9	55.9	14.7	6.6	18.6	5.1
Brazil	10.7	10.2	10.7	10.9	26.7	4.9
Other developing countries	8.3	18.3	7.4	4.4	19.0	3.2
Memoranda items: Group averages						
Maghreb countries	17.0	30.2	16.0	2.6	11.7	2.1
Developing countries	8.0	19.5	7.3	5.0	19.1	3.8
Developed countries	2.8	13.7	1.9	4.0	13.9	3.3

Source: Authors' calculations based on MAcMapHS6-v2 dataset, 2004.

trade and Maghreb trade with partners of primary interest—here, the European Union and the United States.[5]

Sectoral Decomposition

The sector decomposition in our study identifies the product categories most important to the Maghreb region (see table 7.4). The six agricultural sectors in the model include fruits and vegetables, which are major agricultural exports for Algeria and Morocco and, when combined with olive oil, account for half of Tunisia's agricultural exports. The agricultural sectors in the model also tend to be highly protected globally, including by the European Union (table 7.2). Regarding the industrial sectors in the model, fuels and mining products lead the foreign exchange earnings of

---

5. MAcMap zero tariffs between Morocco and Algeria correctly reflect official preferential margins between the two countries, but they do not reflect nontariff barriers to trade such as closed borders due to political tensions between the two countries. See chapter 11 in this book.

Table 7.3 Bilateral applied rates of tariff protection among the European Union, United States, and Maghreb countries, 2004 (percent)

| | Importer | | | | | | | |
	European Union	United States	Algeria	Libya	Mauritania	Morocco	Tunisia	World
Exporter								
Agriculture								
European Union		4.4	19.6	15.0	11.1	41.3	62.3	10.6
United States	19.1		10.7	11.6	9.2	37.3	38.5	18.7
Algeria	5.9	5.1		13.0	16.3	0.0	94.7	12.6
Libya	5.1	0.9	9.6		5.9	0.0	16.3	6.5
Mauritania	0.2	0.1	29.6	0.9		0.4	42.6	9.0
Morocco	3.9	2.2	0.0	0.0	15.7		32.1	9.6
Tunisia	33.3	2.1	25.5	8.8	12.2	17.9		20.2
World	10.3	3.6	16.0	13.1	9.2	41.3	50.7	
Industry								
European Union		2.2	13.4	22.7	9.3	12.3	11.5	2.6
United States	2.2		11.4	20.3	7.7	17.2	20.0	3.9
Algeria	0.0	0.7		37.4	11.0	0.0	5.6	1.5
Libya	0.7	0.8	9.8		8.8	0.0	3.5	1.5
Mauritania	0.0	0.3	6.1	0.4		0.9	20.7	1.6
Morocco	0.0	5.6	0.0	0.0	3.1		9.4	3.6
Tunisia	0.0	5.8	16.0	6.6	4.7	10.5		3.8
World	1.3	2.0	13.0	21.7	8.7	17.3	16.9	

Source: Authors' calculations based on MAcMapHS6-v2 dataset, 2004.

Algeria, Libya, and Mauritania. The major exports of Tunisia and Morocco are mainly concentrated in unskilled labor–intensive manufactures. The sectoral decomposition also includes five service sectors: construction, domestic trade and transportation, business services, other private services, and government services.

The tariff data in tables 7.2, 7.3, and 7.4 indicate that the Maghreb countries are highly protected economies. The average level of protection across all products is 17 percent, more than double the average protection among developing countries as a group (table 7.2). Within the region, Libya, Tunisia, and Morocco enforce the highest overall rates of protection, which range between 19 percent and 21 percent. Maghreb country exports face much lower rates of protection. The discrepancy in import and export protection is common to many developing countries, in part because of preferential access to markets in major developed countries granted under FTAs and nonreciprocal trade agreements such as the US Generalized System of Preferences and African Growth and Opportunity Act. However, for some Maghreb countries, such as Algeria and Libya, good market access may be the result of their specialization in exports of

Table 7.4   Applied tariffs on Maghreb imports from the European Union and United States, 2004 (percent)

Sector	Algeria	Libya	Mauritania	Morocco	Tunisia
	Imports from the European Union				
Agriculture					
Grains	3.8	11.8	1.8	59.0	78.6
Other crops	9.2	5.1	9.9	11.9	37.5
Livestock and meat products	17.5	13.8	11.1	72.6	77.7
Oilseeds and vegetable oils	19.1	9.3	4.5	15.7	44.2
Vegetables and fruit	20.1	21.8	15.7	44.6	139.7
Processed food products	26.4	18.9	13.8	28.7	50.7
Industry					
Fishing	28.1	3.5	18.3	43.5	40.8
Coal, oil, and gas	6.7	71.6	5.4	1.2	4.8
Mineral products	19.7	20.2	19.2	19.1	19.1
Textiles	24.6	14.3	13.9	26.7	17.7
Wearing apparel	30.0	24.1	19.7	44.6	27.8
Leather products	17.9	13.0	9.8	36.9	22.4
Wood and paper	18.6	12.6	7.7	31.3	23.8
Petroleum and coal products	21.1	2.2	12.5	0.5	6.0
Chemicals, rubber and plastics	12.9	10.0	4.7	13.7	8.1
Metals	15.9	9.3	8.1	13.6	15.4
Motor vehicles and transport equipment	9.6	65.9	8.2	13.7	10.3
Electronic equipment, machinery	10.7	17.0	7.0	5.5	9.1
Other manufactures	25.5	40.2	18.9	9.7	24.8
Utilities	15.0	0.0	16.6	0.0	0.0
	Imports from the United States				
Agriculture					
Grains	3.7	8.7	7.1	78.1	49.2
Other crops	6.3	0.8	5.7	6.0	6.6
Livestock and meat products	19.2	26.4	14.1	45.5	63.0
Oilseeds and vegetable oils	6.7	10.8	5.3	12.6	17.3
Vegetables and fruit	25.7	27.7	19.9	48.0	155.9
Processed food products	25.6	15.1	12.1	36.8	54.9
Industry					
Fishing	29.4	3.9	18.3	47.0	40.9
Coal, oil, and gas	5.3	21.9	5.0	17.5	18.2
Mineral products	14.4	14.3	12.8	24.2	27.7
Textiles	22.9	13.2	11.8	32.8	28.2
Wearing apparel	30.0	20.0	20.0	50.0	42.0
Leather products	19.1	13.1	15.5	42.6	38.2
Wood and paper	13.9	7.9	7.1	32.5	27.9
Petroleum and coal products	20.9	2.4	12.6	36.6	8.3
Chemicals, rubber and plastics	13.1	9.3	5.3	21.9	23.8
Metals	15.9	9.4	8.9	23.6	24.7
Motor vehicles and transport equipment	4.2	50.1	3.0	11.2	17.3
Electronic equipment, machinery	9.3	20.4	7.3	9.8	16.9
Other manufactures	27.6	48.3	19.6	32.0	38.3
Utilities	5.5	9.5	13.0	24.7	19.1

Source: Authors' calculations based on MAcMapHS6-v2 dataset, 2004.

primary products that face little protection globally, such as fuels and petroleum products.

Agricultural protection in the Maghreb is particularly high with respect to intra-Maghreb trade (table 7.3). Algeria imposes tariffs of 30 percent and 26 percent on agricultural imports from Mauritania and Tunisia, respectively, but an average tariff of only 16 percent on agricultural imports overall. By contrast, protection of industry in the Maghreb is generally lower—except in Libya—and discrimination against intraregional trade is less prevalent.

Regarding imports from the European Union and the United States, vegetables, fruits, livestock, meat products, and grains are among the most highly protected sectors in Morocco and Tunisia (table 7.4). Algeria, Libya, and Mauritania apply relatively high tariffs on imports of vegetable and fruits as well as processed food products from the European Union and United States. Protection of unskilled labor–intensive other manufacturing is relatively high in Algeria, Libya, and Mauritania. Wearing apparel, also intensive in unskilled labor, ranks among the most protected sectors in Algeria, Libya, Mauritania, and Morocco. By contrast, the Maghreb countries face high tariffs on only a few exports to the European Union and the United States (table 7.5), though these include grain exports. Maghreb oilseeds and vegetable oils also are subject to high tariffs in the European Union, and Maghreb exports of textiles and wearing apparel face relatively high rates of protection in the United States.

In sum, the Maghreb countries appear to enjoy relatively open access to foreign markets while maintaining highly protected domestic markets. As a consequence, establishing a series of FTAs between the Maghreb countries and the European Union or the United States might not increase Maghreb exports sufficiently to finance greater regional imports and increase real income. It remains, however, to apply the Mirage model to quantify the static and dynamic impacts of different Maghreb integration scenarios on trade and national income.

Trade Liberalization Options and Impacts for Maghreb Countries

We apply the Mirage model to the same scenarios for Maghreb integration considered in the preceding gravity model analysis (see chapter 6). The first scenario involves south-south integration under the AMU, specifying a functioning regional free trade area that permits the free circulation of goods in the Maghreb. The second involves north-south integration, realized by a number of stylized bilateral and regional FTAs between selected Maghreb countries, on the one hand, and the European Union and the United States—both separately and combined—on the other hand. The final scenario analyzes multilateral trade integration represented by a full trade liberalization scenario, in which all countries—the Maghreb countries,

Table 7.5   Applied tariffs on Maghreb exports to the European Union and United States, 2004 (percent)

Sector	Algeria	Libya	Mauritania	Morocco	Tunisia
	Exports to the European Union				
Agriculture					
Grains	155.5	155.5	0.0	35.5	100.0
Other crops	0.2	0.4	0.0	0.3	1.6
Livestock and meat products	17.9	2.4	0.0	8.8	9.0
Oilseeds and vegetable oils	59.2	0.0	0.0	60.0	64.3
Vegetables and fruit	2.7	3.7	0.3	1.9	2.4
Processed food products	1.5	7.1	0.2	1.6	2.1
Industry					
Fishing	0.0	5.2	0.0	0.0	0.0
Coal, oil, and gas	0.0	0.0	0.0	0.0	0.0
Mineral products	0.0	0.0	0.0	0.0	0.0
Textiles	0.0	4.4	0.0	0.0	0.0
Wearing apparel	0.0	9.3	0.0	0.0	0.0
Leather products	0.0	0.7	0.0	0.0	0.0
Wood and paper	0.0	0.0	0.0	0.0	0.0
Petroleum and coal products	0.0	3.2	0.0	0.0	0.0
Chemicals, rubber, and plastics	0.0	1.5	0.0	0.0	0.0
Metals	0.0	0.1	0.0	0.0	0.0
Motor vehicles and transport equipment	0.0	0.5	0.0	0.0	0.0
Electronic equipment, machinery	0.0	0.1	0.0	0.0	0.0
Other manufactures	0.0	0.1	0.0	0.0	0.0
Utilities	0.0	0.0	0.0	0.0	0.0
	Exports to the United States				
Agriculture					
Grains	8.3	8.3	0.0	2.9	2.6
Other crops	0.1	2.0	0.0	0.3	1.0
Livestock and meat products	2.6	0.4	0.0	1.1	2.2
Oilseeds and vegetable oils	3.9	14.7	0.0	0.9	0.1
Vegetables and fruit	8.3	7.7	0.0	3.4	8.4
Processed food products	3.6	1.1	0.1	1.7	2.0
Industry					
Fishing	0.3	1.4	0.0	0.0	0.2
Coal, oil, and gas	0.2	0.4	0.0	0.0	0.4
Mineral products	0.1	0.0	0.0	0.1	1.3
Textiles	10.0	5.9	10.4	13.3	11.1
Wearing apparel	12.4	15.6	9.9	11.5	10.6
Leather products	1.5	1.1	0.0	8.9	8.4
Wood and paper	0.3	0.6	0.0	0.1	0.0
Petroleum and coal products	1.9	2.4	0.0	1.6	1.6
Chemicals, rubber, and plastics	1.0	1.4	0.1	0.0	0.1
Metals	0.4	0.1	0.0	0.2	0.1
Motor vehicles and transport equipment	3.0	0.4	0.0	0.3	0.5
Electronic equipment, machinery	1.1	1.1	0.0	0.1	0.0
Other manufactures	2.3	3.6	0.0	0.4	1.2
Utilities	0.0	0.0	0.0	0.0	0.0

Source: Authors' calculations based on MAcMapHS6-v2 dataset, 2004.

the European Union, and the United States—fully liberalize their protection against each other. The final scenario of economic integration through multilateral trade integration could not be carried out in the gravity model analysis. It is important, however, because it provides a first-best yardstick by which to judge the efficacy of the bilateral and regional FTA scenarios.

Static Analysis

Our static analysis abstracts from the dynamic features of the Mirage model and assumes perfect competition in all sectors. Trade policy changes are assumed to occur instantaneously. The economic impacts that the model estimates reflect changes to trade and other variables arising from the tariff reforms of each Maghreb integration scenario relative to the state of the world before the tariff changes.

Impacts on Total Exports

Under the AMU scenario the changes in total exports simulated by the model are modest, ranging from 0.5 percent in Morocco to 4.4 percent in Tunisia (table 7.6). The limited EU bilateral FTAs with the three major Maghreb countries—Algeria, Morocco, and Tunisia—can result in considerable export gains: according to the model, around 43 percent for Tunisia, 37 percent for Morocco, and 8 percent for Algeria. They also result in greater export gains than the limited US bilateral FTAs with the same three Maghreb countries. When the EU and US bilateral FTAs are extended to allow Mauritania and Libya simultaneous free access to the Algerian, Moroccan, and Tunisian markets, export gains for all Maghreb countries are greater, though only marginally so. In general these simulation results show that Maghreb exports face higher initial tariffs in the European Union than they do in the United States. Export gains for Morocco and Tunisia are larger under the EU bilateral FTAs because of the relatively high EU tariffs on fruits, vegetables, oilseeds, and vegetable oils.

When the EU and US bilateral FTAs are expanded to become free trade areas—that is, regional FTAs combining full Maghreb regional integration with reciprocal free trade with the European Union or United States—additional export gains are small for the three major Maghreb countries, but more significant for Libya and Mauritania. However, the hypothesized EU-US-Maghreb FTA is the most beneficial to total Maghreb exports, second only to the trade benefits of full trade liberalization (table 7.6).

Impacts on Bilateral Trade

The EU-Maghreb FTA diverts imports from the United States, but mainly creates trade in exports for the European Union and the Maghreb countries

Table 7.6 Static analysis: Impacts on exports, terms of trade, and national income under Maghreb integration scenarios (percent)

Country	Arab Maghreb Union	EU and US bilateral FTAs				EU and US regional FTAs			
		EU-Maghreb		US-Maghreb		EU-Maghreb	US-Maghreb	EU-US-Maghreb	Full trade liberalization
		Limited	Extended	Limited	Extended				
Total exports									
Algeria	1.2	8.1	8.9	1.0	2.1	8.8	2.1	8.6	10.6
Libya	1.3	-0.1	2.2	0.0	1.3	11.0	1.4	9.0	13.1
Mauritania	0.6	0.0	0.6	0.0	0.5	4.1	0.8	3.8	4.3
Morocco	0.5	37.1	37.5	4.4	4.8	37.4	4.8	39.8	47.8
Tunisia	4.4	42.7	45.9	4.0	8.2	45.4	8.2	-1.0	47.8
Terms of trade									
Algeria	0.1	-0.9	-0.8	-0.1	0.0	-0.9	0.0	-1.1	-1.3
Libya	0.1	0.0	0.2	0.1	0.2	-0.7	0.1	-0.9	-0.4
Mauritania	0.0	0.1	0.2	0.0	0.0	-1.1	0.0	-1.4	-2.2
Morocco	0.0	-6.0	-5.9	-0.7	-0.6	-6.0	-0.6	-6.1	-8.1
Tunisia	-0.1	-2.0	-1.8	-0.7	-0.8	-2.0	-0.8	-0.3	-4.1
National income									
Algeria	0.0	-0.8	-0.8	-0.2	-0.2	-0.8	-0.2	-0.9	-0.6
Libya	-0.1	0.0	0.0	0.0	-0.1	-1.3	-0.1	-1.3	-1.1
Mauritania	-0.1	0.1	-0.1	0.0	-0.1	-1.0	-0.2	-1.1	-0.6
Morocco	0.0	-0.3	-0.3	-0.3	-0.3	-0.3	-0.3	-0.1	0.8
Tunisia	0.2	1.0	1.4	-0.5	-0.2	1.4	-0.2	-0.1	2.6

FTA = free trade agreement

Source: Static MIRAGE model results.

Table 7.7   Static analysis: Impacts on bilateral trade of EU and US regional FTAs with the Maghreb countries (percent)

Exporting country	Importing country						
	European Union	United States	Algeria	Libya	Mauritania	Morocco	Tunisia
EU-Maghreb FTA							
European Union		−0.3	38.5	53.9	19.2	73.4	56.1
United States	0.2		−20.3	−12.7	−15.2	−24.3	−25.2
Algeria	9.3	4.0		7.3	12.5	−3.5	173.2
Libya	7.3	8.0	29.4		−8.9	−10.2	243.0
Mauritania	3.3	4.8	4.0	−1.9		16.8	98.9
Morocco	48.1	19.9	−20.5	−9.4	74.7		81.2
Tunisia	63.8	−4.5	71.3	−2.6	16.2	47.6	
EU-US-Maghreb FTA							
European Union		11.1	33.3	51.2	16.9	70.9	−1.3
United States	12.3		6.2	−7.5	1.0	56.3	−2.2
Algeria	9.5	8.8		5.8	12.9	−6.5	8.4
Libya	9.2	13.1	29.1		−7.3	−12.2	12.2
Mauritania	3.2	7.1	0.5	−3.9		14.2	0.9
Morocco	48.6	43.9	−21.0	−10.6	72.0		25.0
Tunisia	0.2	1.1	−39.7	−36.5	−22.7	−33.7	

FTA = free trade agreement

Source: Static MIRAGE model results.

(upper panel of table 7.7). Except for Tunisia's trade with the United States, Maghreb exports to both the European Union and the United States increase. Trade in the Maghreb is also enhanced, but Libya's increased imports from the European Union and Algeria must be weighed against its reduced imports from the United States and the other Maghreb countries.

Expanding the EU-Maghreb FTA to include the United States increases US trade (lower panel of table 7.7). Tunisia's exports to the United States grow at the expense of its exports to other FTA partners. Tunisia increases its imports from the region and decreases its imports from the European Union and the United States. The other Maghreb countries show the same pattern of trade changes with the European Union as found for the EU-Maghreb FTA, but increased trade with the United States comes at the expense of intra-Maghreb trade.

Impacts on Terms of Trade and Real Income

Morocco and Tunisia generally see their terms of trade worsen under the Maghreb integration scenarios (table 7.6). However, this does not translate into real income losses for Tunisia, except under the FTAs involving the United States. Full trade liberalization results in terms of trade losses for the Maghreb countries owing to induced increases in world agricultural prices and lost trade preferences, particularly in the EU market. Terms of trade losses under the FTAs result from trade diversion effects that reflect the substitution of goods from inefficient producers for erstwhile imports from efficient producers. The US FTAs appear to result in smaller terms of trade losses than do the EU FTAs.

Overall the static analysis results suggest negative but small impacts on the Maghreb's terms of trade and real income. The Maghreb countries are not likely to gain much from south-south integration. The north-south FTAs benefit the Maghreb countries in GDP and exports gains, but also divert more trade and negatively affect terms of trade and real income. The impacts are greater and more substantial for the agrarian economies of Morocco and Tunisia than they are for the oil-exporting economies of Algeria, Libya, and Mauritania.

Dynamic Analysis

In our dynamic analysis we simulate the Mirage model following a sequential and dynamic recursive set-up. The model is first solved for one period; then the values of the model variables determined at the end of the first period are used as the initial values in the next period. In addition, selected sectors in the model—including textiles, wearing apparel, petroleum and coal products, and all services except domestic trade and transport—are assumed to be imperfectly competitive.[6]

The dynamic Mirage model generates a baseline extending from 2001 to 2020 based on World Bank projections of GDP and population levels through 2020.[7] In our application of the model the timeline to implement changes in tariffs and other policy instruments spans 2009 to 2018 and the simulation results reflect deviations from the baseline at the end of the period, 2020.

Modeling Complementary Policies

As mentioned above, the dynamic analysis considers the additional impacts of several complementary economic reforms expected to accompany Maghreb economic integration in the long run. Before presenting

---

6. Introducing imperfect competition is costly in terms of computational complexity in the Mirage model. Thus only a few sectors of the model are assumed to involve imperfect market conditions (i.e., aspects of monopolistic competition).

7. World Bank, *World Development Indicators 2007*, available at www.worldbank.org (accessed August 5, 2008).

the results, we briefly outline these complementary reforms and how they appear in the model.

Services Trade Liberalization. Services constitute an important and growing component of global trade. Barriers to trade in services are difficult to quantify because they emanate from domestic laws and regulations that vary widely across countries. These barriers restrict or prevent service firms from operating efficiently in foreign markets.

Our study depicts barriers to trade in services as quantitative restrictions on imports of construction, business services, trade and transportation, government services, and other services. Although these restrictions are imposed by the importing countries, they act as taxes on the service exports of partner countries, reducing the number of service firms abroad. We expect that lowering or eliminating the export taxes improves competition by increasing the number of exporting firms and reducing the price of imported services. We also expect liberalizing services to generate larger economic gains for service-importing countries than for service-exporting countries (Decreux and Fontagné 2006; Berisha-Krasniqi, Bouët, and Mevel 2006).

CEPII has collected data on the protection of services from two sources. The first source uses bilateral gravity equations to estimate the ad valorem equivalent of trade barriers in services (Park 2002). The second source is a set of trade restrictiveness indices constructed by the Australian Productivity Commission (Kalirajan 2000, McGuire 1998). Figure 7.1 presents the structure of protection for services in Maghreb countries based on these two sources. Computing the levels of protection as simple averages of the protection indices reported by the two sources, figure 7.1 shows that trade and transportation as well as the category of other services are less protected in the European Union and the United States than they are in the Maghreb.[8] Construction and business services are highly protected in all countries, especially the United States and Morocco. The dynamic analysis assumes that protection rates for services in the Mirage model are reduced by 50 percent to complement the EU-US-Maghreb FTA.

Trade Facilitation. The World Trade Organization (WTO 2008) specifies that negotiations in trade facilitation "shall aim to clarify and improve relevant aspects of Articles V, VIII, and X of the GATT [General Agreement on Tariffs and Trade] 1994." More specifically WTO members in the negotiations are directed to clarify and improve GATT Article V (freedom of transit), Article VIII (fees and formalities connected with importation and

---

8. Data on services trade for Libya and Mauritania are not available. The structure of the services barriers in these two countries was assumed to be similar to those of Algeria and Tunisia, respectively.

Figure 7.1   Protection of services by country and sector, 2006

percent

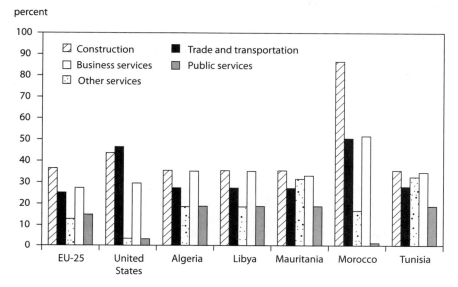

Source: Centre d'Etudes Prospectives et d'Informations Internationales.

exportation), and Article X (publication and administration of trade regulations), with a view to further expediting the movement, release, and clearance of goods, including goods in transit. In other words, trade facilitation aims to reduce the cost of transacting trade.

In the Mirage model, trade facilitation costs are modeled as iceberg costs: For every 100 units of a product exported, only x percent arrive at the destination. This loss is the result of cumbersome administrative requirements and procedural delays in processing goods through customs. According to studies cited in Berisha-Krasniqi, Bouët, and Mevel (2006), the potential losses from cumbersome customs requirements and delays can amount to between 1 and 15 percent of the value of international trade. Developing countries usually adopt less efficient trade facilitation measures than do developed countries, and consequently exports to developing countries face higher trade facilitation costs. In addition, trade facilitation costs are higher in agricultural and food sectors than in industrial sectors, mainly due to sanitary and phytosanitary controls and the expiration of perishable products (Berisha-Krasniqi, Bouët, and Mevel 2006). To reflect these considerations, the model estimates trade facilitation costs at 2 percent and 3 percent of the value of international trade for industry and agro-food sectors, respectively, in developed countries, and 5 and 7.5 percent, respectively, in developing countries. The dynamic analysis accounts for increased trade facilitation by reducing trade costs in the Maghreb countries by 50 percent in conjunction with the adoption of an EU-US-Maghreb FTA. Finally, given the current highly inefficient indirect trade route of energy products between Algeria and Morocco, we reduce the trade costs of oil and gas exports from Algeria to Morocco by an additional 15 percent of the value of bilateral exports.

Increased Domestic Investment. Finally, to assess the potential positive impact of trade liberalization on domestic investment, we follow the example of the steady-state variant of the Harrison, Rutherford, and Tarr (1996) model, in which trade and other economic reforms call for an expansion of physical capital sufficient to bring the real rate of return of capital back to its preliberalization rate. Over the long run, firms react to the new economic environment and accompanying business opportunities by increasing their investment until the returns to capital revert to their initial equilibrium. Because the Mirage model is a neoclassical savings-driven model, we represent this idea by assuming a 5 percent increase in the propensity to save in each Maghreb country in the EU-US-Maghreb FTA.

Table 7.8 summarizes the results of the dynamic analysis. The base scenario is the stylized EU-US-Maghreb FTA considered previously, but now simulated by the dynamic Mirage model. The model incorporates imperfect competition in selected sectors and the elimination of bilateral tariffs on agricultural and industrial goods, implemented linearly over a period of 10 years for the Maghreb countries and 5 years for the United States and European Union. The cumulative impacts of sequentially adding liberalization of trade in services, trade facilitation, and an increase in domestic investment are reported in table 7.8 for the five Maghreb countries individually, the European Union, and the United States.

Impact on Total Exports

In the long run, total exports increase for all countries under the EU-US-Maghreb FTA and the complementary policies contribute positively to the base scenario trade gains. Morocco and Tunisia enjoy the largest export gains overall, around 38 and 43 percent, respectively (table 7.8). This is due to the relatively high rates of protection for specialized agricultural exports (e.g, olive oil exports) and labor-intensive manufactures in both the European Union and the United States. Morocco and Tunisia also expand their exports to the rest of the Maghreb, where their exports face higher tariffs than the two countries apply to imports from the region. Regarding the benefits of complementary policies, liberalizing services offers the largest stimulus to Algerian, Mauritanian, and Moroccan exports; trade facilitation initiatives contribute most to Tunisian exports; and induced increases in domestic investment result in the largest export gains for Libya.

Table 7.8 Dynamic analysis: Macroeconomic impacts of the EU-US-Maghreb regional FTA sequentially adding complementary economic reforms (percent)

		Plus		
Category	Base: EU-US-Maghreb FTA	Liberalization of services	Trade facilitation	Increased domestic investment
		Algeria		
Real exports	12.3	17.7	19.8	24.5
Real GDP	0.9	2.1	2.7	6.3
Real exchange rate	−1.1	−0.1	−0.5	−1.5
Return to capital	−2.1	−1.9	−1.8	−3.5
Return to land	11.2	10.0	10.1	12.6
Return to natural resources	−3.4	−5.9	−5.3	−2.9
Skilled wages	0.0	4.6	6.2	12.3
Unskilled wages	2.8	4.4	5.1	9.3
Agriculture	6.2	6.9	7.4	11.2
Nonagriculture	1.2	3.2	4.0	8.4
Real national income	−0.1	1.1	1.9	3.3
Allocation efficiency	0.3	0.9	1.0	1.2
Terms of trade	−0.3	−0.4	0.0	−0.4
Capital accumulation	0.8	1.3	1.7	5.2
Other	−0.9	−0.6	−0.7	−2.7
		Libya		
Real exports	15.3	15.7	18.3	30.4
Real GDP	2.9	2.8	3.5	10.3
Real exchange rate	−5.6	−5.9	−6.8	−7.4
Return to capital	−3.3	−2.9	−3.1	−10.0
Return to land	−1.2	−0.8	−1.1	3.1
Return to natural resources	10.3	10.9	13.5	21.4
Skilled wages	1.2	0.6	1.9	12.0
Unskilled wages	−0.9	−0.9	−0.5	6.0
Agriculture	−1.4	−1.3	−1.2	4.8
Nonagriculture	−0.5	−0.6	0.0	6.8
Real national income	1.7	1.8	2.9	7.7
Allocation efficiency	0.3	0.2	0.3	0.4
Terms of trade	−0.6	−0.4	−0.1	−0.7
Capital accumulation	2.6	2.6	3.3	9.7
Other	−0.6	−0.6	−0.6	−1.8
		Mauritania		
Real exports	5.8	9.5	11.8	16.4
Real GDP	−0.1	0.4	1.1	4.2

(table continues next page)

Table 7.8   Dynamic analysis: Macroeconomic impacts of the EU-US-Maghreb regional FTA sequentially adding complementary economic reforms (percent)   *(continued)*

	Base: EU-US-Maghreb FTA	Plus		
Category		Liberalization of services	Trade facilitation	Increased domestic investment
Mauritania				
Real exchange rate	−1.7	−2.0	−2.5	−3.3
Return to capital	−0.2	0.7	1.4	−0.9
Return to land	−5.7	−4.3	−4.9	−3.7
Return to natural resources	−2.9	−0.8	1.0	4.3
Skilled wages	−2.1	−1.3	0.7	3.7
Unskilled wages	−2.9	−1.6	−0.7	1.5
Agriculture	−4.2	−2.8	−2.5	−0.6
Nonagriculture	−2.0	−0.8	0.5	2.8
Real national income	−0.8	0.3	1.7	2.3
Allocation efficiency	0.0	0.2	0.2	0.4
Terms of trade	−0.9	−0.4	0.3	−0.2
Capital accumulation	0.1	0.2	0.6	2.8
Other	0.0	0.3	0.6	−0.6
Morocco				
Real exports	37.8	42.6	47.9	50.5
Real GDP	0.9	1.4	2.0	3.9
Real exchange rate	−5.7	−5.1	−5.4	−5.6
Return to capital	1.5	1.6	1.9	−1.8
Return to land	−13.6	−14.6	−14.8	−13.8
Return to natural resources	−1.5	−2.7	−1.6	0.3
Skilled wages	3.4	4.9	6.8	10.8
Unskilled wages	−2.3	−1.9	−0.9	1.4
Agriculture	−7.5	−7.7	−7.2	−5.3
Nonagriculture	−0.2	0.3	1.4	3.9
Real national income	−0.2	0.2	1.2	1.6
Allocation efficiency	2.0	2.5	2.8	2.9
Terms of trade	−2.5	−2.6	−2.1	−2.2
Capital accumulation	−0.6	−0.5	−0.4	1.2
Other	0.9	0.9	1.0	−0.2
Tunisia				
Real exports	42.7	46.1	53.5	59.4
Real GDP	2.8	3.5	5.0	7.8
Real exchange rate	0.1	0.6	0.9	0.9
Return to capital	0.9	1.2	1.6	−1.8

Table 7.8   Dynamic analysis: Macroeconomic impacts of the EU-US-Maghreb regional FTA sequentially adding complementary economic reforms (percent)   *(continued)*

Category	Base: EU-US-Maghreb FTA	Plus		
		Liberalization of services	Trade facilitation	Increased domestic investment
Tunisia				
Return to land	−1.7	−2.4	−1.2	0.7
Return to natural resources	−15.9	−16.7	−16.6	−14.8
Skilled wages	0.1	1.0	3.6	7.4
Unskilled wages	1.4	1.9	4.0	7.3
Agriculture	1.6	1.7	3.7	6.7
Nonagriculture	1.3	2.0	4.2	7.6
Real national income	1.6	2.2	3.9	4.6
Allocation efficiency	3.8	4.2	5.1	6.2
Terms of trade	−1.6	−1.6	−0.6	−0.7
Capital accumulation	0.6	0.8	1.3	3.4
Other	−1.3	−1.2	−1.9	−4.5
European Union				
Real exports	3.9	7.3	7.7	7.9
Real GDP	0.0	0.2	0.2	0.3
Real exchange rate	0.6	0.7	0.8	0.9
Return to capital	0.1	0.2	0.2	0.3
Return to land	−0.5	−0.5	−0.4	−0.2
Return to natural resources	−1.7	−1.8	−2.0	−3.2
Skilled wages	0.2	0.2	0.3	0.4
Unskilled wages	0.2	0.3	0.3	0.5
Agriculture	−0.1	−0.1	0.1	0.3
Nonagriculture	0.2	0.3	0.4	0.5
Real national income	0.1	0.2	0.2	0.3
Allocation efficiency	0.0	0.2	0.2	0.1
Terms of trade	0.1	0.0	0.0	0.1
Capital accumulation	0.0	0.0	0.0	0.0
Other	0.0	0.0	0.0	0.1
United States				
Real exports	2.6	6.3	6.3	6.4
Real GDP	0.0	0.1	0.1	0.1
Real exchange rate	0.3	0.3	0.3	0.4
Return to capital	0.0	0.1	0.1	0.1
Return to land	1.0	1.1	1.1	1.1
Return to natural resources	−2.5	−2.5	−2.8	−4.6

(table continues next page)

Table 7.8 Dynamic analysis: Macroeconomic impacts of the EU-US-
Maghreb regional FTA sequentially adding complementary
economic reforms (percent)   *(continued)*

Category	Base: EU-US-Maghreb FTA	Plus		
		Liberalization of services	Trade facilitation	Increased domestic investment
		United States		
Skilled wages	0.0	0.2	0.2	0.2
Unskilled wages	0.1	0.2	0.2	0.2
Agriculture	1.1	1.3	1.3	1.3
Nonagriculture	0.1	0.2	0.2	0.2
Real national income	0.1	0.2	0.2	0.2
Allocation efficiency	0.0	0.0	0.0	0.0
Terms of trade	0.0	0.1	0.1	0.1
Capital accumulation	0.0	0.0	0.0	0.0
Other	0.0	0.0	0.0	0.0

FTA = free trade agreement

Source: Dynamic MIRAGE model results.

Impact on Real Income

In table 7.8 not all Maghreb countries realize real income gains from the
EU-US-Maghreb FTA. However, when the impacts of the complementary
policies are included, no Maghreb country loses from the combination of
the EU-US-Maghreb FTA and the supporting economic reform initiatives.
Increased domestic investment promotes real income most in Algeria and
Libya, while the trade facilitation initiative yields the largest real income
gains for Morocco and Tunisia. These income gains represent the net effect of greater import discipline over domestic competitive conditions,
terms of trade changes, the efficiency of domestic resource allocation, and
domestic capital accumulation. All the Maghreb countries experience
terms of trade losses owing to trade diversion effects, but these are offset
by allocation efficiency gains generated by reallocating factors of production to more efficient sectors as imports increase market competition in
some sectors and trade facilitation initiatives reduce trade costs within the
Maghreb. Increased competition in the services sectors also contributes to
substantial gains in resource allocation efficiency in the Maghreb countries. These efficiency gains are positive for all Maghreb countries; they
are particularly sizable for Morocco and Tunisia. Finally the gains from
capital accumulation contribute significantly to net gains in real income
across the Maghreb countries.

GDP and Distributional Effects

The long-run impacts on GDP of the EU-US-Maghreb FTA and complementary economic policy reforms are positive across the Maghreb countries. Libya enjoys the greatest gain in aggregate output (10 percent), followed by Tunisia (8 percent) and Algeria (6 percent). GDP gains are positive but smaller for Morocco and Mauritania.

The primary factors of production do not benefit equally from output gains. GDP gains are associated principally with increased returns to landowners in Algeria and natural-resource owners in Libya. The gains to labor favor skilled workers in all countries, but they do not benefit unskilled workers in Libya, Mauritania, or Morocco.

Our Mirage model cannot measure the potential impacts of an EU-US-Maghreb FTA and policy reforms on poverty in the Maghreb countries. Some insights, however, can be drawn from the effects of the FTA and policy reforms on the various classes of labor. Given that the poor in developing countries are mostly unskilled workers and often found in rural households, the negative impacts on real returns to unskilled labor in agriculture in Morocco, Libya, and Mauritania suggest that the gains from regional integration under the EU-US-Maghreb FTA are not especially pro-poor. Only in Algeria do the results suggest a win-win outcome, as unskilled workers in agriculture enjoy higher returns than unskilled workers outside of agriculture.

Eliminating the Wedge on Oil and Gas Shipments from Algeria to Morocco

As part of the trade facilitation initiatives, opening the border between Algeria and Morocco under the EU-US-Maghreb FTA allows energy products to be shipped directly between the two countries. Thus the cost of shipping oil and gas from Algeria to Morocco is reduced by an additional 15 percent. This cost saving further increases energy exports from Algeria to Morocco, from 37.6 percent (the increase without eliminating the price wedge) to 53.6 percent (the increase after eliminating the price wedge). No other appreciable changes in the Mirage model variables result from eliminating the energy import price wedge that Morocco bears.

Conclusion

Using a Mirage model of the world economy, the MAcMap protection dataset, and an augmented version of the GTAP 6.2 database, our static analysis of the prospective impacts of various Maghreb integration schemes and complementary economic policy reforms leads us to several conclusions. South-south integration in the region leads to little trade creation. North-south integration with either the European Union or the

United States leads to trade creation but also diverts some Maghreb trade from customary channels. Full trade liberalization stimulates much more trade but also exposes net food-importing Maghreb countries to higher agricultural prices and lost trade preferences.

That said, our findings are subject to important caveats related to the circumstances of the Maghreb countries and the limitations of our static model. The Mirage model does not account for the benefits of greater competition and possible increasing returns to scale under regional or wider economic integration. It also does not account for FDI and trade in services, two important forces that would likely be stimulated by greater openness and complementary economic reforms in the Maghreb.

To partially overcome these limitations, we apply a dynamic version of the Mirage model that includes imperfect competition and augments Maghreb economic integration with complementary policies that liberalize trade in services, advance trade facilitation, and increase domestic investment. In the dynamic analysis, the prospective impacts of a comprehensive EU-US-Maghreb FTA and supporting policy reforms in the Maghreb countries are substantial in terms of increased real income and GDP. Export gains are relatively modest for the oil-exporting Maghreb countries without the complementary reforms. Tunisia and Morocco are the big winners in terms of expanded exports, mainly to the European Union and United States. Still, the oil-exporting Maghreb countries also gain significantly from the complementary policy reforms, especially in terms of their GDP and real income. Finally, although adverse terms-of-trade effects occur with greater Maghreb regional and global integration, they are offset by allocation efficiency gains stimulated by the procompetitive effects of greater import competition, complementary policy reforms, and increased domestic investment.

References

Bchir, Mohamed Hedi, Yvan Decreux, Jean-Louis Guerin, and Sébastien Jean. 2002. *MIRAGE: A Computable General Equilibrium Model for Trade Policy Analysis.* CEPII Working Paper 2002-17. Paris: Centre D'Etudes Prospectives et d'Informations Internationales.

Berisha-Krasniqi, Valdete, Antoine Bouët, and Simon Mevel. 2006. *The Doha Agreement and the Developing Countries: Decomposing the Sources of the Real Income Variations.* Report submitted to the Centre D'Etudes Prospectives et d'Informations Internationales.

Bouët, Antoine, Yvan Decreux, Lionel Fontagné, Sébastien Jean, and David Laborde. 2006. Tariff Data. In *Global Trade, Assistance, and Production: The GTAP 6 Data Base,* ed. B.V. Dimaranan. West Lafayette, IN: Center for Global Trade Analysis, Purdue University.

Decreux, Yvan, and Lionel Fontagné. 2006. *A Quantitative Assessment of the Outcome of the Doha Development Agenda.* CEPII Working Paper 2006-10. Paris: Centre d'Etudes Prospectives et d'Informations Internationales.

Decreux, Yvan, and Hugo Valin. 2007. *MIRAGE: Updated Version of the Model for Trade Policy Analysis: Focus on Agriculture and Dynamics.* CEPII Working Paper 2007-15. Paris: Centre d'Etudes Prospectives et d'Informations Internationales.

Dimaranan, Betina V., ed. 2006. *Global Trade, Assistance, and Production: The GTAP 6 Data Base.* West Lafayette, IN: Center for Global Trade Analysis, Purdue University.

Harrison, Glenn, Thomas Rutherford, and David Tarr. 1996. Increased Competition and Completion of the Market in the European Union: Static and Steady-State Effects. *Journal of Economic Integration* 11, no. 3 (March): 332–65.

International Food Policy Research Institute and International Fund for Agricultural Development. 2007. *Impact of Trade Liberalization on Agriculture in the Near East and North Africa.* Rome: International Fund for Agricultural Development.

Kalirajan, Kaleeswaran. 2000. *Restrictions on Trade in Distribution Services.* Productivity Commission Staff Research Paper. Canberra: AusInfo.

McGuire, Greg. 1998. *Australia's Restrictions on Trade in Financial Services.* Productivity Commission Staff Research Paper. Canberra: AusInfo.

Park, Soon-Chan. 2002. *Measuring Tariff Equivalents in Cross-Border Trade in Services.* Working Paper 02-15. Seoul: Korea Institute for International Economic Policy.

USTR (United States Trade Representative). 2008. Expanding Algeria's Exports under the GSP Program. Power Point presentation by Marideth Sandler, Office of the US Trade Representative, Executive Office of the President. April.

WTO (World Trade Organization). 2008. Agriculture: Work in the WTO—Current Negotiations. Available at www.wto.org (accessed August 5, 2008).

8

A Unified North Africa on the World Stage: Overview of Maghreb Sector Studies

FRANCIS GHILÈS

North Africa has been gripped for more than a generation by a number of political and economic fears. Morocco argues that it cannot possibly allow its energy supplies to depend on the goodwill of Algeria, which, due to its resources and proximity, would be the obvious supplier. Algeria for its part fears that its neighbors—Morocco and to a lesser degree Tunisia—are only interested in expanding their export markets and preying on Algeria's growing oil and gas wealth. These reciprocal economic fears feed on unsolved political issues and on one another; they also play on the internal characteristics of the regimes, which have mastered using fear of the other to slow down any serious evolution toward more democratic forms of government or a more equitable sharing of national wealth. Governance in the Maghreb has improved much more slowly than the pace witnessed in other countries, notably in Asia.

North Africa's fears often have been encouraged from abroad as the region has been caught up in the broader swirl of international affairs. For much of the 1970s Europe and the United States did not look kindly upon Algeria's support for the Palestine Liberation Organization. When Algeria bought weapons from the former Soviet Union, France was happy to arm

Francis Ghilès is a senior fellow at the European Institute of the Mediterranean, where he specialises in security, energy, and broader political and economic trends in North Africa and the Western Mediterranean.

Morocco and Libya to put pressure on Algeria to stop purchasing arms. Today the high price of oil and gas—and the knowledge that Algeria has abundant reserves of both—has put the country back in the driver's seat in North Africa: It can act as a facilitator or spoiler on many fronts. Algeria has been a reliable exporter of gas to Libya, the United States, and Europe for 45 years. By 2020 it will have become the European Union's second-largest source of imported gas after Russia. Meanwhile, Algeria, Morocco, and Tunisia have all used the heightened fear of Islamic terrorism to further their own internal agendas and ensure that the West turns a blind eye to their lack of respect for greater freedoms of speech and greater transparency in economic matters—in other words, for the due process of law.

North African countries thus have become pawns in a broader game they do not control, a game that today includes the United States, Europe, Russia, China, and India. Fifty years ago there existed a deep feeling of Maghreb solidarity, symbolized by the Appel de Tanger for Maghreb unity, which the leading politicians of the day signed in April 1958.[1] Today each country has built a nation state on the classic European model, to the detriment of regional sentiment.

The absence of any long-term political vision for North Africa has encouraged the flight of capital and of educated and less-educated people who cannot hope to find good investment opportunities and jobs in economies that are growing too slowly. Many younger North Africans—two-thirds of the population is under the age of 25—despair of their countries' and the region's future as they watch Europe integrate while China and India grow in wealth, power, and influence on the world stage. Rates of economic growth need to improve significantly over the next decade as a huge bulge of young people enter the labor market; the future may become very bleak, not only for the region but for the world, if the generational transition needed to meet this challenge is unsuccessful. That sea change is not only about economics, but greater prosperity would help.

To date, North Africa has avoided the serious conflicts that forced Europe, after two bloody world wars, to build a common economic market and a common dream of a shared future. However, military expenditure has soared while investment in education and infrastructure is desperately needed. The unresolved legal status of the Western Sahara has stifled all attempts to bring Morocco and Algeria closer.

The European Union has offered the Maghreb the prospect of a free trade zone, one of the main pillars of the Barcelona Process, which was launched in 1995. However, today the European Union appears at worst scared of its southern-rim Mediterranean neighbors and at best skeptical of the need to engage them in serious debate. Meanwhile it erects rigid barriers against further immigration, often giving the impression of being

---

1. Francis Ghilès, "El Maghreb Paga El Precio de su Desunion" ["The Maghreb Pays the Price for Disunity"], *El Pais*, June 5, 2008. See also Ghilès (2008a).

an Old Europe with no great ambitions for the future. Unlike Asian countries and the Americas, Europe hardly dares dream of a Mediterranean Union. Southern-rim countries, not least in North Africa, are equally wary. The sector studies presented in this volume demonstrate the tantalizing prospects that opening all frontiers in North Africa could offer—and the leveraged effect this could have on trade and investment flows with the wider world. To date, however, except for the growing presence of Tunisian entrepreneurs in Algeria, this prospect remains a mirage.

We are faced with a beauty contest between Algeria, Tunisia, and Morocco as each attempts to prove its value to the West, Russia, and China. Each tells the West that it has come closest to Western norms of good economic and political governance. The West, meanwhile, is very keen on how terrorism might best be contained. The mantra of terrorism and the security of oil and gas supplies sometimes appear to be the only prisms through which the media and Western governments view the region. The threat of al Qaeda cannot be dismissed, but the main source of social violence lies in the deep discontent among young people who are faced with poor employment opportunities, expensive housing, and growing income disparities in systems addled by corruption. In Europe at least, another major concern is stemming the flow of immigrants, be they legal or not.

Today, despite its troubled recent past, North Africa is producing more and more entrepreneurs who are looking to the future and wish to engage with the world. They tire of old political quarrels, as does the younger generation whose voice goes unheeded in international forums. Also, as mentioned above, entrepreneurs and the younger generation—in which women are playing an ever greater role—are mindful of the rise of China and India, which both have encouraged diasporas to aid their own economic development. There is a lesson here for the Maghreb (Ghilès 2007c, 2008a). Ten percent of Morocco's and Algeria's population live and work abroad, often carrying European and North American passports. Such binational young entrepreneurs who are tempted to set up shop in their former motherlands would be perfect bridge builders between two worlds—and two civilizations—that we are often told are in conflict. They despair, however, of the slow pace of reform and what they see as antiquated systems of governance and the European Union's virtual ignorance of their existence.

Giving entrepreneurs a greater role is vital: Industry not only creates many jobs, but also manufactures a lobby for enforceable contracts, the rule of law, and ultimately, representative government. However, the Barcelona Process overlooked the role of private entrepreneurs and there are still no well-established forums in which private and state entrepreneurs can meet on a regional basis. Too many meetings see European officials peddle their democratic wares and lecture the Maghreb on women's rights while Maghreb officials ask EU countries to atone for their colonial sins and shell out more money. By contrast, when businessmen meet, the tone is altogether more positive: They realize that the opportunities to build joint ventures with European, US, Asian, and Russian companies offer hope for the future (Ghilès 2006a, 2006b, 2007b). But the positive contribution of entrepreneurs is ignored by many political leaders on both shores and by the media, which often treat North Africa as if it were little more than a den of Islamic terrorists and illegal immigrants where one can nonetheless buy energy and go on cheap holidays. They do not seem to realize that North Africa is a young region whereas Europe is increasingly gray, running the risk of marginalization in the longer term as its population declines. The Union for the Mediterranean has the merit of putting the Mediterranean at center stage; it may help Europe realize that it must look south.

Sector Recommendations

For the Maghreb—a region of 80 million people, rich in oil, gas, agricultural products, and tourism, and sitting on the doorstep of the world's largest market—the real challenge is to integrate more fully and quickly into international flows of trade and investment. Were all five Maghreb countries to do so, they would have to adapt more quickly to international norms of economic, legal, and even political governance.[2] Such an evolution can only come about through a process of mutual stake building among the different countries, particularly Algeria and Morocco, which would suggest cross holdings in equity in the energy and banking sectors. We thus make a number of suggestions that could, in the short and medium terms, encourage greater links between North African countries and the rest of the world.

Energy

Energy remains the strategic key. Sonatrach, Algeria's state oil and gas company, could agree to sell greater quantities of gas to Morocco through the existing Maghreb-Europe Pedro Duran Farell Pipeline that runs from Algeria to the Iberian peninsula. As matters stand, Morocco levies a 7 percent transit fee paid in kind on the throughput of Algerian gas. At first it sold the gas it received from the transit fee to Spanish companies; today it uses some of it—0.5 billion cubic meters—for the Tahaddart combined-cycle thermal plant, and will soon use all the transit fee gas when the Aïn Beni Mathar combined-cycle thermal plant is completed. As a confidence-

---

2. The sector studies contain limited reference to Libya and Mauritania because data are not available, but the recommendations should apply to those two countries as well.

building measure, Sonelgaz, the state Algerian gas company, could be invited to invest capital in this new venture.

The Moroccan state electricity company, Office National de l'Electricité, had envisaged building a combined-cycle plant to produce electricity at Al Wahda; it thought that it would buy gas from the pipeline paying the same cost and freight prices paid by Spanish buyers who received liquefied natural gas from Algeria. Algeria refused this deal, but such a project could be relaunched. To boost confidence further, Sonatrach could be invited to invest capital in the underwater section of the Pedro Duran Farell pipeline, which runs under the strait of Gibraltar, as it already holds a 50 percent stake in the underwater section of the Trans-Med Pipeline (Enrico Matteï), which since 1983 has carried gas from Algeria to Italy through Tunisia and under the strait of Sicily.

Multiproduct pipelines—liquefied petroleum gas, gasoline, and diesel—could link different centers of gas bottling and distribution situated on either side of the Algeria-Morocco border. This would not only help meet local needs, but also curtail the smuggling of oil and gas products that currently plagues the industry. Pipelines could be built that feed off the Maghreb-Europe pipeline to supply major Moroccan cities such as Fez. Electricity connections among the three countries could be developed and used much more rationally than is the case today.

Finally, connecting the different north-south gas lines—the Pedro Duran Farell and Enrico Matteï, plus the Medgaz, which is under construction and will carry gas directly from western Algeria to Almeria in southern Spain, and the planned Galsi pipeline, which will carry gas from eastern Algeria directly to the Italian mainland via Sardinia—could increase the volume of gas trade in the western Mediterranean to 18 million tons of oil equivalent by 2020. This would represent 20 percent of all energy requirements in the Maghreb.

Europeans will have to alter their perceptions of North Africa so that the region's oil and gas producers are not seen simply as suppliers of raw materials (Ghilès 2007a). North African producers must also appreciate that energy can act not only as a great catalyst for Maghreb cooperation, but also as a tool of development, a way to combat climate change—a looming menace for Algeria, Tunisia, and Morocco—and a means of producing another commodity that is becoming increasingly scarce: water.

Banking and Insurance

The banking systems of Algeria, Morocco, and Tunisia have features in common. The share of bank credit devoted to the public sector is high and the percentage of people holding bank accounts is low. The flow of capital escaping the region is higher than the total worker remittances and foreign direct investment that the region receives. Individuals of high net worth have little trust in the systems in which they operate. Yet entrepreneurs who are close to the ruling elites benefit from modern banking services and low interest rates. In short, the banking systems facilitate practices that hinder economic development.

To convert to productive use the large volume of unused liquidity currently held in the banking system, new financial instruments could be created that are common to the three main Maghreb countries. Inspiration could be drawn from the Association of Southeast Asian Nations Plus Three, which created the Asian Bond Initiative and Asian Bond Fund. Creating a North African equivalent to the United Kingdom's Financial Times Stock Exchange index (FTSE100) or France's Continuous Assisted Quotation (CAC40) would also help draw financial markets closer. Beyond this, ensuring full currency convertibility for the three countries would ensure greater transparency. The inevitable privatization of the Algerian banking system could offer an opportunity to create two regional banks with shareholdings in the three countries; these banks' prime task would be to encourage and engineer mergers and acquisitions across North Africa. Finally, establishing a triple-A rated Mediterranean financial agency would help to bring these initiatives and others under one roof and signal the strong interest of the European Union and the United States in a faster pace for Maghreb economic development.

Greater efforts should be made to understand the flow of remittances to North Africa from North Africans in Europe. Policymakers are wrong to assume that migrant populations aspire to integrate fully into either Europe or their former motherlands; they often seek to straddle both, and as mentioned above, there are thus lessons to be learned from the Chinese and Indian diasporas.

Transport

The most obvious actions to improve transport in the Maghreb would be to reopen road and rail services between Algeria and Morocco—which would require only a few weeks' work—and to increase the frequency of flights between Algiers and Casablanca. These would at least turn the frontier into a manageable and open line of demarcation, rather than an area where illegal immigrants from southern Saharan countries float around in a no man's land.

The motorways being built in all three countries need to be connected, both near the coast and inland. Such links would help boost trade and investment. Where air traffic is concerned, a joint air safety regulation authority would be a good start. Morocco has adopted an open skies policy. Tunisia is open to low-cost carriers. Encouraging Algeria to move in a similar direction would reinforce what is already a very active north-south volume of traffic. Ports could cooperate far more than they do today and promote transshipment, which would insert them more fully into the global value chain.

Food Industries

Food industries offer many opportunities for regional cooperation. As patterns of production and consumption are similar across the Maghreb and proximity could be a great asset, economies of scale could be exploited if transport links between countries are reestablished and upgraded. Vertical integration should draw on the relative advantages of each country: water in Morocco, energy in Algeria, and more advanced capacity to transform raw food products in Tunisia. Multinational food processing companies already consider the Maghreb as a unit; merging private companies that operate within the region offers many opportunities to build on this perception. Greater value could be added to products such as dates, olive oil, and camel milk.

Opening up frontiers would also help rid the region of smuggling and encourage each government to promote coherence among the policies they pursue on product control and the subsidies they enact for food production and consumption. Beyond this, joint policies could be enacted regarding water conservation, broader protection of a fragile and often overfished coastline, and other areas of importance for agriculture and tourism. As the climate changes, such considerations should weigh ever more on authorities' minds.

Conclusion

The above measures would deliver great benefits to the Maghreb: faster economic growth, new jobs, modernized legal systems, and greater freedom. Some benefits can be realized quickly; others will take a few years. Whatever the case, a more stable and confident North Africa could take its destiny in hand and profit fully from the greater flows of trade, investment, and knowledge that the early 21st century offers. The United States and Europe should encourage such reforms because a common economic market and a common dream in the Maghreb of a shared future would help lay to rest some of the fears expressed in Washington and European capitals as to the region's capacity to contain terrorism and emigration. North Africa could become a highly respected partner for the European Union, the United States, and other countries in the world.

Europe has tended to see the southern-rim Mediterranean countries as more of a threat than an opportunity; inward direct investment to the Maghreb, however, is increasing and the region attracts a little more than 4 percent of world investment flows, just above its population weight.

Such investment has quintupled in five years despite the ongoing net flight of capital from the region. The investors are largely from Europe but come increasingly from the Persian Gulf, India, China, and Brazil. Their presence is needed to deepen the trends under way.

Two thousand years ago, the Mediterranean was a hub of world trade. In a region so beholden to history, it is worth concluding with the words of two leading statesmen who lived at the time of the splendor of al Andalus; the words ring as true today as they did 600 years ago. The Maghreb statesman and philosopher Ibn Khaldun (1332–1406) said in the *Muqaddimah* that it was "thanks to trading with foreigners that the needs of the people, the profits of merchants, and the wealth of countries grew" (Ibn Khaldun 1974). The chancellor of Florence, Colucci di Pietro Saluti (1331–1406), remarked that "the pilgrimage is a holy act, justice even more so but the holiest act of all in our eyes, is trade." North African leaders and their European counterparts would do well to ponder such wise words and act on them. Private entrepreneurs and some state companies are already doing so.

References

Ghilès, Francis. 2006a. Cómo Conseguir un Tigre Magrebí [How to Get to a Maghreb Tiger]. Paper presented at a conference entitled From the Cost of Non-Maghreb to a North African Tiger, sponsored by the European Institute of the Mediterranean (IEMed) and El Centro International de Toleda para la Paz (CITpax), Madrid, Spain, May 25–26.

Ghilès, Francis. 2006b. L'Afrique du Nord Sans Frontières ou Comment Relever le Défi de la Mondialisation [North Africa without Borders, or How to Step Up to the Challenge of Globalization]. *AFKAR-IDEAS*, no. 11 (July–August): 20–23.

Ghilès, Francis. 2007a. Algeria, a Strategic Gas Partner for Europe. *Politica Exterior*, no. 118 (July/August).

Ghilès, Francis. 2007b. L'Afrique du Nord et l'Europe, une Interdépendance Recherchée et Acceptée [North Africa and Europe, an Interdependence Sought and Accepted]. Paper presented at a conference on North Africa, sponsored by the European Institute of the Mediterranean (IEMed) and El Centro International de Toleda para la Paz (CITpax), Barcelona, Spain, November 22–23.

Ghilès, Francis. 2007c. Promoting the Role of Citizens with Dual Nationality as Economic and Social Bridge-Builders with North Africa. Paper presented at a conference on security through science, sponsored by the North Atlantic Treaty Organization, February 16–17, Barcelona, Spain.

Ghilès, Francis. 2008a. La Diaspora Asiatique: Une Utopie Maghrébine [The Asian Diaspora: A Utopia for the Maghreb]. *Economia* 3 (June/September): 32–36.

Ghilès, Francis. 2008b. Le Cout du Non Maghreb Marginalise l'Afrique du Nord [The Cost of Not Having Maghreb Marginalizes North Africa]. Paper presented at a conference of the Union des Jeunes Euro-Maghrébins, Oujda, Morocco, April 26–27.

Ibn Khaldun. 1974. *The Muqaddimah: An Introduction to History.* Translated by Frank Rosenthal. Pantheon Books.

9

The Maghreb Energy Sector: Situation and Perspectives

MUSTAPHA FAÏD

The Maghreb energy situation is characterized by several dynamic factors that suggest, at the same time, serious potential for instability and great opportunity for cooperation. Energy consumption is highly disparate among Maghreb countries and far below that in the countries of the northern Mediterranean; that said, consumption is projected to increase rapidly, linked to Maghreb population growth. Energy concerns dominate the countries' external trade balances, though energy trading among them is almost totally absent, but potential for intraregional trade is high. With genuine and balanced cooperation among players, the Union for the Mediterranean could contribute to creating an integrated economic entity in the Maghreb with energy playing the lead role.

Energy Situation

The five Maghreb countries differ from one another in several ways with respect to energy, particularly the type of energy used, the level of energy consumption, and the availability of hydrocarbon resources.

Mustapha Faïd is president of SPTEC Conseil, a Paris-based consulting firm specializing in oil and gas issues. He was general manager of Observatoire Méditerranéen de l'Energie from February 2007 to June 2008.

Table 9.1 Consumption of primary energy in the Maghreb, selected years (million tons of oil equivalent)

Country	1971	1980	1990	2000	2006
Algeria	3.7	12.2	23.9	29.3	34.0
Libya	1.7	7.2	11.5	17.0	18.7
Mauritania	0.2	0.4	0.6	1.0	1.3
Morocco	2.4	4.8	6.7	9.8	12.6
Tunisia	2.0	3.8	5.5	7.6	8.9
Total	10.0	28.3	48.2	64.6	75.4

Source: Observatoire Méditerranéen de l'Energie.

Table 9.2 Primary energy consumption in the Maghreb, 2006

Country	Consumption (million tons of oil equivalent)	Population (millions)	Per capita consumption (tons of oil equivalent)
Algeria	34.0	33.3	1.0
Libya	18.7	6.0	3.1
Mauritania	1.3	3.1	0.4
Morocco	12.6	30.5	0.4
Tunisia	8.9	10.1	0.9
Total/average	75.4	83.0	0.9

Source: Observatoire Méditerranéen de l'Energie.

Energy Consumption

The Maghreb countries' energy consumption reached 75 million tons of oil equivalent (mtoe) in 2006, up from less than 10 mtoe in 1971, an annual growth rate of nearly 6 percent over the period (table 9.1). Algeria consumes the largest share with 44 percent (34 mtoe), followed by Libya with 25 percent (19 mtoe), Morocco with 17 percent (13 mtoe), Tunisia with 12 percent (9 mtoe), and Mauritania with 2 percent (1 mtoe). Annual energy consumption per capita varies considerably from country to country (table 9.2): more than 3 tons of oil equivalent (toe) per capita in Libya but only about 1 toe in Algeria and Tunisia and barely 0.4 toe in Morocco and Mauritania.

Average primary energy consumption per capita amounts to 0.9 toe in the Maghreb; by comparison, consumption is over three times larger for the northern Mediterranean countries at 3.2 toe per capita. This discrepancy underlines the importance of energy issues to the development of the Maghreb countries, individually and as a group.

Figure 9.1 Consumption of primary energy in the Maghreb by energy type, 2006 (percent)

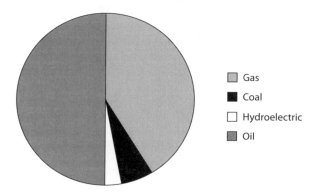

☐ Gas
■ Coal
☐ Hydroelectric
■ Oil

Source: Observatoire Méditerranéen de l'Energie.

Table 9.3   Oil consumption in the Maghreb, 1971–2006
(millions of tons)

Country	1971	1980	1990	2000	2006
Algeria	2.3	5.5	9.7	10.0	11.6
Libya	0.7	4.6	7.4	12.7	13.2
Mauritania	0.2	0.2	0.3	0.5	1.0
Morocco	1.8	3.9	5.1	6.6	7.6
Tunisia	1.3	2.5	3.2	3.8	4.0
Total	6.2	16.8	25.7	33.6	37.4

Sources: Observatoire Méditerranéen de l'Energie; BP Statistical Review of World Energy 2007.

Fossil fuels are the dominant form of energy used in the Maghreb, representing 97 percent of total energy consumption (figure 9.1).

Oil

In 2006 oil consumption stood at almost 38 mtoe, half of total primary energy consumption. Because of their large hydrocarbon resources, Libya and Algeria are the largest oil consumers in the region, at over 13 million tons and nearly 12 million tons, respectively. Consumption totaled less than 8 million tons in Morocco, 4 million tons in Tunisia, and only 1 million tons in Mauritania (table 9.3).

Table 9.4 Consumption of natural gas in the Maghreb, 1971–2006 (million tons of oil equivalent)

Country	1971	1980	1990	2000	2006
Algeria	1.2	6.5	13.5	18.7	21.6
Libya	0.9	2.5	4.1	4.2	5.3
Mauritania	n.a.	n.a.	n.a.	n.a.	n.a.
Morocco	n.a.	n.a.	n.a.	n.a.	0.5
Tunisia	0.0	0.4	1.2	2.7	3.7
Total	2.1	9.3	18.8	25.6	31.1

n.a. = not available

Sources: Observatoire Méditerranéen de l'Energie; CEDIGAZ.

Natural Gas

In 2006 consumption of natural gas reached 31 mtoe—34 billion cubic meters (Gm^3)—41 percent of total primary energy consumption in the Maghreb. Algeria, Libya, and Tunisia have all created transport and distribution networks for natural gas and consume, respectively, 21.6 mtoe, 5.3 mtoe, and 3.7 mtoe (table 9.4).

The distribution network in Algeria supplies more than 2.2 million customers, a coverage rate of 38 percent at the end of 2006. Libya consumes $5.9\ Gm^3$ and is developing its national pipeline network while continuing to convert power stations to natural gas. Tunisia's consumption for 2006 was $4\ Gm^3$. Increased capacity of the Enrico Matteï pipeline, which transports Algerian gas to Italy and Slovenia, also increased the availability of natural gas on Tunisia's local market. Morocco has only been using natural gas since January 2005. Consumption is now up to $0.6\ Gm^3$ of Algerian gas thanks to the first combined-cycle power plant in Tahaddart (near Tangiers).

Coal

Coal consumption is only 4.3 mtoe in the Maghreb, roughly 6 percent of total primary energy consumption (table 9.5). Morocco is the main consumer of coal in the region. However, production is in sharp decline in the Jerada coal mines in the west of the country and Morocco has to import most of the coal it uses to produce electricity. Algeria and Tunisia consume very little coal, less than 1 mtoe combined.

Table 9.5   Coal consumption in the Maghreb, 1971–2006
(million tons of oil equivalent)

Country	1971	1990	2000	2006
Algeria	0.2	0.6	0.5	0.8
Libya	n.a.	n.a.	n.a.	n.a.
Mauritania	n.a.	n.a.	n.a.	n.a.
Morocco	0.3	10.1	2.6	3.4
Tunisia	0.1	0.1	0.1	0.1
Total	0.6	10.8	3.2	4.3

n.a. = not available

Sources: International Energy Agency; Observatoire Méditerranéen de l'Energie.

Table 9.6   Consumption of renewable energies, 1971–2006
(million tons of oil equivalent)

Country	1971	1980	1990	2000	2006
Algeria	0.01	0.01	0.02	0.08	0.08
Libya	0.10	0.13	0.13	0.14	0.17
Mauritania	0.05	0.16	0.24	0.53	0.25
Morocco	0.13	0.26	0.32	0.44	0.47
Tunisia	0.67	0.82	1.04	0.94	1.00
Total	0.96	1.38	1.75	2.13	1.96

Source: Observatoire Méditerranéen de l'Energie.

Renewable Energy

Consumption of renewable energies is very low, less than 2 mtoe in 2006, of which half is consumed by Tunisia (table 9.6).

Electricity

Electricity consumption reached 91.4 terawatt hours (TWh) in 2006 (table 9.7). Average annual growth in electricity consumption exceeded 8 percent between 1971 and 2006. The share of electricity consumption for each of the Maghreb countries is as follows: 38 percent for Algeria (34.4 TWh), 26 per-

Table 9.7   Electricity consumption in the Maghreb, 1971–2006
(terawatt hours)

Country	1971	1980	1990	2000	2006
Algeria	2.2	7.1	16.1	25.4	34.4
Libya	0.5	4.8	10.2	15.5	24.0
Mauritania	0.1	0.1	0.2	0.3	0.4
Morocco	2.3	5.3	9.6	13.7	19.2
Tunisia	0.9	2.9	5.8	10.6	13.5
Total	6.0	20.2	41.9	65.5	91.4

Source: Comité Maghrébin de l'Electricité (COMELEC).

cent for Libya (24.0 TWh), 21 percent for Morocco (19.2 TWh), 15 percent for Tunisia (13.5 TWh), and less than 1 percent for Mauritania (0.4 TWh).

Energy Resources

The Maghreb is clearly rich in natural resources—particularly oil and natural gas reserves—but those resources are not spread evenly among the region's countries.

Oil and Natural Gas

Hydrocarbon reserves in the Maghreb amount to more than 7 billion tons of oil and nearly 6,000 Gm³ of natural gas. In 2006 the Maghreb countries produced a little over 175 million tons of oil and 102 Gm³ of natural gas (table 9.8). At current levels of production, the Maghreb has 40 years of oil reserves and 58 years of natural gas reserves remaining. These resources are mostly concentrated in Algeria and Libya. Libya has the largest reserves of oil with 5.4 billion tons, while Algeria only has 1.5 billion tons—18 years of production at the current rate. However, Algeria dominates natural gas reserves with 4,500 Gm³ against 1,300 Gm³ in Libya. Algeria and Libya combined hold 87 percent of oil reserves and 71 percent of natural gas reserves for the entire Mediterranean region. Together with Egypt, which holds 23 percent of the Mediterranean gas reserves, the three countries control 93 percent of such reserves.

Renewable Energy

Maghreb countries benefit from significant renewable energy resources, in particular solar and wind power. Sunshine hours vary between 2,650 and 3,400 hours per year. Average annual irradiation varies from 1,300

Table 9.8   Oil and natural gas reserves and production, 2006

Country	Oil Reserves Millions of tons	Oil Reserves Percent	Oil Production (millions of tons)	Oil Reserves/ production (years)	Natural gas Reserves Gm³	Natural gas Reserves Percent	Natural gas Production (Gm³)	Natural gas Reserves/ production (years)
Algeria	1,545	19	86	18	4,504	54	85	53
Libya	5,399	67	86	63	1,316	16	15	89
Tunisia	90	1	3	27	70	1	3	28
Maghreb total	7,034	87	175	40	5,890	71	102	58
Rest of the Mediterranean	1,032	13	60	17	2,390	29	61	39
Total for the Mediterranean	8,066	100	235	34	8,280	100	163	51

Gm³ = billion cubic meters

Sources: BP Statistical Review of World Energy 2007; CEDIGAZ; Observatoire Mediterranéen de l'Energie.

kilowatt hours per square meter per year ($kWh/m^2/year$) on the coastal zones to 3,200 $kWh/m^2/year$ in the south and desert zones. Average wind speed in the region fluctuates between 6 and 11 meters per second.

The potential for harnessing solar and wind energies is significant in the region—6,000 megawatts in Morocco, for instance—but it is not yet exploited. Despite political support for renewable energy in most Maghreb countries and wide recognition of the benefits, many institutional, regulatory, and financial obstacles remain.

Energy Trading

Energy trading among Maghreb countries remains extremely weak considering the countries' needs, availability of resources, and proximity.

Oil and Petroleum

Table 9.9 summarizes the trade of oil and petroleum products among Maghreb countries in 2005. The most striking feature is the negligible level of intra-Maghreb trade in the oil sector: only 1.8 million tons, under 3 percent of the total of 70 million tons traded to and from the region. One could think that the countries of the Maghreb deliberately ignore each other.

Algeria does not sell any of its oil to its neighbors and exports only 1 million tons of liquefied petroleum gas to Morocco, 4.6 percent of total Algerian exports of petroleum products. Morocco imports only 10.6 percent of the petroleum products it needs from Algeria and brings in the remaining 6.7 million tons from outside the Maghreb. Tunisia imports around 0.8 million tons of oil from Libya, just 18.3 percent of total Tunisian imports and less than 2 percent of total Libyan exports. Tunisia exports more than 1.3 million tons of petroleum products to countries outside the Maghreb.

Natural Gas

Tunisia and Morocco are transit countries for Algerian pipelines to Italy and Spain, and for this service they are able to levy a share. In 2006 the share amounted to 1.8 Gm^3, or 2.9 percent of the total gas exported by Algeria.

In Tunisia the Enrico Matteï gas pipeline, which was brought into service in 1983, will have its capacity increased to 32 Gm^3 a year. As the transit levy is 5 percent, Tunisia will benefit by up to 1.6 Gm^3 a year. Furthermore, the Tunisian company STEG has a contract to buy 0.5 Gm^3 of Algerian gas a year.

In Morocco the Pedro Duran Farell (Maghreb-Europe) gas pipeline, which came into service in 1997 to supply Spain and Portugal, has a ca-

Table 9.9   Oil flows between Maghreb countries, 2005 (million tons of oil equivalent)

Importer	Exporter							
	Algeria	Libya	Morocco	Tunisia	Total Maghreb	Rest of the Mediterranean	Rest of the world	Total
Algeria		0	0	0	0	402	450	852
Libya	0		0	0	0	0	29	29
Morocco	975	37		0	1,012	490	6,167	7,669
Mauritania	0	0	0	0	0	0	0	0
Tunisia	0	779	12		791	191	3,278	4,260
Total Maghreb	975	816	12	0	1,803	n.a.	n.a.	n.a.
Rest of the Mediterranean	20,159	45,372	0	1,317	66,848	n.a.	n.a.	n.a.
Rest of the world	140	779	0	0	919	n.a.	n.a.	n.a.
Total	21,274	46,967	12	1,317	69,569	n.a.	n.a.	n.a.

n.a. = not available

Sources: International Energy Agency; BP Statistical Review of World Energy 2005.

Table 9.10   Electric interconnections between Maghreb countries, 2006

Interconnection	Voltage (kilovolts)	Year of commissioning
Ghazaouet, Algeria ↔ Oujda, Morocco	225	1988
Tlemcen, Algeria ↔ Oujda, Morocco	225	1988
Djebel Onk, Algeria ↔ Metlaoui, Tunisia	150	1984
El Aouinet, Algeria ↔ Tajerouine, Tunisia	225	1984
El Aouinet, Algeria ↔ Tajerouine, Tunisia	90	1952
El Kala, Algeria ↔ Fernana, Tunisia	90	1956
Mellousa, Morocco ↔ Tarifa, Spain	400	1996/2006
Medenine, Tunisia ↔ Abukamash, Libya	220	2003
Tobruk, Libya ↔ Saloum, Egypt	220	1998

Source: Comité Maghrébin de l'Electricité.

Table 9.11   Electricity flows between Maghreb countries, 2006
            (gigawatt hour)

Importer	Exporter						Total
	Algeria	Libya	Morocco	Tunisia	Egypt	Spain	
Algeria		n.a.	136	135	n.a.	n.a.	271
Libya	n.a.		n.a.	n.a.	123	n.a.	123
Morocco	159	n.a.		n.a.	n.a.	1,899	2,058
Tunisia	141	n.a.	n.a.		n.a.	n.a.	141
Egypt	n.a.	91	n.a.	n.a.		n.a.	91
Spain	n.a.	n.a.	27	n.a.	n.a.		27
Total	300	91	163	135	123	1,899	2,710

n.a. = not available

Source: Comité Maghrébin de l'Electricité; Observatoire Méditerranéen de l'Energie.

pacity of 12.7 Gm³ a year. The transit charge is 7 percent, so Moroccan levies can claim up to 0.9 Gm³ a year. Morocco only recently decided to use gas in its new combined-cycle power plant at Tahaddart, which requires 0.6 Gm³ a year.

Electricity

Tables 9.10 and 9.11 show electricity trading among the Maghreb countries for 2006. Flows remain extremely low—only 0.7 TWh, less than 1 percent of the total electricity consumption of these countries. Electricity interconnections developed in the Maghreb remain vastly inferior to the potential of the region because the lines were intended for zero-sum two-way transactions over a period of time, essentially to meet emergency needs. Even though construction of the interconnection line between Tunisia and Libya was completed in 2003, there has not yet been any trade between the two countries. The only significant trading relation is between Morocco and Spain. Morocco imports 1.9 TWh from Spain, around 10 percent of its needs and nearly 12 times the amount it buys from Algeria (table 9.11).

Summary

Intra-Maghreb energy trade is very low, mostly due to a lack of trust among the region's countries. Algeria sells very little energy to its neighbors. It exports only 1 million tons of petroleum products to Morocco, around 5 percent of its oil exports. It sells 0.5 Gm^3 of natural gas a year to the Maghreb generally, less than 1 percent of its natural gas sales. Finally, it trades less than 0.6 TWh of electricity with its immediate neighbors, less than 2 percent of its production. Libya exports less than 1 million tons of oil—less than 2 percent of its energy trade—to Tunisia and does not export any natural gas there. Morocco's energy trade with Maghreb neighbors amounts to only 1 million tons, or 11 percent of its total energy trade. Tunisia's trade with other Maghreb countries represents barely 14 percent of its total energy trade.

Socioeconomic Data

Developments in the Maghreb's energy sector occur in the context of economic growth that is not quite keeping pace with the region's rising population. Domestic demand for energy is likely to increase, putting more pressure on each country's external trade balance.

Population

In 2006 the population of the Maghreb totaled 83 million inhabitants (table 9.12). Algeria is the most highly populated country (over 33 million), closely followed by Morocco (31 million). Together they represent nearly 77 percent of the Maghreb's population. Table 9.12 outlines the region's population growth from 1971 to 2020. Numbers more than doubled between 1971 and 2006, from 38 million to 83 million. The largest increases occurred in Algeria (more than 19 million) and Morocco (15 million).

The population of the Maghreb is young and numbers are expected to exceed 100 million by 2020, an annual rate of increase of 1.3 percent over the period. This will inevitably entail a large increase in energy consumption, especially electricity.

Table 9.12   Population growth in Maghreb countries, 1971–2020 (millions)

Country	1971	1980	1990	2000	2002	2004	2006	2010p	2020p
Algeria	14.2	18.8	25.3	30.5	31.4	32.4	33.3	35.2	39.9
Libya	2.1	3.0	4.3	5.3	5.5	5.7	6.0	6.7	8.2
Mauritania	1.3	1.6	2.0	2.6	2.8	3.0	3.1	3.6	4.5
Morocco	15.4	19.3	23.9	27.8	28.5	29.1	30.5	32.3	36.8
Tunisia	5.2	6.4	8.2	9.6	9.8	9.9	10.1	10.7	12.1
Total	38.1	49.1	63.7	75.8	78.0	80.1	83.0	88.5	101.5

p = projection

Sources: World Bank, *World Development Indicators 2007*; UNCTAD, *Trade and Development Report*, 2007.

Economic Growth

As table 9.13 shows, in 2006 the GNP of the five countries totaled nearly $200 billion. Algeria accounted for the largest share (36 percent), followed by Morocco (26 percent), Libya (24 percent), Tunisia (13 percent), and Mauritania (less than 1 percent).

GNP growth rates for Maghreb countries are mediocre. For 2007 the estimates are 3.1 percent for Algeria and 2.3 percent for Morocco. Tunisia and Libya did much better, with rates of 6.3 and 6.8 percent, respectively. In 2008 the GNP growth rate for Libya is expected to reach 9 percent. The rest of the Maghreb countries will maintain modest rates.

Over the longer term, the GNP of the Maghreb should reach around $324 billion (constant dollars) in 2020 while the population is expected to increase by 20 million inhabitants. Average annual GNP growth rates are projected at between 3.5 and 4.0 percent for Maghreb countries over the next 15 years, which is relatively modest in the context of population growth of 1.3 percent per year. Energy needs are likely to rise sharply even with modest economic growth, as the increase in population will be a considerable factor. In addition, the energy intensity record—the amount of energy consumed (mtoe) to produce one unit of GNP at current dollars—is particularly high for Algeria (0.48) and Libya (0.39). The average energy intensity for the Maghreb is 0.39.

The Place of Energy in Trade Balances

Merchandise trade balances for Maghreb countries differ widely. Algeria and Libya exhibit surpluses, in large part due to hydrocarbon exports. Morocco, Tunisia, and Mauritania incur large deficits.

Table 9.14 reports the Algerian merchandise trade balance. Hydrocarbon exports account for almost 98 percent of Algeria's total exports, signaling

Table 9.13   Gross national product figures and projections, 1970–2020 (billions of current dollars)

Country	1970	1980	1990	2000	2001	2002	2003	2004	2005	2006	2007e	2008p	2010p	2020p
Algeria	4.9	42.3	62.0	54.8	56.2	58.9	62.9	66.2	69.6	70.8	73.0	76.6	87.7	127.7
Libya	4.0	35.5	28.9	34.5	36.0	37.2	40.6	42.7	45.3	47.7	50.9	55.4	53.3	67.3
Mauritania	0.2	0.7	1.0	1.1	1.1	1.1	1.2	1.2	1.3	1.4	1.5	1.5	1.6	2.1
Morocco	4.0	21.0	28.9	37.1	39.4	40.7	42.9	45.1	46.2	49.9	51.0	54.1	59.5	80.6
Tunisia	1.4	8.7	12.3	19.4	20.4	20.7	21.9	23.2	24.1	25.5	27.1	28.6	30.9	45.9
Total	14.0	108.0	133.0	147.0	153.0	159.0	170.0	178.0	187.0	195.0	204.0	216.0	233.0	323.6

e = estimate; p = projection

Source: World Bank, *World Development Indicators 2007.*

Table 9.14   Algerian merchandise trade balance, 2007

	Exports		Imports		Balance
Category	Millions of dollars	Percent	Millions of dollars	Percent	(millions of dollars)
Consumption goods	33	0.1	4,009	14.6	–3,976
Energy	55,705	97.7	313	1.1	55,392
Equipment goods	46	0.1	10,097	36.8	–10,051
Food products	87	0.2	4,827	17.6	–4,740
Primary products	170	0.3	1,277	4.7	–1,107
Semifinished products	978	1.7	6,919	25.2	–5,941
Total	57,019	100	27,441	100	29,577

Source: Agence Nationale de Promotion des Exportations, www.promex.dz.

Table 9.15   Moroccan merchandise trade balance, 2007

	Exports		Imports		Balance
Category	Millions of dollars	Percent	Millions of dollars	Percent	(millions of dollars)
Consumption goods	4,106	30.1	5,525	18.9	–1,419
Energy	288	2.1	5,833	20.0	–5,545
Equipment goods	1,572	11.5	6,377	21.8	–4,805
Food products	2,463	18.1	3,005	10.3	–542
Primary products	1,425	10.4	1,776	6.1	–351
Semifinished products	3,783	27.7	6,719	23.0	–2,936
Total	13,638	100.0	29,235	1.0	–15,598

Source: Centre Marocain de Promotion des Exportations, www.cmpe.org.ma.

an extreme dependence on oil and natural gas. The share of food in total imports is almost 18 percent, around $5 billion of food products annually.

Morocco's merchandise trade deficit totaled $16 billion in 2007 (table 9.15). Energy imports amounted to over $5 billion, 20 percent of total imports and around 35 percent of the trade deficit.

Tunisia's merchandise trade deficit was around $4 billion in 2007 (table 9.16). The share of energy in total imports was about 12 percent, somewhat less than the share for Morocco. However, thanks to local resources, Tunisia manages a slight surplus in energy trade. Food exports represent only 6 percent of total exports and do not entirely balance food imports.

Libya's merchandise trade balance in 2005 exhibited a surplus of $21 billion (table 9.17). Libya is very similar to Algeria in that hydrocarbon exports represent more than 95 percent of total exports. This raises the same

Table 9.16   Tunisian merchandise trade balance, 2007

Category	Exports Millions of dollars	Exports Percent	Imports Millions of dollars	Imports Percent	Balance (millions of dollars)
Consumption goods	5,568	37.3	1,936	10.3	3,632
Energy	2,416	16.2	2,311	12.3	105
Equipment goods	2,103	14.1	5,001	26.6	−2,898
Food products	896	6.0	1,323	7.0	-427
Primary products	1,038	6.9	375	2.0	664
Semifinished products	2,924	19.6	7,871	41.8	−4,947
Total	14,945	100.0	18,818	100.0	−3,872

Source: Institut National de Statistique.

Table 9.17   Libyan merchandise trade balance, 2007

Category	Exports Millions of dollars	Exports Percent	Imports Millions of dollars	Imports Percent	Balance (millions of dollars)
Energy	27,526	95.3	55	1.0	27,471
Food products	29	0.1	1,319	17.0	−1,290
Manufactured goods	1,242	4.3	6,369	81.0	−5,127
Chemical products	751	2.6	322	4.0	429
Machinery and transport equipment	29	0.1	3,612	46.0	−3,583
Other manufactured products	462	1.6	2,277	29.0	−1,815
Metals and mining	58	0.2	71	1.0	−13
Primary agricultural products	29	0.1	47	1.0	−18
Total	28,884	100.0	7,853	100.0	21,031

Source: UNCTAD, *Trade and Development Report*, 2007.

concern as for Algeria: an extreme dependence on hydrocarbons. The proportion of food imports is also large, almost 17 percent of total imports or around $1.3 billion of food products annually.

Mauritania had a merchandise trade deficit of around $1 billion in 2005 (table 9.18). Energy imports are small and account for 10 percent of total imports.

The Maghreb as a whole is an important trading region; merchandise transactions amount to $200 billion a year, of which 43 percent relate to

Table 9.18   Mauritanian merchandise trade balance, 2005

Category	Exports Millions of dollars	Exports Percent	Imports Millions of dollars	Imports Percent	Balance (millions of dollars)
Energy	n.a.	n.a.	132	10.0	−132
Food products	324	47.0	135	10.0	189
Manufactured products	16	2.4	1,050	79.0	−1 033
Chemical products	1	0.1	32	2.0	−31
Machinery and transportation equipment	6	0.9	891	67.0	−885
Other manufactured products	10	1.5	128	10.0	−118
Metals and mining	344	50.0	3	0.2	342
Primary agricultural products	2	0.3	3	0.2	−1
Total	687	100.0	1,324	100.0	−637

n.a. = not available

Source: UNCTAD, *Trade and Development Report,* 2007.

hydrocarbons. Total exports reached nearly $115 billion in 2006. Algeria and Libya together accounted for nearly 75 percent of regional exports. Tunisia accounted for some 13 percent of total exports and Morocco for 12 percent. Maghreb imports reached around $85 billion, with Morocco representing nearly 35 percent of the regional total, followed by Algeria (32 percent), Tunisia (22 percent), Libya (9 percent), and Mauritania (less than 2 percent).

Scenarios and Perspectives in the Mediterranean Context

The projected rise in energy demand throughout the Maghreb underlines the need for extra capacity in the region. It also emphasizes the complementarities in resources and needs throughout the region, and thus the benefits of efficient trade flows between the countries.

Energy Demand Projections

Table 9.19 shows growth projections for each type of energy in the Maghreb through 2020. Considerable growth in energy consumption is predicted between 2006 and 2020, from 75 mtoe to 128 mtoe. This is mostly linked to the development of electricity generation, which will consume

Table 9.19 Demand for energy in the Maghreb, 2006–20

Country	Primary energy (mtoe)			Oil (million tons)			Natural gas (mtoe)			Renewable energy (mtoe)			Coal (mtoe)			Electricity (TWh)		
	2006	2010p	2020p	2006	2010p	2020p	2006	2010p	2020p	2006	2010p	2020p	2006	2010p	2020p	2006	2010p	2020p
Algeria	34.0	40.0	61.8	11.7	13.0	15.0	21.5	26.0	45.5	0.1	0.1	0.4	0.7	0.8	0.9	34.4	46.1	85.5
Libya	18.7	23.5	28.5	13.2	12.3	13.3	5.3	11.0	15.0	0.2	0.2	0.2	0.0	0.0	0.0	24.0	35.0	48.3
Mauritania	1.2	1.4	1.7	1.0	1.2	1.2	0.0	0.0	0.0	0.3	0.3	0.4	n.a.	n.a.	n.a.	0.4	0.5	0.7
Morocco	12.6	16.6	20.0	7.6	8.4	9.5	0.6	2.3	5.2	0.5	0.6	0.7	3.4	4.0	4.2	19.2	27.4	37.3
Tunisia	8.9	12.6	16.1	4.0	6.8	7.6	3.7	4.5	7.0	1.0	1.2	1.4	0.1	0.1	0.1	13.5	16.3	28.4
Total	75.4	94.1	128.1	37.4	41.7	46.6	31.1	43.8	72.7	2.0	2.4	3.2	4.3	4.9	5.3	91.4	125.3	200.1

p = projection
mtoe = million tons of oil equivalent
TWh = terrawatt hours

Sources: International Energy Agency; BP Statistical Review of World Energy 2007; Observatoire Méditerranéen de l'Energie; CEDIGAZ; and authors' estimates.

31 mtoe in fossil fuels (coal, oil, and gas)—nearly 40 percent of primary energy demand in the Maghreb in 2020. Oil consumption in the Maghreb will increase somewhat, from 38 million tons in 2006 to nearly 47 million tons in 2020. Consumption of natural gas should increase sharply between 2006 and 2020, from 34 Gm^3 (31.1 mtoe) to 80 Gm^3 (72.7 mtoe). Requirements for electricity generation will double between now and 2020, from 17 to 34 Gm^3. Consumption of renewable energy is projected to increase from 2.0 mtoe to only 3.2 mtoe between 2006 and 2020. Important sources of renewable energy exist in the region, but they are likely to remain poorly exploited unless there is a big push from the Union for the Mediterranean. Demand for coal, which is mainly used to generate electricity, should increase from 4.3 mtoe in 2006 to 5.2 mtoe in 2020. This increase is concentrated in Morocco, where consumption will rise from 3.4 mtoe in 2006 to 4.2 mtoe in 2020.

As is noted above, demand for electricity is expected to rise very steeply. According to national companies, total electricity generation in the Maghreb countries should rise by 8 percent per year to reach 200 TWh by 2020. The largest increase is expected in Algeria, where capacity should more than double over the same period. An increase in capacity of more than 24 TWh is expected in Libya and 18 TWh in Morocco. The increase in Tunisia will be around 15 TWh. To accommodate electricity needs in the region, the Maghreb will need to develop additional capacity of over 23,000 MW. Almost 50 new units, each with a capacity of 500 MW, will need to be built—on average, three new power stations per year. From now until 2020, Maghreb countries will need to invest between 15 billion and 20 billion euros to construct and renovate power stations. The investment is considerable at a time when the oil, gas, and electricity industries are all experiencing higher costs for engineering and construction and a significant shortage of skilled manpower.

By using interconnections among countries and increasing intra-Maghreb electricity trade, the region can help satisfy its increased demand and better guarantee the reliability of networks. Better use of existing electric interconnections and gas infrastructure can be a start in promoting energy trade among Maghreb countries and establishing, over the long term, an integrated regional market. A cooperative approach will optimize investment and reduce the financing demands for new capacity.

Energy Trade Potential

The following sections present estimates of intra-Maghreb energy flow increases that could easily be achieved either with existing infrastructures (perhaps renovated) or through projects already under construction or planned.

Algeria-Morocco

Energy trade between Algeria and Morocco could be increased rapidly and significantly. Morocco could import between 35 and 40 percent of its petroleum needs from Algeria. The two countries could trade 3.5 million tons by 2020 using coastal shipping or, preferably, a multiproduct pipeline constructed between the frontier storage facilities at Remchi in Algeria and Oujda in Morocco. Algeria could increase its imports of lubricants from Morocco. Oil transactions could be multiplied by three to four times in 10 years.

Existing natural gas infrastructure between the two countries already allows Morocco to collect 0.9 Gm^3 of gas annually as a transit charge on deliveries sent to Spain and Portugal. The capacity of the gas pipeline could be increased by adding a 5-to-6 Gm^3 compression station, which would respond to increased demand both in Morocco and elsewhere. This would allow Morocco to increase the size of its service fee levy to 1.25 Gm^3. In addition, Morocco could contract a further 2 to 3 Gm^3 of Algerian gas, or 50 percent of its estimated additional needs, by 2020. Morocco would then receive 3 to 4 Gm^3 of gas from Algeria, 50 to 70 percent of its estimated needs for 2020.

Regarding electricity, the third interconnection line being developed between Morocco and Algeria, as well as the 400 kilovolt project throughout the Maghreb, should easily allow an increase of transactions to 4 TWh.

Algeria-Tunisia

Tunisia could import up to 50 percent of its natural gas needs from Algeria, tripling the amount currently imported to 3.5 Gm^3 a year. A levy of up to 1.5 Gm^3 could be collected as transit charges. A further 2 Gm^3 could be imported as part of a contract. The remaining demand could be met through national production and imports from Libya. Gas infrastructure between Tunisia and Algeria already exists; progress on the Libya-Tunisia project, which has been pending for some time, could be accelerated. Tunisia could also satisfy 20 to 30 percent of its oil requirements by importing from Algeria (1.5 to 2 million tons).

Regarding electricity, a fifth interconnection line is being built between Tunisia and Algeria. The ELTAM line along the Maghreb is being upgraded to 400 kilovolt, which will allow transactions to the level of 6 TWh.

To summarize, more than 18 mtoe could be traded between the Maghreb countries by 2020, representing 15 percent of the total energy requirements of the region: petroleum products in the amount of 8.5 million tons (18 percent of total Maghreb oil needs, namely 47 million tons); natural gas in the amount of 9.5 Gm^3 (12 percent of Maghreb natural gas needs, namely 80 Gm^3); and electricity in the amount of 15 TWh (7.5 percent of total demand in the Maghreb, namely 200 TWh).

Sustainable Development

Sustainable development in the Mediterranean requires implementing vigorous policies to conserve energy and better exploit renewable energy. Two collaborative regionwide projects need to be considered: an integrated solar project and applying the Kyoto Protocol's Clean Development Mechanism (CDM).

Integrated Solar Project

An integrated solar project would focus on developing a large number of sites across the Maghreb to produce electricity from solar power (photovoltaic and solar concentrator) and locally manufacturing solar panels, solar concentrators, and other equipment and accessories. On a large enough scale, this project would satisfy both cost criteria and conditions for financing. Such an initiative would benefit from the expertise of northern Mediterranean companies and from the Maghreb's human and technical resources.

The project would affect the economic and social development of rural zones substantially, improving technology for pumping water and thus irrigation for agriculture; it would also establish small units of transformation, storage, and refrigeration that could increase the tourist appeal of these semideserted regions. Finally, it would help Maghreb countries better retain their rural populations, reduce urban concentrations, and diminish tensions over energy sources and the environment.

Clean Development Mechanism

Sustainable development would help fight pollution, which affects all large cities in the Maghreb, and climate change, to which the region is extremely vulnerable. Applying the CDM of the Kyoto Protocol could contribute to financing efficient renewable energy projects. Unfortunately, unlike other regions—Latin America, China, and India—the Mediterranean has been slow to take advantage of this mechanism.

To benefit from the CDM, a regional carbon fund could be set up with the collaboration of northern Mediterranean energy companies. This fund would invest in CDM projects and encourage an energy policy adapted to the Maghreb, while simultaneously helping the northern Mediterranean countries to reach their targets for reducing greenhouse gas emissions in line with the Kyoto Protocol and its successor agreement.

Diversifying Energy Supply in the Maghreb: The Nuclear Option

The pressure of energy demand means that no option should be ignored. Renewable energy forms should obviously be used to the maximum, but they will not be sufficient to replace thermal production methods in the electricity sector. The nuclear option is being considered seriously in the Maghreb. Morocco, Algeria, Tunisia, and Libya are all separately studying the possibility of including nuclear power in their energy choices and are elaborating protocols of cooperation with several other countries.

Nuclear power development is a complex field that is particularly sensitive to issues of security. It requires massive investment that cannot be achieved without close cooperation with international companies that have the requisite technology and expertise, notably to handle radioactive waste. Developing nuclear power to generate electricity should take place in a regional context, allowing Maghreb countries to pool their human, technical, and financial capabilities and at the same time benefit from the expertise of their partners.

Training and Research and Development

Efficient and lasting partnerships will not exist without investing in training and research and development. It is essential to plan for specialized training institutes and joint research centers. Several regional institutes should be set up to train engineers and technicians in fields related to hydrocarbon, electricity, and nuclear industries, as well as renewable energy and sustainable development sectors. Instructors and specialists should come from every country and the diplomas delivered by training courses should be recognized across the entire Euro-Mediterranean region. Maghreb institutes should be publicly supported to develop research programs in subjects of common interest.

The Challenge for the Union for the Mediterranean

Twelve years after the start of the Barcelona Process, the gap between European countries and the developing countries of the southern Mediterranean is as large as ever. This calls for a fresh spur to cooperation between the Mediterranean's northern and southern shores. One of the greatest challenges facing the creation of a Euro-Mediterranean partnership will be to alter fundamentally the European perception of North African countries as simply suppliers of raw materials or as market opportunities. Meanwhile, Maghreb countries should not stick to old individualistic attitudes but consider the advantages of a regional approach, not only from geostrategic and economic points of view, but also in terms of the strong workforce formed by a young population.

The question arises regarding whether the energy sector could act as a catalyst to initiate the process toward an integrated economy with a high and sustainable level of growth and more widespread cooperation around the Mediterranean. The uneven division of energy resources among Mediterranean countries suggests a basis for well thought out and acceptable forms of interdependence.

Recommendations

Based on the above figures, recommendations for the Maghreb consist of developing energy trading generally within the region and specifically building power stations to service both the Maghreb and European countries.

Developing Energy Trading

Above all else, the development of energy trade is essential. The potential is enormous if countries can find the political will and are prepared to encourage business in the right direction. The following paragraphs suggest measures that could be achieved realistically in the short term.

Multiproduct pipelines—liquefied petroleum gas, gasoline, and diesel—could be constructed to connect the storage and distribution facilities on either side of the borders between Algeria and Tunisia and between Algeria and Morocco. This initiative would not only meet the growing needs of the border regions, but also end the considerable informal trade in petroleum products across the borders. Natural gas consumption could be increased, in particular in Morocco, in the electricity, tertiary, and domestic sectors. A gas pipeline already runs through Moroccan territory and branches could be created that connect it to large urban centers. Constraints on electricity could be eased by maximizing the use of existing electric interconnections between countries and by upgrading them to increase transactions both within the Maghreb and with Europe. In addition, a 400 kilovolt line running from Morocco to Egypt would reinforce electricity networks efficiently across North Africa.

Direct undersea north-south connections could be constructed between Morocco and Spain, between Algeria and Spain via the Medgaz pipeline, between Algeria and Italy via the Galsi pipeline, between Tunisia and Italy, and even between Libya and Italy. These connections would allow partners to use complementary supply and demand situations better and optimize investments at a regionwide level, reducing costs for individual countries. The connections would also provide more reliable and secure supplies of electricity to Maghreb countries.

Partnerships for Building Power Stations

Despite the important progress in rural electrification that Maghreb countries have made in recent years, access to electric power is still not universal and much remains to be done. The difference in production capacity between the southern and northern Mediterranean countries demonstrates the level of effort still required. Maghreb countries should eventually enjoy the same amount of secure power per capita that the European Union does.

The anticipated development of both electric generation capacity and transport networks will require total investment of about 15 billion to 20 billion euros for the Maghreb countries by 2020. The question is whether Maghreb countries can raise such sums given their economic situation, the small amount of public funds available, the lack of creditworthiness, and the country risk premiums that lenders demand.

All North African countries from Morocco to Egypt should establish a global plan to build electricity power stations with joint-venture companies. This is one of the most crucial challenges facing the Mediterranean. Fortunately, natural gas is widely available. Reforms enacted over recent years in several countries have opened energy markets to the private sector. This should allow them to enter into partnership projects. Mediterranean cooperation would improve the institutional and financial conditions needed to finance local energy projects. Nuclear power also remains an option. Some power stations could be coupled with desalination plants, as the desalination of seawater is crucial for the future of North Africa. Other power stations could be dedicated, in part, to exporting electricity.

The main goal should be universal access to reliable electric power. Improvement of interconnections should be a priority, as it will allow better exploitation of complementary relations, not only among the Maghreb countries, but also between North Africa and the European market. Power projects should not only seek to optimize production and availability in the Maghreb, but also exploit opportunities to export gas and electricity to the north.

Conclusion

The grand idea is for Maghreb countries to agree on a global plan, based on their mutual interests, for building power plants, refineries, and transport and distribution infrastructure, as well as developing wind and solar power. Growth in demand for energy in the Maghreb—particularly electricity—will be considerable over the next 15 years. This will be one of the key factors affecting the economic and social development of Maghreb countries. However, growth runs the danger of being slowed by problems in financing the necessary infrastructure.

A global plan would be based on joint-venture companies bringing together operators in Maghreb countries and European players, both to develop integrated projects that would respond more efficiently to energy needs and to export gas, electricity, and other petrochemical products to Europe and other markets. Reforms enacted independently by various Maghreb countries over recent years have encouraged the opening of energy markets to the private sector; these should be extended to attract more firms to the energy sector.

Cooperation on a Mediterranean scale would facilitate the establishment of appropriate institutional structures and adequate finance. In the context of balanced cooperation, the Union for the Mediterranean could make a major contribution to economic integration. Discordant voices have already been raised, notably in Algeria, where the project is criticized for not being a political agreement. But the project remains important and it is imperative to make the correct strategic, economic, and political choices. Without a doubt, the energy sector could be a driving force for establishing the Union for the Mediterranean, based on complementary supply and demand, a balance of relationships, and a regard for solidarity.

Given the inequalities between the Mediterranean's north and south, the scale of investment needed, and the human and technical resources to be mobilized, cooperation is necessary and desirable in the Maghreb's energy sector. The economic policies of the Maghreb countries should be formed with a long-term vision of regional solidarity and cooperation; otherwise the region will remain prey to numerous contradictions that foment instability.

10

Maghreb Banks
and Financial Markets

ABDERRAHMANE HADJ NACER and GUILLAUME ALMÉRAS

For years, North African governments have made strenuous efforts to restructure their financial sectors and bring them into line with international standards, with the help in particular of the World Bank and the European Union. In 2003 Egypt adopted a new banking law aimed at stabilizing its financial sector by reinforcing the prudential ratios of banks, improving their standards of governance, and raising minimum capital requirements. The following year, a restructuring plan launched several reforms: debt forgiveness, withdrawal of the state from the banking sector, and privatization (open to foreign investors) of two of the four leading state banks.

Similar reforms are being enacted with varying degrees of speed and vigor elsewhere. Table 10.1 gives an overview of the top 15 North African banks. Tunisia is a laggard: With 20 credit institutions, 18 offshore banks, and 9 foreign banks with representative offices, Tunisia might seem to be oversupplied with banking services, but the sector remains dominated by state-owned banks, in particular Société Tunisienne de Banque and Banque de l'Habitat. Algeria is undeniably undersupplied in terms of branch networks, market share held by private banks, and methods of payment. There are hardly more bank branches in Algeria now than at the

Abderrahmane Hadj Nacer is the former governor of the central bank of Algeria. He ran the department of economic affairs at the presidency of Algeria from 1985 to 1989. Guillaume Alméras is a partner at BGV Consulting in Paris, where his fields of expertise are international banking and development finance.

Table 10.1 Top 15 banks in North Africa, 2006

Bank	Rank in Africa	Country	Tier 1 capital (millions of dollars)	Assets (millions of dollars)	Profits (millions of dollars)	Return on equity (percent)	Return on assets (percent)
Groupe Banque Populaire	6	Morocco	1,711	16,002	409	24	1.8
Attijariwafa Bank	7	Morocco	1,538	19,573	363	23.6	1.9
National Bank of Egypt	9	Egypt	1,179	34,107	89	7.5	0.2
BMCE	12	Morocco	748	10,060	158	21.1	1.5
Banque Misr	14	Egypt	584	18,490	38	6.5	0.2
Commercial International Bank	15	Egypt	538	6,632	168	31.2	2.5
Banque du Caire	16	Egypt	510	7,943	22	4.3	0.3
Arab International Bank	18	Egypt	474	3,833	22	4.6	0.6
Crédit Populaire d'Algérie	22	Algeria	400	6,494	147	36.7	2.3
Société Tunisienne de Banque	24	Tunisia	338	3,620	17	5	0.5
Bank of Alexandria	25	Egypt	315	5,764	196	62.2	3.4
BIAT	21	Tunisia	276	3,186	20	7.2	0.6
SG Marocaine de Banque	33	Morocco	271	3,790	73	27	1.9
BNA	34	Tunisia	269	3,463	n.a.	n.a.	n.a.
AAIB	36	Egypt	258	4,918	77	30	1.5

n.a. = not available

Source: African Business/Africa Banker, October 2007.

time of independence in 1962, despite a threefold increase in the population. The seemingly never-ending privatization process of the Crédit Populaire illustrates how much progress needs to be made if international standards are to be met. The spotlight was turned on this process when Santander withdrew its takeover bid because the Spanish bank believed the dice were loaded. Recently, Algeria has also experienced two unfortunate private banking initiatives, both of which resulted in the spectacular collapse of newly founded private banks, El Khalifa and Banque Commerciale et Industrielle d'Algérie.

In 2005 the public sector accounted for 30 percent of bank loans in Morocco, 32 percent in Tunisia, and almost 88 percent in Algeria. Banks with foreign capital controlled 34 percent of the Tunisian market and 21 percent of the Moroccan market, but only 10 percent of the Algerian market. Despite this, the Algerian market today attracts the attention of the largest international institutions, in particular Gulf banks, which, for the moment, have not developed Islamic banking much beyond Egypt.

The Egyptian banking landscape remains in a state of transition. The first two objectives—consolidating institutions and opening internationally—have been partly achieved. The number of financial institutions decreased from 61 in 2004 to only 40 at the end of 2006. However, this number is still excessive because the objective was to retain only 26 institutions. Regarding international openness, the two leading Egyptian private banks, National Société Générale Bank and Bank of Alexandria, have come under French and Italian control, respectively; that said, these two banks only attract 10 percent of deposits despite their large branch networks. The two leading state-owned banks, which account for half the branches in the country, attract roughly half the deposits but supply less than 40 percent of the loans. Moreover, they are highly specialized by sectors: hydrocarbons for the National Bank of Egypt and textiles for Misr Bank.

Banking reforms today have been most successful at the eastern and southern ends of the Mediterranean rim. Moroccan and Turkish banks are very profitable and their performance indicators often outshine their European counterparts. In 2006 the Turkish banks had an average return on equity (RoE) of 19 percent, an operating ratio of 46 percent, and a ratio of reserves against nonperforming loans of 89 percent. The same year, in Morocco, the average RoE of banks was 16 percent, although Attijariwafa Bank reached almost 20 percent and Banque Centrale Populaire 24 percent, both with operating ratios of 49 percent. The average reserve ratio for Moroccan banks was 74 percent. By comparison, the RoE of Santander, the most profitable bank in Europe today, is 17 percent.

Morocco's banking sector is thus characterized by the strength of its banks, which it wants to turn into national champions. The three leaders—Attijariwafa Bank, Groupe Banque Populaire (which is majority state-owned at the holding level), and Banque Marocaine du Commerce Extérieur (BMCE)—account for 64 percent of loans and almost all deposits, of which 60 percent are from emigrant remittances for Groupe Banque Populaire. Attijariwafa Bank and Groupe Banque Populaire own more than half of all bank branches. The progress of the Moroccan banks is particularly visible in regulation and new activities. In 2007 they adopted part of the Basel II directive with respect to capital ratios. Attijariwafa and Banque Centrale Populaire have begun to record modest yet significant gains in capital markets.

Leading Moroccan institutions are developing an international presence, mostly southward on the African continent. Attijariwafa opened several branches in Senegal and could expand into Burkina Faso, Gabon, and Equatorial Guinea. Banque Centrale Populaire is considering a move into Mauritania. The BMCE has a presence as a commercial bank in Senegal (BMCE Capital). Attijariwafa has a presence in Tunisia (Banque du Sud) and, like the BMCE, has applied for a license in Algeria. Finally, with its Spanish shareholder Santander, Attijariwafa is developing partnerships to deal with flows of emigrant remittances.

In both Turkey and Morocco, international expansion is driven by the saturation of the domestic banking sector, as gaining local market share has become increasingly difficult. Turkey has 49 banks, of which 3 are state owned, 15 are foreign banks, and 13 are commercial and development banks. The five leading institutions attract 83 percent of deposits, but account for only 62 percent of total bank assets and extend only 57 percent of loans.

Market saturation in Turkey and Morocco is paradoxical, as by Western standards neither has a particularly developed banking system. No more than 37 percent of the Moroccan population uses banking services, compared with 98 percent in France. There is one bank branch for every 7,300 inhabitants in Morocco compared with one branch for every 2,400 people in France. Morocco has the highest ratio in the region, but a third of the branches are concentrated in and around Casablanca. The profitability of Turkish and Moroccan banks can best be explained by the relatively restricted development of these two banking markets.

In Morocco, banks finance themselves in large part through short-term deposits. In 2006 interest paid was 3.43 percent for six months, on average. The funds are then reinvested in treasury bills and bonds, with rates ranging from 2.57 percent for 13 weeks to 4.63 percent for 20 years, and in loans, with an average rate of return of 7.08 percent (11.53 percent for consumer credits).[1] The margins on loans appear to be so wide because access

---

1. See Bank al Maghrib (2006). These figures are not unusual for emerging countries. Chilean banks, the best performing among emerging countries from a banking standpoint, were making loans at 4 percent interest in 2004.

Table 10.2   Market capitalization to GNP ratio for selected countries, 2006 (percent)

Country	Ratio
Algeria	n.a.
Brazil	0.56
Egypt	0.73
India	0.75
Israel	1.31
Jordan	1.89
Lebanon	0.34
Libya	n.a.
Malaysia	1.43
Morocco	0.68
Romania	0.29
South Korea	1.07
Syria	n.a.
Tunisia	0.13
Turkey	0.34

n.a. = not available

Source: Central Intelligence Agency (CIA) World Factbook.

to credit remains a privilege; at the same time, the margins raise doubt over the intensity of competition in the banking sector.

North African banks are too liquid, as is often the case in emerging markets. They do not use all the funds they collect in lending activity. Weakness in credit extension resembles other emerging countries. The ratio of domestic credit to GDP is 66 percent in Morocco, 65 percent in Tunisia, and around 13 percent in Algeria. By comparison, the ratio reaches 123 percent in the United States and 167 percent in the European Union; the figure for South Korea is 76 percent, and for Brazil only 41 percent.

As table 10.2 shows, capital markets remain poorly developed, even nonexistent in Algeria and Libya, although the stock exchange in Morocco has an emerging profile that attracts foreign investors, who account for 30 percent of Moroccan stock market capitalization. Morocco's emerging profile includes the presence of speculation, visible in the remarkable appreciation of the Moroccan All Shares Index (MASI) on the Casablanca stock exchange, which rose by 71 percent in 2006 against an increase of 21 percent for Tunisia's Tunindex in 2006.

By contrast with Morocco's stock market, the bond and traded debt markets are apathetic. In 2006 only 4.1 billion Moroccan dirhams in bonds

Table 10.3 Public debt to GNP ratio for selected countries, 2007 (percent)

Country	Ratio
Algeria	10
Brazil	44
Egypt	105
India	59
Israel	83
Jordan	67
Lebanon	188
Libya	5
Malaysia	41
Morocco	64
Romania	19
South Korea	33
Syria	37
Tunisia	55
Turkey	58

n.a. = not available

Source: Central Intelligence Agency (CIA) *World Factbook.*

were issued in Morocco, which originated from two issuers. In the same year, 1.3 billion dirhams of treasury notes were issued. Outstanding treasury debt was 10.3 billion dirhams.

The weakness of financial markets in the region can be linked to the limited role of institutional investors, in particular the feeble development of insurance companies, not so much in number as in size. Egypt has 21 insurance companies, of which three, together with one reinsurance company, control 70 percent of the market. But the market accounts for only 2 percent of GDP. In Algeria the insurance market accounted for a paltry 0.6 percent of GDP in 2005, despite the existence of 16 companies, of which 7 are state-owned. In such conditions governments have no choice but to finance their debt through banks and therefore deposits. Apart from Algeria and Libya, Maghreb countries have high levels of public debt (table 10.3).

In sum, there is a stranglehold on the extension of credit. First, financial markets lack depth. Second, company accounts are generally opaque, due to the wide use of double accounting that allows the flight of profits and a corresponding reduction of equity capital. This is both the cause and the consequence of restricted access to credit. Many small and medium-sized companies have learned to manage without bank loans and thus are not inclined to increase transparency; various legal measures have been introduced in response. The Tunisian Financial Security Law of October 2005 mandates auditing for joint-stock companies. The World Bank recommendations of credit ratings and establishing a credit bureau are being pursued.

In the meantime, nonperforming loans remain high, at 11 percent in Morocco and 19 percent in Tunisia compared with fewer than 4 percent in France. In reaction, banks require prohibitive guarantee levels. The estimated average for the Middle East and North Africa region is 230 percent of the extended loan, one of the highest in the world. Banks demand that guarantees be in the form of personal assets, for the most part real estate or, for foreign currency transactions, a cash equivalent. Many private individuals and business are thus excluded from the credit market because they cannot meet the guarantee requirements. This system penalizes the development of the economy as a whole and hobbles the growth of banks, as banks often have to content themselves with sharing the mortgage on speculative real estate, such as apartment buildings or tourist infrastructure.

The above practices are hardly conducive to developing a true credit culture. Banks tend to base their decisions on the face value of the personal assets offered as guarantees rather than on evaluations of the projects and their attendant risks. This effectively turns banks into simple holders of security. As a result, they do not develop the technical expertise to evaluate business risks or engage in financial engineering that would meet the needs of the business community. Lack of transparency in the balance sheets of firms means that the true cost of risk is barely reflected in bank lending rates.

Inadequate legal systems—poorly protected property rights, lapses in land registry entries, opaque lease arrangements—often make it difficult for banks to enforce the loan guarantees. Banks thus accumulate many unpaid debts, but the legal procedures to resolve disputes are long and expensive, and their outcome is often uncertain. Faced with such constraints, it is hardly surprising that banks limit the offer of credit in quantity (many businesses do not qualify), quality (few long-term arrangements), and terms (mandatory personal asset guarantees and cash collateral for international trade transactions).

For the moment, despite considerable efforts to modernize the system and a few successes, banks are not in a position to promote economic development in North Africa. This was the situation of French banks at the end of the 19th century; one response was the rise of popular savings institutions independent of established banks (e.g., Caisse d'Epargne, a savings bank). Today, the situation of Moroccan banks suggests parallels. Though the majority of the country's population is rural, only 6 percent of loans were directed to the farming sector in 2006. Industry received 28 percent of loans and the service sector 66 percent.

Moreover, across the entire region, the tendency is toward forms of pure usury where consumer credit and microcredit are concerned. With interest rates that easily reach 50 percent annually, repayment is extremely fast. The popularity of microcredit assumes results that are not confirmed by available data, notably regarding job creation. In Morocco, 12 microcredit associations have 1 million clients (they estimate their market at 3.2 million clients), of which 66 percent are women, but they create less than 5,000 jobs per year (Bank al Maghrib 2006). Yet Morocco has one of the most developed microcredit markets in the world. The microcredit emanates essentially from private foundations, unlike in other countries, where it is supported by semipublic initiatives. In Tunisia, the Banque Tunisienne de Solidarité gives assistance at preferential rates of 5 percent a year using the network of post office branches. Tunisia distinguishes itself from other countries in the region because most microcredit borrowers have completed high school or have university degrees.

Mortgage financing has grown fastest in Morocco, where real estate speculation is significant in large towns. The level of outstanding debt increased by 24 percent in 2005 and 28 percent in 2006, and the share of variable-rate indebtedness among individuals reached 42 percent of total indebtedness in 2006.

The entrepreneurial profiles of North African countries are characterized by a large proportion of small and medium-sized enterprises (SMEs) and especially very small businesses. Family firms dominate the agricultural and service sectors. Several lending organizations such as the European Investment Bank (EIB) are beginning to develop loan refinancing for SMEs.

A goal of the Mediterranean banks is to make banking services more widely available. Until recently the lack of efficient methods for depositing and withdrawing funds has been a considerable obstacle to extending credit to both firms and individuals. Banking activity in the region is first and foremost characterized by long queues at counters. Cash still dominates debit and credit cards, checks, and above all, wire transfers; however, this creates a profitable environment for banks, as it makes their clients captive and limits the market share that any new entrant can hope to gain.

North African banks should seek to extend loans. In Morocco, short-term credits, consisting of debit accounts and cash credits, still exceed capital goods financing and account for 54 percent of credit. Banking services are essentially short term, especially for private banks. The World Bank (2006) has underlined that three-quarters of investment in the region is self-financed and 12 percent is supported by bank loans, the lowest level in the world.

To mitigate the lack of long-term finance, development banks were created in many countries, but have now either been converted into universal and privatized banks—such as the Banque Tuniso-Koweïtienne, which was acquired by a French savings banks—or still struggle to find their place. The fundamental problem stems from difficulties in attracting and transforming savings. This is relevant to both national and international savings remitted by emigrants.

Emigrant Remittances

In quantitative terms, remittance flows in the Mediterranean remain difficult to assess precisely, be it in sending or receiving countries. In Algeria no proper structure has been put in place to collect these funds.

Despite the interest that emigrant remittances attract today, notably from large international lenders such as the EIB or the African Development Bank (AfDB), the most available and reliable figures are those of Morocco, surely one of the best organized countries in the world in this respect. Nearly 4 billion euros have been transferred to Morocco every year for the past five years, half of this amount from France. Out of the total 4.3 billion euros received in 2006, 3 billion euros went through banks.[2] Total remittance flows represent 22 percent of current revenues reported in the Moroccan balance of payments. These flows are more than 50 percent of export revenues, exceeding revenues from either tourism or phosphates.[3]

Total annual remittance flows from Europe to Algeria, Morocco, and Tunisia are estimated at 10 billion euros. Flows from Europe to the larger Mediterranean area stand at around 20 billion euros. In parallel, new remitting countries are emerging, such as Canada, and others are playing a larger role, such as the Gulf states. In France, at least 41 percent of emigrants transfer money back to their home countries, sending, on average, between 15 and 25 percent of their income in roughly eight transfers a year. Recipient households receive on average 2,470 euros per year.

Despite their size, remittance flows have attracted little interest in the Maghreb. It was originally assumed that the transfers would progressively dry up as families regrouped abroad and most emigrants gave up on the idea of returning home. Yet, for the past six years, the amounts transferred have been growing significantly, at a rate of 15 percent per year. In Morocco, over the past seven years, only 2002 recorded a decrease, a fall of 12 percent. This same phenomenon can be observed elsewhere. Money is no longer sent back simply to support the family. It is saved and invested as emigrants attempt to profit from differentials in purchasing power between the two shores.

All of the above calls for a fresh look at the behavior of migrant populations, in particular those born in Europe, who may not aspire to integrate fully in either their country of origin or their country of adoption,

---

2. Office des Changes du Maroc, Transfers, 2007, available at www.oc.gov.ma (accessed May 20, 2007).

3. Nevertheless these transfers would appear to be very inferior to the revenues generated by the Moroccan production of cannabis, estimated at 12 billion euros per year. Generated by trafficking routes in Europe, it remains difficult to assess what proportion of these revenues is remitted back to Morocco and what percentage of transfers they represent. According to the United Nations Office on Drugs and Crime (UNODC 2005), Moroccan farmers earned $214 million in 2004 from cultivating cannabis.

but rather seek to straddle the two. Instead of reducing transfers, economic development in North African countries may increase them.

On the other hand, there is a considerable mass of capital originating in North African countries—estimated roughly at around 7 billion euros per year—that has been invested in Europe or the United States for lack of adequate investment targets locally. Thus, although emigrant remittances are the prime source of foreign exchange, domestic savings flee the Maghreb region for lack of opportunities and any confidence in local markets. This phenomenon constitutes another structural brake on development.

The dominant reason for emigrant remittances remains family support, demonstrated by the fact that in Morocco remittance fluctuations follow harvest fortunes. The direct beneficiaries of the transfers still use the money mainly for daily consumption expenses (51 percent). Nevertheless, the share allotted to investment is increasing and is estimated to account for 20 percent of the transfers. According to the AfDB (2007), 40 to 70 percent of emigrants over the age of 35 invest some of the remittances they send. Funds used for investment purposes are invested in real estate (83 percent), commerce (12 percent), industry (3 percent), and agriculture (2 percent). However, the productive use of remittance funds is doubly compromised. First, the majority of the funds disappear from the banking circuit. Second, there are few useful investment instruments in North African economies apart from real estate.

No formula has been worked out that allows transferred funds to be deployed directly for productive investment. One can only point to the disappointing results of the institutions created for this purpose, such as Desiyab in Turkey (1976), the Syrian Expatriate Fund, and Bank al Amal in Morocco (1989). Many of the conditions necessary for success—guaranteed convertibility, fiscal advantages, state support for investments—appear to be in place, yet these institutions largely fail to meet the needs of emigrants. It is erroneous to believe that large numbers of emigrants can engage directly in productive investment: Banks are crucial to intermediation. International lenders make the same mistake when they suggest channeling funds using microfinance institutions or communities as recipients.

The majority of transfers remain outside the banking system because access to banking services is restricted and no single banking institution has sufficient networks on both sides of the Mediterranean to organize the collection and distribution of funds on a large scale. In these circumstances, most transfers are handled by money transfer companies such as Western Union, which have agreements with local banks and post offices on both sides of the Mediterranean. The fees charged are often accused of being prohibitive. Fees for transfers to Algeria or Tunisia are around 8 percent and can reach 16 percent of the sum transferred. According to the AfDB (2007), 70 percent of emigrants and 90 percent of recipients were unaware of these costs. Some transfers are in cash or use informal channels, and are thus expensive and risky. However, informal channels can be advantageous when there is a significant disparity between the official exchange rate and that of the free market; disparities of around 10 percent can be observed in Morocco. This is another reason why currency convertibility should be adopted.

Banks on both sides of the Mediterranean could remedy the situation by agreeing to connect their networks on an account-to-account basis. This would considerably reduce the cost of transfers while allowing funds to remain within the banking system. Such systems have already been set up between several institutions—notably between Spain and Morocco and between Portugal and France—but a consortium approach has yet to be developed on a scale appropriate to the Mediterranean. Mediterranean cooperation is observable in other sectors, however, such as telecommunications: In response to the needs of emigrant populations, two Moroccan telecommunications companies, Maroc Telecom and the Moroccan Sahan group, formed the Mobisud consortium with SFR, a French company.

An account-to-account linkage is the only formula that would permit the large-scale mobilization of emigrant savings. It responds well to the targeted needs of emigrants, particularly for real estate projects. At least a part of remitted funds might be used to create a market for long-term financial instruments, a market now lacking in the Maghreb. In turn, this market could become a source of long-term financing of infrastructure, among other uses. A genuine Euro-Mediterranean financial arena could eventually emerge from this foundation.

A Bank of the Mediterranean?

The idea of creating a Bank of the Mediterranean, modeled on the European Bank for Reconstruction and Development, which works with East European countries, has often been raised, but the Ecofin Council rejected it in 2003. This decision reflected diverging priorities among EU countries as well as budgetary constraints. The current inclination is to create a Mediterranean financial agency that would administer a fund to develop business and a fund dedicated to infrastructure. Those instruments would partly replace the EIB's Neighborhood Investment Facility.

Creating a financial agency could revive private investment in the Mediterranean partner countries and support SME financing. It also would centralize various initiatives involving European public aid. A multilateral management strategy could be developed by opening up the agency's capital to outside actors, such as individual countries of the European Union and the Mediterranean, and investors from the Gulf states. If created, the agency should develop innovative financing strategies and get involved in emigrant transfers, as discussed. A partnership between the agency and banking institutions on both shores would gather funds in amounts that far exceed those advanced by the European Union.

The agency would certainly be able to improve administration of financing for projects and infrastructure. However, the financing needs for foreseeable large-scale projects, such as the Horizon 2020 project for pollution control in the Mediterranean, far exceed the funds that the agency might have at its disposal. It would therefore be necessary to mobilize government borrowings by various Mediterranean states for major undertakings.

Following the example of the Association of Southeast Asian Nations Plus Three (ASEAN+3), the agency should help to develop bond and stock markets in the Mediterranean partner countries. This would provide an alternative to bank intermediation and address the need for long-term financing and capital-intensive projects. Such markets would allow international investors to use local currency in their financing. Moreover, the market would facilitate the creation of specialized savings products in terms of objective and maturity—liquid savings, real estate savings, health and retirement savings—that require the management of assets in forms that yield higher returns than are currently available.

Beyond this, it is possible to imagine the creation of a Maghreb version of France's Continuous Assisted Quotation (CAC 40) stock market index. In October 2007, the Subsahara Africa 50 Index was launched, grouping the 50 strongest stock market capitalizations of 11 countries, headed by Nigeria (40 percent) and Kenya (20 percent). The capitalization of those stock markets has greatly increased over the last years, from $15 billion in 2002 to $100 billion in 2007, but for the most part they remain far below the size of the Maghreb stock markets.

An ambitious extension of the financial agency concept might entail a regional financial institution with supranational powers. It would have three aims: to transform unused liquidity into long-term financial instruments that could contribute in all three countries to the modernization of the financial system; to turn the inevitable privatization of the Algerian banking system into an opportunity to create two regional banks with shareholdings in the three countries, the prime task of which would be to encourage and engineer mergers and acquisitions across North Africa; and to ensure full currency convertibility.

Recommendations and Conclusion

Excepting Mauritania and Libya, where everything remains a work in progress, the three other North African countries have overhauled their financial systems. Today, each of these countries has modernized systems of payment and all are progressively aligning their standards for monitoring bank risk to international norms. At one extreme, the Moroccan banking system has been thoroughly modernized and banks offer a quality of service equivalent to that of European or US banks. At the other extreme, the banking system in Algeria, as it operates in 2008, has regressed beyond the standards of the 1960s.

All in all, the reforms to date have not substantially modified the banking landscape. They have failed to significantly increase access to loans for businesses and individuals. The reforms must be continued, and even accelerated, in the case of Tunisia and Algeria.

The three banking systems display common features. The share of bank credit devoted to the public sector is high and the percentage of people holding bank accounts is low. The flow of capital escaping the region is higher than the combined total of workers' remittances and foreign direct investment (FDI). High net-worth individuals, including entrepreneurs, have little trust in the systems in which they operate. Yet entrepreneurs who are close to the ruling elites benefit from modern services and low interest rates.

North African banks are traditionally too liquid. But seeing this feature in isolation can be misleading. The moment these banks try to expand, they rapidly use up their resources. This is precisely the case today. FDI is flowing into the region and the investing firms often apply for loans in local currency. As a consequence, since the fourth quarter of 2007, Moroccan banks have experienced very real cash flow problems (Bank al Maghrib 2008). In sharp contrast to the nonbank financial markets in the region, which are shallow and reflect the weakness of institutional investors, North African banks are flourishing. But despite the efforts of recent decades, banks do not play the role they could in developing the economies of North Africa.

Two recommendations can be made concerning the development of financial systems in North Africa. First, countries should loosen the conditions for access to credit. Second, they should encourage the accumulation of banking resources in the form of household savings. In this respect, two initiatives should be launched in the context of Mediterranean economic integration.

First, a Euro-Mediterranean finance agency should be created that would be dedicated to supporting SMEs and guaranteeing risk to facilitate bank refinancing and lines of credit. The procedures could be inspired by models such as the US Small Business Administration or French Oséo and established on a Euro-Mediterranean scale. Second, the largest private European and North African banks should agree to connect their networks and thus form a consortium to bring emigrant money into the banking system and encourage savings. This unprecedented approach would use the accumulated resources in concert with multilateral public lenders to develop investment vehicles and guarantee funds. The modalities of such a public-private partnership would need to be precisely defined.

Apart from the banks, two recommendations relate to other financial markets in the region, which remain underdeveloped. The insurance sector is in great need of reform, particularly regarding rationalization of policies, privatization, and consolidation of many small players. It is particularly important to encourage the emergence of substantial insurance companies to add depth to financial markets.

Stock and bond markets need to be developed. Reforms should concentrate on building bridges to European and Gulf stock markets to encourage the double or triple quotation of local businesses, revising quotation conditions to encourage the entry of foreign investors in local markets, creating bonds and public-private stock funds on the model of those developed by ASEAN+3, and establishing a North African Dow Jones index.

Operations should be consolidated for microfinance institutions, allowing them to enhance their productivity and the security of their operations. Joint back offices could be created. Stronger links should be put in place with both national and international banking networks, especially for emigrant money.

Finally, at a microeconomic level, two measures are essential, in line with numerous recommendations made by the World Bank and others, namely, creating credit bureaus and overhauling the instruments of risk quotation. Each country should concentrate on broad-brush measures to reduce nonperforming loans. These include buying some of the debt from banks at a steep discount, securitizing some of the debt with the support of specialized international banks, and engaging international factoring professionals to sort out many of the present difficulties.

References

AfDB (African Development Bank). 2007. *Remittances by Migrants, a Development Challenge*. Abidjan.

Bank al Maghrib. 2006. *Annual Report*. Rabat.

Bank al Maghrib. 2008. *Monetary Report* (March). Rabat.

UNODC (United Nations Office on Drugs and Crime). 2005. *Morocco Cannabis Survey 2004*. New York.

World Bank. 2006. *MENA Economic Development and Prospects*. Washington.

11

Opportunities for Logistical Improvements through Maghreb Integration

HASSAN BENABDERRAZIK

The sobering failure of North African countries to deal peacefully with their differences is only too obvious on either side of the Algerian-Moroccan border. Closed frontier checkpoints, unused rail tracks leading nowhere, and unfinished motorways celebrate the failed dream of the Arab Maghreb Union (AMU) launched in Marrakech 19 years ago. What might convince people to stand up for an ambitious project to integrate the region? Have the many years in which AMU countries pursued their own path undermined the rationale for true integration? At the borders—more so on the Algerian-Moroccan border, less so on the Algerian-Tunisian one—many age-old trade and family links have now faded away to be replaced by smuggling.

Meanwhile, ever stronger north-south ties have blossomed, as Algeria, Morocco, and Tunisia have vied to strengthen their ties with important European partners and countries beyond. New roads, harbors, and railroads following a north-south logic have profoundly changed the economic landscape of North Africa, opening the question of whether such developments have rendered the AMU concept obsolete. We concentrate

Hassan Benabderrazik founded and directed the consulting group AgroConcept from 1985 to 1998. He was secretary general of the Moroccan Ministère des Affaires Générales from 1999 to 2001 and of the Ministry of Agriculture from 2001 to 2004.

139

on regional infrastructure, transport, and logistics, using economic analysis to assess opportunities for cooperation and common development.

Numerous papers and studies have looked at the relationships between infrastructure and development in the context of economic integration (e.g., Agenor and Moreno-Dodson 2006, Calderon and Serven 2004, Tanzi 2005 and 2006). The literature addresses two issues: the nature of infrastructure as a network, in which the value of the service provided is proportional to the number of feasible connections created, and the intensity of use as a measure of the actual economic payoff. An empty road or an idle port is a bad investment, but greater use multiplies its social benefits.

This chapter focuses on the changing transportation landscape in Algeria, Morocco, and Tunisia resulting from regulatory reform designed to improve competitiveness. A brief summary of the milestones of the process illustrates the progress made and what remains to be done. Although the countries concerned diverge in how much they export and hence their logistical performance, all three have modernized their institutional frameworks for port operations and road, rail, and air transport. Those reforms were motivated by the need to improve efficiency through both competition and public-private partnerships. The increased use of containers, logistical platforms, and integration into global value chains has contributed to modernizing the transportation sector.

Good logistics entail the proper use of transport networks to ensure well functioning supply chains. The logistics concept encompasses transport by all modes, management of storage facilities, information networks to process documents quickly and efficiently, and customs and banking services. A strong logistical chain coupled with the efficient use of infrastructure offers great potential to reduce costs, as logistics account for 18 to 20 percent of GDP in Mediterranean countries. Cost reductions of 25 percent through proper management are quite common. Such reductions result from using transport lines optimally, relying on logistical platforms to group and distribute, exploiting transshipment to secure the best routes and costs, and relying on information processing for electronic data interchange (EDI).

There are numerous opportunities to optimize infrastructure usage and logistical cost through Maghreb integration, but these have little relevance without meaningful trade volumes among Maghreb countries. There can be no serious logistical cost reductions when trade is virtually blocked because of closed borders. How much would trade increase if borders were opened? Achy (2006) suggests a tenfold increase; the World Bank (2006) predicts a much smaller gain. Contrasting views on the potential trade growth among North African countries agree on one point, however: Trade between North Africa and Europe will remain key. The sheer size of Europe's market, its proximity, the trade concessions it has granted to North African countries, and the cooperation and investments it offers all suggest a sustained expansion of north-south trade. This explains the initial question concerning the relevance of the AMU project. In a globalized environment, with trade routes, infrastructures, and logistics dictated by the needs of Euro-Mediterranean trade, does a Maghreb integration project still make sense?

Transport Reforms in the Region

When the North African countries became independent more than a generation ago, they inherited an institutional framework that regulated transport and infrastructure modeled on the French system. This model assumed that competition was a recipe for failure and a waste of resources.

In air transport, national carriers shared the benefits of a duopoly with a fixed grid of supply and prices. Public agencies supplied and managed airports and air services and were financed through monopoly taxes or direct public subsidies.

In road transport, governments set up a public monopoly of freight forwarding. All requests for road freight were processed by public agencies that allocated freight to licensed transporters without regard for quality and punctuality. Each route had its own licensed operators; the official agency set prices. Fears of destructive competition were used to justify this extensive state intervention: Governments were eager to avoid price wars and overinvestment in capacity by the private sector and thus imposed licenses and quotas to regulate supply. Roads were planned, built, and maintained by governments and financed by the central budget.

Where maritime transport was concerned, state companies operated lines connecting their main ports to French ports in pool conferences, sharing capacity and setting prices. In Morocco, the Office Chérifien des Phosphates set up Marphocean for specialized phosphoric acid transport; in Algeria, Sonatrach had its own fleet of liquefied natural gas tankers. Chartered ships were used for bulk and general cargo. As with roads, state agencies built, maintained, and managed ports that were financed by the central budget. Dockers worked in closed shops. Stevedores were in charge of handling, loading, and unloading. Such systems did not look kindly on innovations such as roll-on-roll-off container terminals or specialized quays.

Finally, rail transport was characterized by public monopoly. State bodies were in charge of the railways' infrastructure development, finance, maintenance, and management.

By the beginning of the 1980s the shortcomings of the rigid transport framework were becoming increasingly obvious. In Morocco's road transport sector a large number of informal private transporters took over the sclerotic Office National des Transports organization and handled more than 90 percent of traffic. The result was increased fragmentation, weak quality control, and equipment that was ill adapted to needs. Many large industrial companies set up their own fleets to insure quality, increasing fragmentation further. More or less the same situation prevailed in Algeria with the dominance of its transport authority. In Tunisia, until liberalization in the 1980s, the authorities set up regional monopolies that created a fragmented sector with many small suppliers and no large-scale operators. In Europe and Asia, improved logistics were regarded as a strategic means to leverage competitiveness. Countries on the southern Mediterranean shores, however, found themselves unable to adapt to the new paradigm.

In air transport, national carriers operated with high costs, high tariffs, and low rates of utilization, which negatively affected tourism. As for maritime transport costs, cartel pricing, poor management of ports, and long delays in customs inspections combined to make trans-Mediterranean transport one of the most expensive in the world.

In the 1990s the poor state of affairs in transport finally led the authorities to initiate sweeping reforms. Tunisia and Morocco led the way; Algeria followed with a short lag.

Railway Transport

Encouraged by the World Bank, governments adopted the new standard model of providing railway services by separating infrastructure from transport, administratively speaking, and allowing for competition. Governments tried to use public-private partnerships to extend the railway network but with little success.

Road Transport

The governments of Algeria, Morocco, and Tunisia liberalized freight and imposed a licensing scheme to improve technical and managerial practices. Though protracted, these reforms encouraged competition, even if they did not address the fragmented nature of the market and the poor quality of service. As multinationals began operations in Morocco in the 1990s, they brought with them second-, third-, and fourth-party logistics firms. New cross-docking platforms reinforced large-scale distribution in Morocco.

International road transport is vital for exports such as garments or fresh fruits and vegetables as it allows door-to-door delivery and small shipments. It also fits with the supply chain requirements of large-scale distribution and allows exports to benefit from geographical proximity. The resilience of the textile industry in North Africa as it faced the end of the Multi Fiber Arrangement and new competition from Asia owes much to the flexibility and punctuality of semitrailers. However, even after due recognition of the importance of local firms, governments have been unable to increase their share in total road transport above 10 percent.

Air Transport

Morocco entered an open skies agreement with the European Union in 2004. This agreement was a cornerstone of a Moroccan policy that aims to attract 10 million tourists by 2010. It allowed an impressive expansion of the number of airlines operating in Morocco and a sharp reduction in travel costs. The increase in air traffic gave fresh impetus to airport authorities and the national carrier to turn Casablanca Mohammed V Airport into a hub for northern and western Africa.

Port Management

Important steps toward liberalizing ports have been taken in the Maghreb. The state monopoly in Morocco was dismantled and ownership and commercial operations were separated. This reform allowed the Moroccan government to set up Tangiers-Med, a project that included plans for a transshipment harbor, a multimodal logistical center, and a very large industrial zone. In Algeria, port services are now open to private operators and each port is run individually by either the Chamber of Commerce or a state company. A container terminal has been built in Bejaia, Algeria, in partnership with Protek, the Singapore port operator. Dubai Ports World has expressed interest in managing container terminals in Algiers. Tunisia has followed the same course, as the government has looked for private partners to develop a cruise port in La Goulette through a build-operate-transfer arrangement and proposed different concessions to adapt the capacity of ports in Rhades, Zarzis, and Gabès.

Shipping Companies

State shipping companies have been restructured and some privatized, as was the case for Comanav in Morocco. National authorities promoted some competition and the share of goods transported through national carriers dropped significantly. The three countries are involved in the European Motorways of the Sea initiative to define heavy-duty sea lines and simplify the process of transport through EDI and a global positioning system–based tracking mechanism.

Customs Reforms

Morocco and Tunisia have pursued customs reform with the aim of reducing the time spent for customs inspection. EDI systems have been set up in Tunisia (SINDIA Tradenet) and Morocco (SADOK) to reduce delays

Table 11.1   Logistics performance index country rankings, 2007

Indicator	Algeria	Morocco	Tunisia
Logistics performance index	140	94	60
Customs	148	101	39
Infrastructure	139	77	44
International shipments	139	64	55
Logistics and competence	139	119	88
Tracking and tracing	109	130	60
Domestic logistical cost	33	133	30
Timeliness	103	95	105

Source: Arvis et al. (2007).

in the paperwork accompanying imports and exports. The Tunisian system is the most ambitious, bringing together banks, freight forwarders, port authorities, customs, maritime agents, importers and exporters, the ministry of trade, and customs agents.

Measuring Logistics Performance

All the above reforms should have boosted logistical efficiency. However, international benchmarks show that a long road lies ahead to attain parity with other regions. Table 11.1 is an extract from a World Bank report on trade logistics in the global economy (see Arvis et al. 2007). The authors constructed a composite index of logistics performance (LPI) and ranked 150 countries accordingly. Tunisia takes the lead in North Africa: It is ranked 60th out of 150 countries. Morocco follows in the 94th position. Algeria is among the bottom 10 countries. Analysis of the individual components of the index shows that customs procedures are dragging down Algeria and Morocco, and to a lesser extent, Tunisia. Algeria's performance also reflects its reliance on oil and gas exports and the corresponding neglect of logistics for other exports as well as imports generally.

Opportunities for Integration

The closed border between Morocco and Algeria, which has been maintained for almost 25 years, has profoundly affected trade flows, trade routes, and logistics in the region. It pushed trade flows toward a north-south pattern, increasing reliance on the European market. Exporters now know more about the requirements of consumers in Europe than those of consumers in neighboring countries. Logistics firms are likewise more familiar with the norms and regulations governing customs and inspections in Spain and France than those in Algeria and Tunisia. When Maghreb governments consider investing in infrastructure, Europe takes precedence over neighbors. However, that North African countries are relatively ill informed about the regulations and procedures of their immediate neighbors does not imply an absence of opportunities to integrate; it simply underlines the obstacles ahead.

Infrastructure

A simple rule of thumb for infrastructure is that its value rises in proportion to its use and its use is dictated by its convenience. For transport infrastructure, extending the network is essential. Value and convenience are increased by the number of connections available and this network effect is unrelated to the cost of investment. From this point of view, closing a border is, in economic terms, a real disaster. Valuable rail infrastructure simply sits idle, reducing its utility to that of a cul de sac instead of a vector for increased trade and improved competitiveness.

The same logic applies to motorways. Morocco's national network stops at Oujda and the East-West Algerian motorway stops at Maghnia or Tlemcen. Algerian and Tunisian entrepreneurs cannot use any of the connections to Morocco and Spain and vice versa. Passengers bear some of the cost of this disruption, reducing their ability to use the road network.

To overcome the border's closure each country has invested in independent infrastructure, such as the ports of Nador in Morocco and Ghazaouet in Algeria. Oujda, the capital of eastern Morocco, lies 70 kilometers inland, but is closer to Ghazaouet than to Nador. Shipping goods from Oujda through Ghazaouet rather than Nador would have allowed for economies of scale and saved expenditure on new infrastructure.

Hub-and-Spoke Opportunities

Increasing connections and usage are a constant objective of harbor and airport managers. Following a hub-and-spoke model offers a solution for operators of small transport nodes: Instead of competing frontally to increase the number of network connections, small operators can connect to hubs and plan their shipping of containers and passengers. Using this model, even small harbors and airports can offer a large number of destinations and origins. The model also allows for economies of scale when the hub can accommodate quick transshipment and large ships, offering lower costs than a direct connection can.

Maritime Ports

The first transshipment harbor ready to receive ultra-large carriers (post-Panamax) located in a southern-rim Mediterranean country began to operate near Tangiers in 2007. It expects to attract traffic from around the world and respond to the logistical requirements of global value chains, thereby bringing foreign direct investment to Morocco. Renault-Nissan was the first major car company to commit to a spot in the industrial park, followed by parts manufacturers. Medhub, the largest logistical platform in the region, is very close and connected by rail and highway to the port.

Once connected by rail, sea feeders, and highways to Algeria and Tunisia, the new port could become a regional hub facility, improving the competitiveness of all firms that participate in global value chains. Developing national transshipment ports instead of using Tangiers-Med facilities would certainly imply less traffic in the region and higher logistical costs to firms.

Airports and National Carriers

The three national fleets of Algeria, Morocco, and Tunisia are dwarfs in the global world of air transport, in relation to both established world airlines and emerging global alliances. For Air Algérie, Tunis Air, and, to a lesser extent, Royal Air Maroc, the size of their networks and markets made them feeders to global hubs, notably Emirates in Dubai and British Airways in Heathrow. Air France cannibalized part of their traffic by excluding the Maghreb carriers from its hub at Charles de Gaulle. Instead they use the second Paris airport, Orly, which has few international connecting flights. The net result is that transit passengers are channeled to Air France when they begin their journey.

For West African traffic, Royal Air Maroc has a stronger hand. Casablanca's location, connections to West Africa and North America, and dense network with Europe allowed the city to develop a hub for western and northern Africa, eventually challenging Paris's domination. An alliance that brings under the same wing all three Maghreb national airlines could—and should—use Casablanca to increase its market share on the North Atlantic route.

Multimodal Transport and Logistical Platforms

All North African countries lag in logistical development. Systems of local transport, storage, and distribution in Algerian and Moroccan internal markets are outdated and challenging to modernize. Tunisia stands in a somewhat better position. All three countries, however, need to pursue internal reforms to streamline production and distribution systems; logistical platforms should play an important role. A logistical platform is a tool to deal efficiently with space and time constraints and make supply-chain management more flexible. A platform could group or ungroup goods and mix product types and origins in shared containers, increasing the efficiency of transport and the quality of service.

Interconnection has the potential to improve the competitiveness of all three economies through an efficient distribution process and, more important, links among suppliers. A connected network of suppliers could more easily climb the value added chain, such as through higher quality automotive parts made in Tunisia, Morocco, and Algeria.

Logistics as Optimizer

Third-party logistics insure the optimization of supply chain costs by internalizing different functions: transport, storage, assembling, packing, customs processing, tracking, and document processing. They optimize by exploiting price differences related to underused capacities, such as empty seats, idle space, quays, and berths, and immobilized trucks. In so doing they are crucial to increasing the benefits of infrastructure development. We can draw on two individual and virtuous examples of such development in the recent history of the region. First, when ports were congested in Algeria, the Algerian National Office of Cereals relied on wheat imports unloaded in Casablanca and transported by rail to millers in Algeria. Second, the imbalance in general cargo trade in Algeria—high import demand, but low exports of general cargo—has led to a steady return of empty boxes and containers from Ghazaouet back to Morocco. Empty boxes are not expensive to fill, creating incentives for exports from Oujda if and only if the border is opened. These examples show the pervasive benefits that shared infrastructure offers through good logistics.

Concluding Remarks

As stated previously, there are no gains in logistics without trade. The essence of logistics is to lower transaction costs; without transactions there can be no cost reductions. Trade across the land border between Morocco and Algeria is currently proscribed. This closure has led to a curious state in which all exchanges between the two countries either transit through Spanish and French harbors or are smuggled. This precludes better knowledge of consumer needs in both countries and obstructs investment that could arise from the combination of talents and resources on both sides of the border.

Smugglers know how to play on the differences in subsidies ranging from foodstuffs to pharmaceuticals and gas. They know the moneychanger game of speculation and hoarding as well as the bureaucratic rules on foreign currencies. They are aware of the appeal of Moroccan caftans and accessories to the fashion cognoscenti in Algiers, Tlemcen, and Oran. They know which mechanical parts are in short supply in Morocco and how keen Moroccan palates are, leading to a high demand for confectionary goods in Morocco. These anecdotal examples support what gravitational models predict: huge opportunities for trade owing to common cultural values and consumer preferences. However, the models tell only half of the story. North African entrepreneurs spend a lot of time and money attempting to identify precise needs and opportunities for trade and investment. Because North African consumers have very similar tastes, this knowledge can fuel locally based development, trade, and investments. It could allow open economies—due to their commitments to the World Trade Organization, European Union, United States, and Arab League—to benefit from integration without resorting to the standard strategy of a customs union and the risk of trade diversion alongside trade creation. North African entrepreneurs could and should use their clout and knowledge to take advantage of increased market size resulting from open borders.

Two complementary tools can certainly help to link producers: clusters, with a shared pool of qualified workers and suppliers in design, engineering, equipment, and inputs, such as textiles in Tunis or agricultural products in Agadir; and networked firms, working for global value chains and leveraging gains in logistical development within the region along the lines outlined in this chapter. All these developments need good logistics, not the other way around.

References

Achy, Lahcen. 2006. *Le commerce en Afrique du Nord: Evaluation du potentiel de l'intégration régional en Afrique du Nord* [*Trade in North Africa: Evaluation of the Potential for Regional Integration in North Africa*]. Report CEA-AN/RABAT/CIE/XXI/3/I. Rabat: United Nations Economic Commission for Africa.

Agénor, Pierre-Richard, and Blanca Moreno-Dodson. 2006. *Public Infrastructure and Growth: New Channels and Policy Implications.* Policy Research Working Paper 4064. Washington: World Bank.

Arvis, Jean-François, Monica Alina Mustra, John Panzer, Lauri Ojala, and Tapio Naula. 2007. *Connecting to Compete: Trade Logistics in the Global Economy, The Logistics Performance Index, and its Indicators.* World Bank Report. Washington: World Bank and International Bank for Reconstruction and Development.

Calderon, Cesar, and Luis Serven. 2004. *The Effects of Infrastructure Development on Growth and Income Distribution.* Policy Research Working Paper 3400. Washington: World Bank.

Tanzi, Vito. 2005. *Building Regional Infrastructure in Latin America.* Integration and Regional Programs Department Working Paper SITI-10. Washington: Inter-American Development Bank.

Tanzi, Vito. 2006. *The Production and Financing of Regional Public Goods.* Integration and Regional Programs Department Occasional Paper SITI-08. Washington: Inter-American Development Bank.

World Bank. 2006. *Is There a New Vision for Maghreb Economic Integration?* World Bank Report 38359. Washington.

12

Updating the Maghreb Project:
The Case of Food Industries

OMAR ALOUI

Does the Maghreb integration project have value in the context of global-ization and a Euro-Mediterranean free trade zone? If so, what should be done in the short-to-medium term to propel the project forward? This chapter analyzes these issues from the vantage point of the Maghreb's food processing industries, which account for a large share of employ-ment, trade, and consumer expenditure in North African economies. The first part briefly explores theoretical concepts. The second part presents some stylized facts about the region's food industry and trade. The chap-ter concludes with a short list of recommendations.

The conventional trade diversion approach is still the dominant analyt-ical framework for both politicians and scholars thinking about regional integration in Maghreb countries. This approach is, however, obsolete; the region offers huge trade-creation potential due to globalization and Euro-Mediterranean initiatives. This potential—which arises from geo-graphical proximity, similar resource bases, and common consumption patterns—is particularly important in the food industries. Proximity reduces the costs of vertical and horizontal integration as well as discov-ery processes, which are all engines of trade. Trade figures, while incom-plete, show interesting trends that confirm the potential for gains from horizontal and vertical integration. Meanwhile, agricultural production

Omar Aloui is a professional economist and manager of a leading consulting firm in food policy and agricultural studies based in Rabat, Morocco.

Table 12.1 Traditional and new trade theories related to determinants of trade

	Traditional theories			New trade theory	
Determinants	Factor endowments	Productivity differences	External economies of scale	Internal economies of scale	
Trade patterns	Interindustry trade			Vertical differentiation	Horizontal differentiation
Specialization	Along comparative advantage		Through agglomeration	Along the quality spectrum	In varieties
Adjustment	Important		Potentially important		Weak
Costs	Change in factors prices among industries within countries		Potential income divergence among countries		

can create spillover effects among Maghreb countries for regional public goods, such as water, health, and biodiversity.

We identify five entry points as opportunities to develop a Maghreb integration project in the food sector. As political economic theory teaches, regional integration is a multiactor building process. Not only stakeholders but also public opinion and lobbying activities from external bodies are crucial.

Theoretical Framework

From a conventional point of view, regional integration in the Maghreb has low value because of trade diversion effects. However, a debate over Maghreb integration must account for trade creation effects based on economies of scale and proximity factors as well as regional public goods and their spillover effects.

Economies of Scale and Proximity as Engines of Integration

Scale economies and intraindustry trade are considered to be the new engines of growth in evaluating regional integration processes. Intraindustry trade of similar products—that is, horizontal trade—between countries with comparable economic structures and endowments of production factors is a phenomenon outside the familiar Heckscher-Ohlin model (Helpman and Krugman 1985). Such horizontal trade encourages the exchange of varieties. Table 12.1 captures the traditional and the new theory arguments related to trade determinants.

Regional Public Goods and Cooperation

A public good is defined essentially by three characteristics. First, it is a commodity or service that can be consumed by one person without diminishing the amount available for consumption by another person (nonrivalry). Second, it is available at zero or negligible marginal cost to a large or unlimited number of consumers (nonexclusiveness). Third, it does not bring about disutility to any consumer now or in the future (sustainability).

A regional public good is an international public good that displays spillover benefits to countries in the neighborhood of the producing country. Countries can benefit greatly from cooperating in the production of regional public goods when they share common resources such as rivers, fishing grounds, hydroelectric power, rail connections, or the environment. In the presence of economies of scale or neighborhood externalities, market solutions are generally suboptimal; failing to cooperate can be very costly. Regional cooperation is not the same as regional integration, though integration may foster cooperation.

Food Industries

Evidence collected from the literature and the data shows that food industries are highly sensitive to both economies of scale and the presence of regional public goods. This is because agriculture is a multifunctional activity that plays a triple role: It is an economic process, a way of life, and a provider of environmental services (World Bank 2007b).

The food industry in the Maghreb is affected by a complicated assortment of factors. Horizontal trade is mainly promoted by multinational firms operating in the region. Economies of scale characterize intraregional direct investments in the food industry. Trade based on consumer demands for variety in food products has flourished thanks to informal networks among Maghreb countries. Overuse of coastal resources, water shortages, destruction of pasture land and habitats, and recent animal pandemics are common issues for Maghreb food and agricultural activities. Collaborative regional action offers the best response to all of these concerns, especially as the environmental and health effects spill across borders.

Food Market Context Analysis

Globalization and Euro-Mediterranean initiatives are the main factors affecting regional markets. This context offers both threats and opportunities. The threats have to do with global price uncertainties and asymmetrical liberalization of trade with the European Union. The opportunities are related to special features of the Mediterranean diet and the presence of EU companies in the Maghreb area.

Regional Effects of Globalization

Uncertainties are rising on many fronts, among them the future of the international trade regime for agriculture, genetically modified foods, climate change, high energy prices, the impact of biofuel production on food prices and the environment, and the ability to contain human, animal, and plant diseases. Chinese and Indian growth affect nearly a third of the world's population directly and many more indirectly. China is the largest net importer of grains and oils. As Maghreb countries also are net importers of basic foodstuffs, a rise in food prices threatens the region.

Globalization promotes a diffusion of the Mediterranean diet all over the world, in particular for olive oil, wines, vegetables, and spices. This creates a great opportunity for Maghreb farmers and food industries, but to take advantage of it, Maghreb countries need a dynamic and market-driven new agriculture led by high-value activities. Other important factors include institutional and technological innovations as well as more efficient forms of agricultural production, whether by the state, powerful private actors, or civil society organizations.

Regional Effects of Euro-Mediterranean Initiatives

In 1995 the Barcelona Conference paved the way for the creation of a free trade zone between the European Union and its Mediterranean partners. Tunisia, Morocco, and Algeria signed bilateral association agreements with the European Union in 1995, 1996, and 2002, respectively.

The modalities of liberalization are scheduled in lists of products and gradual timetables for dismantling trade barriers.[1] The European Union committed itself to maintaining existing preferences toward North African countries, but without improving in any significant way access to Europe's market. Algeria, Morocco, and Tunisia agreed to eliminate existing barriers to market access on the majority of nonagricultural products from the European Union. All three countries chose to dismantle tariffs gradually over a maximum period of 12 years. Some highly sensitive products were scheduled in negative lists and are not subject to tariff elimination. However, the association agreements specify that these negative lists are to be reviewed regularly.

The association agreements do not mention any calendar for tariff elimination across the agricultural sector; the concessions deal more with

---

1. All the agreements signed by the European Union have the same structure. The first component concerns political and security cooperation, the second component deals with trade and covers the main commitments of the partners, and the third component addresses economic and cultural cooperation.

quantitative restrictions than tariffs. Significant increases in quotas have been granted to the North African economies on products such as olive oil and cut flowers. The association agreements initially mentioned that agriculture would be further liberalized five years after the agreement came into force, but the increase in quotas is still under negotiation in most North African economies. The positive side of the association agreements lies more in attracting foreign direct investment (FDI), especially from EU countries, an aspect that is not easily modeled but nevertheless could be quite important.

Main Characteristics of Regional Markets

In agriculture and the food industries the World Bank (2006) includes the Maghreb countries in their category of transforming countries, which covers most of Asia, the Middle East, North Africa, and parts of Europe and Central Asia. In this group of countries economic growth is rapid in some sectors, but a large share of poor households remain in rural areas. These countries need to increase the pace of growth in agriculture and related rural nonfarm sectors both to reduce poverty and to confront rising rural-urban income disparities.

In Tunisia in recent years the agricultural sector has enjoyed a stable share of GDP in terms of value added (13 percent), employment (16 percent), export revenues (10 percent), and investment (10 percent). In Morocco agricultural activities represent around 15 percent of GDP and around 20 percent of exports. The sector employs about 40 percent of the total labor force, but around 78 percent in rural areas. In Algeria agricultural activities represent close to 12 percent of GDP and around 2 percent of exports. The sector employs around 22 percent of the total Algerian labor force. Major exports include dates, wine, and potatoes, which amount to around $200 million. Of course, oil and gas account for 98 percent of Algerian exports (World Bank 2007b).

Similarities in Supply Constraints

Supply conditions are constrained by one major factor in the region: water shortage. Table 12.2 shows the intensity of this constraint, particularly in Tunisia and Algeria. The water situation in Morocco seems less dramatic, though it is still a concern. Morocco has a water self-sufficiency ratio of nearly 70 percent, which means that the country has more than two-thirds of the water it needs to feed its people and irrigate its land. This translates into a larger share of agriculture in GDP and exports. However, water scarcity remains a problem in the Maghreb as a whole.

Table 12.2   Agricultural indicators in the Maghreb region

Indicator	Algeria	Tunisia	Morocco
Share of agriculture in GDP (percent)	12.7	12.6	16.7
Water withdrawal by agricultural sector (billions of cubic meters)	3.9	2.2	11
Total virtual imported water embedded in food imports (billions of cubic meters)	10.9	4.1	5.8
Self-sufficiency ratio in water (percent)	34	38	68
Irrigation efficiency ratio (percent)	37	54	37
Share of irrigated land (percent)	6.8	7.5	14

Source: World Bank (2007a).

Similarities in Consumption Patterns

Maghreb food markets are changing from ingredients for traditional meals, intensive in female labor, to processed food preparations, intensive in services and industrial inputs. Several factors are altering global food consumption patterns worldwide, including in the Maghreb: higher income, urbanization, improved transportation, and consumer perceptions regarding product quality and safety. Table 12.3 reveals that the three countries share basic consumption habits. It also shows that Tunisia, with higher levels of urbanization and female participation in the labor force, leads the way in the consumption transition process, while Morocco lags behind.

Still, Moroccan industries are adjusting to new demand conditions, as illustrated in table 12.4 on processed food growth in Morocco.

Domestic Policies

In domestic food policies, Algeria, Morocco, and Tunisia are similar in two ways: They all support farm investment through a variety of subsidies and they all have distorting price subsidies at the consumer level. Consumer price policies differ between countries that tax at the import level and subsidize at the processing stage, as Morocco does, and countries that tax imports less but provide large subsidies for local production, storage, and marketing, as Algeria does.

Extraregional Food Trade

Algeria, Morocco, and Tunisia all heavily rely on foreign supplies and each runs a deficit in agricultural trade balances. However, substantial

Table 12.3 Structure of food intake, 2006 (total per capita kilograms)

Category	Algeria	Morocco	Tunisia
Alcohol (including beer and wine)	10	15	6
Animal fats and products	2	8	3
Beverage crops	10	3	8
Cereals and products, excluding beer	620	613	566
Eggs and products	11	7	20
Fish, seafood and products	9	9	30
Fruits and products (excluding wine)	155	87	233
Meat (slaughtered) and products	50	36	72
Milk and products	314	78	280
Offals edible	3	5	4
Oilcrops (excluding products)	2	3	12
Pulses and products	16	10	20
Spices	1	2	6
Starchy roots and products	112	31	81
Sugar and sweeteners	84	76	88
Treenuts and products	3	1	9
Vegetable oils and products	41	19	57
Vegetables and products	235	113	504

Source: Food and Agriculture Organization FAOSTAT database.

Table 12.4 Value of local production of selected processed food industries in Morocco (millions of dirhams)

Processed food activity	1990	2005
Meat preparations	20	500
Sugar-based products	500	1,600
Drinks	500	2,200

Source: Conseil Général du Développement Agricole, *Situation de l'Agriculture Marocaine,* 2008.

differences exist among them. In 2006 Algerian food exports represented only 2 percent of Algerian food imports, whereas Moroccan and Tunisian food exports represented 62 and 88 percent of food imports, respectively, in the two countries.[2]

2. Figures are from the United Nations Commodity Trade (COMTRADE) Statistics Database, available at comtrade.un.org (accessed July 22, 2008). Moroccan and Tunisian ratios computed with different databases can yield opposite rankings, but the overall situation indicated by these figures is quite robust.

Past political orientations in Algeria favored the development of nonagricultural sectors, which helps explain current trade patterns. For Morocco and Tunisia the trade gap is largely linked to climatic conditions and to a steadily increasing population. Most of the Maghreb countries produce staple goods, such as grains, raw edible oil, and raw sugar, but production levels are insufficient to meet demand; thus the need for imports from abroad.

In addition to staple goods, most of the Maghreb countries have large livestock production and some have well-developed fruit and vegetable sectors. These have been steadily improved by better technology. Currently fruits and vegetables constitute the larger share of Morocco's and Tunisia's agricultural exports.

For decades Maghreb agricultural exports were oriented toward a few EU countries, namely France, Italy, and Belgium, and more recently Spain and Portugal. EU reluctance to increase imports of some products from the Maghreb limits Maghreb exports, notably fresh tomatoes and strawberries. The situation has deteriorated further since the signing of bilateral trade preference agreements between the European Union and Chile and South Africa, the agricultural exports of which are similar to those of Maghreb countries.

To tackle the difficulties they face, Maghreb countries intend to reach beyond traditional markets. Product diversification lies at the heart of reforms, especially for highly prized products, such as fresh green peas, green beans, and melons. Market diversification within and outside the European Union is also on the agenda. More export volumes are now directed toward Africa and the Middle East as well as Canada and the United States. In some cases, trade conventions or agreements with trade partners have facilitated these options.

Maghreb countries have developed their food processing sectors significantly. This was initially in response to the need for staples such as flour, refined sugar, and refined edible oil; thus each country has a milling industry. Additional investments took place as international demand for processed fruit and vegetables increased and as domestic production expanded further. A new generation of processing industries has appeared, encouraged by the involvement of multinational companies, particularly in industries that rely on imported raw products, such as cheese, pasta, or dried foods.

In exports the share of global processed foods is about 20 percent for Morocco and a little less for Tunisia. However, the type of goods exported is different. Tunisia's main exports are processed tomatoes, pasta, and ice cream. Morocco's top exports are food preparations and canned olives.

Intraregional Food Trade

The high level of extraregional food trade contrasts with the low level of intraregional trade. There is a complete disconnect between the two mar-

Figure 12.1   Imports of Morocco, Algeria, and Tunisia by origin country, 2006

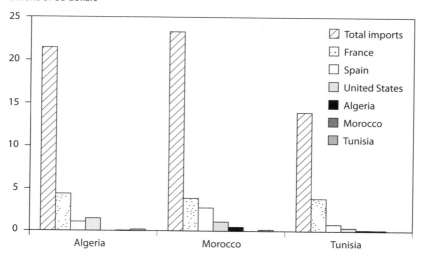

Source: United Nations COMTRADE Database.

kets. Bilateral trade among Maghreb countries as a share of their total trade is often less than 2 percent, despite attempts to boost regional trade through preferential trade agreements (see figure 12.1 and table 12A.1 in the appendix).

The Arab Maghreb Union, the main goal of which was tariff elimination in the region, was never quite implemented because of incompatibilities among national regulations and because of protectionist fears and political tensions. At a bilateral level, several tariff preference agreements were also signed, as between Morocco and Algeria in 1990 and Algeria and Tunisia in 1991. A new agreement is under discussion between Tunisia and Algeria. At a wider level, almost all Arab countries signed the Greater Arab Free Trade Area (GAFTA), which sets tariff exemptions, though GAFTA did not explicitly enter into force in most countries because it lacks well-defined rules of origin. To boost trade flows among their countries, Tunisia, Morocco, Egypt, and Jordan have chosen to sign a new and more elaborated trade agreement, the Agadir Agreement, that entered into force very recently.

Despite the low level of intraregional trade, the potential exists for trade creation within the region, particularly through better integration. The different Maghreb countries, after all, trade different food products. Tunisia has a comparative advantage in domestic primary products such as dates. Other food products are largely traded because local industries have undergone significant vertical integration, as has occurred with olive oil from Tunisia and processed foods from Morocco. The third category of products covers horizontal integration of processed foods based on imported raw material, such as Tunisian pasta and Moroccan cheese.

Recommendations

Food products have been given special treatment in every economic integration initiative worldwide. In some cases this has prompted countries to form a regional unified policy, such as the EU Common Agricultural Policy. Other situations resulted in agricultural exception clauses, such as those found in free trade agreements negotiated within Latin America or the Middle East and North Africa region. New opportunities in the Maghreb are based on proximity factors and regional public goods, but the possibilities are not reflected in trade figures, mainly because of intraregional policy distortions.

In open economies, civil society and private actors influence the decision-making process, notably though lobbying, though this is more or less efficient depending on the country and type of government. A regional integration process cannot be a simple consequence of top-down decision making regarding tariff levels. It should be a multiactor building process that maximizes the Maghreb's potential to produce a common vision and a common strategy to reach this vision. Managing transitions depends crucially on the willingness and capacity of local stakeholders—notably private firms—to cooperate and create regional clusters, innovation systems, or regulatory bodies in the case of regional public-goods provision initiatives. Table 12.5 summarizes potential areas of cooperation among Maghreb countries.

The first area for potential cooperation lies in trading opportunities based on economies of scale, proximity, and similarities in consumption patterns. This entry point is already at work as multinational enterprises (MNEs), such as Unilever, Danone, Nestlé, or Kraft, create regional platform strategies (Van Witteloostuijn 2007). Regional food exports from Morocco to Algeria and Tunisia are exclusively MNE products. This kind of trade creation based on proximity and economies of scale is promoted by FDI and can be rapidly mobilized.

The second entry point offers vertical integration opportunities based on complementarities in factor endowments as much as on proximity factors. Olive oil trade among Tunisia, Morocco, and Algeria is a good example of this opportunity, with raw products coming from the most competitive producer and local firms adding value through their market information and networks.

Table 12.5   Potential areas of cooperation among Maghreb countries

	Entry point	Domains to be covered	Projects
Regional growth	Horizontal integration	Processed products sensitive to economies of scale	Regional FDI facility
	Vertical integration	Olive oil	Common FDI attraction
	Self discovery projects	Camel milk	Public-private partnership projects
	Coordination projects	Food safety Quality insurance Counterfeiting Smuggling	Policy coordination with EU support
Regional public good	Common pool resources	Water Biodiversity Ranges Coastal resources	Cooperation projects with multilateral funding and technical assistance

FDI = foreign direct investment.

The third entry point is based on the self-discovery potential of regional firms. Conducting innovation projects at the regional rather than individual level can reduce the costs and risks for local firms of launching new products and discovering new markets. Region-specific products, such as camel milk, are natural candidates for these projects, as their potential is untapped.

The fourth entry point is based on reducing the spillover effects of heterogeneous food norms and standards. These frictions encourage smuggling and counterfeiting; they also adversely affect food quality and health protection. The divergence in rules can be exploited by border mafias in rent-seeking activity that bridges the gap between low-standard countries and high-standard countries.

The fifth entry point relates to creating a common pool for regional resource conservation, for which border limits have no significance. This sort of project can benefit directly from the experience and support of international organizations, the European Union, and the United States.

These recommendations taken together can go a long way toward integrating the Maghreb's food and agriculture sectors. Granted, the Maghreb—like virtually every other region—faces obstacles to liberalizing what are often sensitive and highly politicized sectors. But the potential gains to each country are worth overcoming these difficulties.

References

Helpman, Elhanan, and Paul Krugman. 1985. *Market Structure and Foreign Trade: Increasing Returns, Imperfect Competition, and the International Economy.* Cambridge, MA: MIT Press.

Van Witteloostuijn, Arjen. 2007. Globalization in the Food Industry: The Impact on Market Structures and Firm Strategies. University of Antwerp, Belgium. Available online at www.foodeconomy2007.org (accessed May 26, 2008).

World Bank. 2006. *World Development Report 2007: Development and the Next Generation.* Washington: International Bank for Reconstruction and Development and World Bank.

World Bank. 2007a. *Making the Most of Scarcity: Accountability for Better Water Management Results in the Middle East and North Africa.* Washington.

World Bank. 2007b. *World Development Report 2008: Agriculture for Development.* Washington: International Bank for Reconstruction and Development and World Bank.

Table 12A.1 Food trade between Algeria, Morocco, and Tunisia using Harmonized System classification, 2006 (millions of US dollars)

Product category	Importer country					
	Algeria	Morocco	Algeria	Tunisia	Morocco	Tunisia
	Partner country					
	Morocco	Algeria	Tunisia	Algeria	Tunisia	Morocco
01 Live animals	n.a.	n.a.	n.a.	n.a.	n.a.	n.a.
02 Meat and edible meat offal	n.a.	n.a.	n.a.	n.a.	n.a.	n.a.
03 Fish, crustaceans, molluscs, aquatic invertebrates, nes	0.20	n.a.	0.00	n.a.	n.a.	n.a.
04 Dairy products, eggs, honey, edible animal product, nes	2.34	n.a.	0.10	1.29	n.a.	0.35
05 Products of animal origin, nes	n.a.	n.a.	n.a.	n.a.	n.a.	n.a.
06 Live trees, plants, bulbs, roots, cut flowers, etc.	0.04	n.a.	0.00	n.a.	n.a.	n.a.
07 Edible vegetables and certain roots and tubers	0.03	n.a.	0.00	n.a.	n.a.	n.a.
08 Edible fruit, nuts, peel of citrus fruit, melons	0.00	1.45	0.05	n.a.	20.32	n.a.
09 Coffee, tea, mate and spices	0.03	n.a.	n.a.	n.a.	0.00	n.a.
10 Cereals	n.a.	n.a.	n.a.	n.a.	n.a.	n.a.
11 Milling products, malt, starches, inulin, wheat gluten	0.02	n.a.	0.01	1.44	n.a.	n.a.
12 Oil seed, oleagic fruits, grain, seed, fruit, etc., nes	0.00	n.a.	0.00	n.a.	0.01	n.a.
13 Lac, gums, resins, vegetable saps and extracts, nes	0.00	n.a.	0.00	n.a.	n.a.	n.a.
14 Vegetable plaiting materials, vegetable products, nes	n.a.	n.a.	0.07	n.a.	n.a.	n.a.
15 Animal,vegetable fats and oils, cleavage products, etc.	n.a.	n.a.	3.04	0.32	1.78	n.a.
16 Meat, fish, and seafood food preparations, nes	0.26	n.a.	0.54	n.a.	n.a.	n.a.
17 Sugars and sugar confectionery	1.35	n.a.	1.65	1.73	0.00	3.47
18 Cocoa and cocoa preparations	0.02	n.a.	0.15	n.a.	0.02	n.a.
19 Cereal, flour, starch, milk preparations, and products	0.06	n.a.	5.18	n.a.	0.85	n.a.
20 Vegetable, fruit, nut, etc. food preparations	0.00	n.a.	4.71	n.a.	0.78	n.a.
21 Miscellaneous edible preparations	2.90	n.a.	2.61	n.a.	0.31	n.a.
22 Beverages, spirits, and vinegar	0.12	n.a.	0.08	n.a.	0.22	6.70
23 Residues, wastes of food industry, animal fodder	n.a.	n.a.	n.a.	n.a.	n.a.	1.70
24 Tobacco and manufactured tobacco substitutes	n.a.	n.a.	n.a.	n.a.	n.a.	n.a.
Total food imports	7.38	1.45	18.18	4.78	24.28	12.22
Total merchandise imports	49.88	445.80	171.58	106.00	133.85	92.00

nes = not elsewhere specified
n.a. = not available

Sources: United Nations COMTRADE Database; International Trade Center.

13

Reviving Maghreb Integration: Recommendations

CLAIRE BRUNEL and GARY CLYDE HUFBAUER

Attempts to revive the Arab Maghreb Union (AMU) have been unsuccessful mostly because of tense political relations among members. However, some cooperation can be observed among Maghreb countries at a bilateral level. Tunisia and Morocco have made good progress in port infrastructure and air traffic rights. The Tunisian project to build a deep water port in Enfidha will complete the Tangiers-Med plan and establish a direct maritime link between Tunisia and Morocco. In November 2007 the two countries signed an air traffic agreement to liberalize the carriage of passengers and cargo, and the Tunisian minister of transport has expressed a willingness to extend the agreement to the rest of the AMU.[1] These and similar initiatives could pave the way for regional integration.

To foster integration, the region needs to develop a strong institutional framework and progress further on trade liberalization and facilitation. The United States and the European Union could be important to promoting the needed reforms, especially as both parties are already involved in various trade and investment agreements as well as aid initiatives with the Maghreb countries.

Claire Brunel is a research assistant at the Peterson Institute for International Economics. Gary Clyde Hufbauer has been the Reginald Jones Senior Fellow at the Peterson Institute for International Economics since 1992.

1. "Bientot Une Ligne Maritime Directe Avec Le Royaume" ["Soon a Direct Maritime Line With the Kingdom"], *Comtex*, February 22, 2008.

US-Maghreb Economic Ties

Table 13.1 summarizes the bilateral trade and investment relations between the United States and each of the Maghreb countries. The extent of economic association with the United States varies widely across the region. At one end of the spectrum stands Morocco, which signed its free trade agreement (FTA) with the United States in 2004; at the other end is Libya, which has no trade or investment agreements with the United States and is not currently eligible for the Generalized System of Preferences (GSP). Libyan economic relations with the United States were nonexistent until the lifting of US sanctions in 2004 and not until June 2006 did the United States remove Libya from the list of states sponsoring terrorism. Economic ties between Libya and the United States are thus new in the making. Libya's recent blockage of a UN resolution sponsored by the United States to condemn violence in the Middle East may again put a strain on political relations.[2] The US Congress recently amended the Foreign Sovereign Immunities Act to allow prejudgment attachment of Libyan government assets, even though Libya has been removed from the US government's list of terrorism sponsors; this move also has strained relations. That said, the United States and Libya are in the final stage of negotiating a trade and investment framework agreement (TIFA).[3]

Tunisia and the United States have signed a TIFA as well as a bilateral investment treaty (BIT). The two parties are contemplating negotiations for an FTA.[4] While economic relations between Algeria and the United States include a TIFA, political relations are fragile. In March 2008 Algeria accused the United States of interfering in its internal affairs by expanding a dialogue with Algerian civil society and welcoming opposition parties to Washington.[5] Mauritania has been designated as a least-developed beneficiary developing country for the GSP program. Mineral fuels—principally oil—accounted for 99 percent of US imports from Mauritania in 2006.

In addition to trade and investment agreements, the United States provides Maghreb countries with technical and financial assistance. The two most important vehicles are the Middle East Partnership Initiative (MEPI) and the Millennium Challenge Corporation (MCC). The MEPI program funds reform in politics, economics, education, and women's empowerment in Algeria, Morocco, and Tunisia. Currently, the MCC only provides

---

2. John Heilprin, "Libya Blocks UN Council From Condemning Fresh Violence in the Middle East," Associated Press Newswires, March 6, 2008.

3. Gary G. Yerkey, "US, Libya 'Very Close' to Signing Bilateral Trade, Investment Agreement," *Bureau of National Affairs*, May 30, 2008.

4. Unpublished reports indicate that Tunisia is also considering FTA negotiations with Japan.

5. "Algeria Officials 'Accuse' US of Interfering in Country's Domestic Affairs," BBC Monitoring Middle East, March 5, 2008.

Table 13.1 Bilateral agreements between the United States and Maghreb nations

Country	Trade and investment framework agreement	Bilateral investment treaty	Free trade agreement	Other bilateral agreements related to trade or investment	Generalized system of preferences (GSP) status
Morocco		Signed in 1985, entered into force in 1991	Signed in 2004, entered into force in January 2006	Agreement on Science and Technology Cooperation (2006)	Not applicable; Western Sahara is a "Non-Independent Countr[y] [or] Territor[y]" that is designated beneficiary developing country (no goods restrictions)
Algeria	Signed in 2001			Investment Incentive Agreement (1990); Agricultural Commodities Agreement (1966); Memorandum of Understanding concerning Cooperation and Trade in the Field of Agriculture; Agreement on Science and Technology Cooperation (2006)	Designated beneficiary developing country (no goods restrictions)
Tunisia	Signed in 2002	Signed in 1990, entered into force in 1993		Agreement on Science and Technology Cooperation (2004)	Designated beneficiary developing country (no goods restrictions)
Mauritania					Designated beneficiary developing country, least-developed beneficiary developing country (no goods restrictions)
Libya		In negotiation			Not applicable

assistance to Morocco and Mauritania. The MCC approved a grant of $697 million over five years for Morocco to fund programs in three sectors, namely agriculture (specifically fruit trees), small-scale coastal fishing, and artisan crafts. In December 2007 the MCC selected Mauritania as the latest eligible country. Mauritania will participate in the MCC's two-year threshold program, which awards smaller grants to progress on specific indicators with the prospect of qualifying for larger grants in the future.

EU-Maghreb Economic Ties

EU relations with the Maghreb countries are governed by the Barcelona Process (see chapter 3). However, another large project is also underway: the proposal by President Nicolas Sarkozy of France to create a Union for the Mediterranean. Originally the union was to involve only those countries bordering the Mediterranean. However, at Germany's request, it was agreed that all EU members and Mediterranean countries would be invited to join.[6] The new project, jointly proposed by France and Germany, significantly dilutes France's original ambitions; however, EU leaders approved the proposal unanimously on March 13, 2008. Though a detailed plan to implement the new initiative has yet to be revealed, the union is meant to revitalize the Barcelona Process. The Union for the Mediterranean was launched on July 13, 2008.

Some concerns have been voiced regarding the union's dual presidency concept and the need to avoid duplicating institutions between the Union for the Mediterranean and the European Union.[7] Most important, the prospect of using EU funds to finance the union is controversial. Some observers also worry that President Sarkozy is using the union to sideline Turkey's accession to the European Union.[8]

Migration remains one of the key issues between the southern Mediterranean countries and the European Union. The Maghreb is both the source of large emigrant flows and a transit platform for migration from the rest of Africa to Europe. Faced with these pressures, Spain is multiplying its immigration agreements with northern and western African coun-

---

6. Countries bordering the Mediterranean are Albania, Algeria, Bosnia-Herzegovina, Croatia, Egypt, Israel, Lebanon, Libya, Montenegro, Morocco, Palestinian Authority, Syria, Tunisia, and Turkey. Jordan and Mauritania could be included as well, although they do not border the Mediterranean.

7. The dual presidency concept of the Union for the Mediterranean calls for a country from the northern bank (a member of the European Union) and a country from the southern bank to share the presidency, which raises potential governance issues.

8. "Nicolas Sarkozy et Angela Merkel veulent convaincre l'UE de l'utilité de l'Union pour la Méditerranée" ["Nicolas Sarkozy and Angela Merkel want to convince the European Union of the usefulness of the Union for the Mediterranean"], Le Monde, March 13, 2008.

tries, including Morocco and Mauritania. The agreements provide for joint patrols, cooperation in training, and liaison officers.[9] Some success in tackling the immigration issue will be important to enlist public support within the European Union for further economic integration with the Maghreb.

Role of Bilateral Agreements

As both the European Union and the United States are working to raise their profiles in the region, it is important to suggest how bilateral trade agreements between one of the major parties and a Maghreb country can promote reforms at a regional level. The following sections detail salient features that the United States or the European Union might insist on, either in the text of a bilateral trade or investment agreement, or in a companion agreement designed to enhance regional integration.

Tariff Barriers

A Maghreb partner of the United States or the European Union could be required to lower or eliminate its own tariffs on selected products imported from other Maghreb countries. The Enabling Clause could be used to justify the World Trade Organization (WTO) consistency of these provisions.[10] Ideally, tariff preferences that a Maghreb country grants to the United States or the European Union through a trade agreement would be extended fully by that Maghreb partner to its Maghreb neighbors. However, after negotiations, the Maghreb preferences might be limited to a subset of products covered by the US or EU bilateral FTA.

Rules of Origin

Rules of origin for shipping merchandise through cross-border supply chains can be particularly cumbersome when a country is a partner in several bilateral trade agreements. In the context of the Euro-Med Partnership, Algeria, Morocco, and Tunisia apply full cumulation among them-

---

9. "Spain in the Fight against Illegal Immigration," Parliament of the United Kingdom documents, available at www.parliament.uk (accessed on March 4, 2008).

10. In its decision, titled "European Communities—Conditions for the Granting of Tariff Preferences to Developing Countries," the Appellate Body ruled that the Enabling Clause did not require that countries grant identical tariff preferences to all developing countries, but instead that the level of preference be based on the specific development, financial, and trade needs of the developing countries in question; available at www.ejil.org (accessed April 15, 2008).

selves and diagonal cumulation with the other pan-European countries. Those provisions could be extended to Libya and Mauritania as well, especially as they are working toward full participation in the Barcelona Process.

The United States and any of its Maghreb partners, starting with Morocco, could negotiate agreements similar to the qualified industrial zones (QIZ) agreement with Egypt and Jordan. The QIZ agreement allows duty-free entry to the United States for Egyptian goods produced in the zones that use Jordanian inputs.[11] QIZs for other Maghreb countries, starting with an extension of the US-Morocco agreement, could help the Maghreb integrate regionally and with the global economy. As a larger-scale version of the QIZ agreement, the United States could allow for the cumulation of inputs across the Maghreb in meeting rules of origin. This approach could be coupled with a requirement that Maghreb countries lower their own tariff barriers for shipments within the region.

Aid for Technical Assistance and Capacity Building

Dennis (2006a) shows that the benefits of a regional trade agreement between Middle East and North Africa countries could triple if accompanied by trade facilitation measures. Detailed models for Morocco and Tunisia suggest that flexibility in the markets for capital, labor, and land would increase the payoff from trade liberalization by a multiple of six (Dennis 2006b). Rigidities in factor markets include delays in securing finance, controls on land and construction, and restrictions on majority ownership by foreign firms. These econometric findings reflect a poor business climate throughout the Maghreb. Comparing regulation and reforms in 178 economies, the World Bank's *Doing Business 2008* report finds that Algeria, Morocco, and Mauritania rank in the bottom third while Tunisia barely makes the top half.[12] Mauritania is the lowest ranked of the Maghreb countries. Among Mauritania's business handicaps are limited access to financing, an inflexible labor market, low educational attainment, and corruption and taxation levels that are among the highest in the world.[13]

The European Union has improved the business climate in Eastern Europe by accelerating reforms. It might do the same for the Maghreb through the framework of the Union for the Mediterranean. Bilateral US

---

11. To qualify, a good must be "substantially transformed" and must have at least 35 percent of its value added in the QIZ factories.

12. Libya is not included in the report.

13. Enterprise Surveys Country Profile: Mauritania, *World Bank Enterprise Surveys*, 2006. Available at www.enterprisesurveys.org (accessed April 20, 2008).

and EU trade agreements with individual countries could likewise contribute. Creating systems for independent administrative and judicial review of customs determinations could be a starting point, but much else can be done.

As the World Bank (2006) argues, investment and services are particularly important to Maghreb economic integration. To this end, the United States and European Union should encourage harmonization of investment and regulatory regimes throughout the region to the highest standards set forth in bilateral trade agreements. In addition, they should promote sector-specific investment and regulatory reforms, particularly for the service sectors. For example, the Euro-Med Partnership is seeking to complete the integration of electricity markets in the Maghreb.[14] Only some countries have linked their electricity grids, such as Algeria and Tunisia. Morocco and Algeria are in the process of setting up a joint venture to link the Algerian power grid to the European Union via Morocco.[15] The ultimate goal is to connect all North African countries to the EU single energy market. The project would promote electricity generation at low-cost plants and reduce the amount of spare capacity across the Maghreb. A trans-Maghreb power grid would also provide energy security for the region. But much remains to be done. Integration could likewise be fostered for natural gas at both the production and distribution levels.

As another example, Maghreb partners could be asked to open their insurance and leasing sectors not only to US and EU firms, but also to other Maghreb countries. Regulatory regimes for insurance and leasing could be harmonized across the Maghreb. Finally, the United States and the European Union could extend so-called fifth freedom rights to air carriers based in the region,[16] provided the home nations accorded similar rights to other regional carriers.

Instruments similar to the Economic and Technical Cooperation (Ecotech) agenda of the Asia Pacific Economic Cooperation (APEC) forum

---

14. In December 2003 in Rome, Algeria, Morocco, Tunisia, and the European Commission (as nonparticipant promoter) signed a protocol of agreement for the progressive integration of the electricity markets of the three Maghreb countries into the EU electricity internal market. The long-term objective is to sign a Euro-Maghreb energy community treaty that also would include Libya and Mauritania. See "Establishment of the 'Rome Euro-Mediterranean Energy Platform' within the Framework of the Euro-Mediterranean Energy Cooperation," decree of the Minister of Productive Activities of the Government of Italy, October 15, 2004. Available at http://ec.europa.eu (accessed on March 23, 2008).

15. "Algeria Plans Power Export to Spain Via Morocco," Reuters, May 10, 2008.

16. Fifth freedom rights are the rights of an airline of one country to land in another country, drop off some passengers and pick up others, and continue traveling to a third country, rather than returning to its own country.

could facilitate capacity building and technical cooperation in the Maghreb.[17] The United States and European Union could assist in harmonizing standards throughout the region following the precedent established in the US–Association of Southeast Asian Nations (ASEAN) TIFA and applied to pharmaceutical and agricultural products. Likewise, while much of the Maghreb transportation infrastructure is relatively good, the United States and the European Union could encourage the World Bank to initiate selected projects to improve ports, airports, roads, and pipelines. Technical and financial assistance for transportation infrastructure should focus on transnational networks. In April 2008 the ten western Mediterranean countries—Portugal, Italy, Spain, France, Malta, and the five AMU members—signed a memorandum of understanding introducing a series of infrastructure projects, including a high-speed train and motorway across North Africa.

Improving the Efficiency of Intraregional Shipments

The last set of features concerns the need to decrease the time and cost of shipments to Maghreb neighbors. At US or EU insistence, a Maghreb country might agree to streamline its customs procedures to ensure the faster release of goods, not only for goods arriving from the United States or Europe, but also for goods arriving from its Maghreb neighbors. New procedures should strictly follow the principles of the Kyoto Convention, which state that customs authorities must maintain formal consultative relationships with importers and that customs formalities must be specified in national legislation and be as simple as possible.

Consistent with these principles, Maghreb customs authorities should permit express shipments by qualified traders and open all borders for certified truckers. The authorities could publish applicable laws and regulations on the Internet and permit electronic submission of customs information before the arrival of shipments, whether by land, sea, or air. Each Maghreb partner should apply risk management principles for customs control so that officers only inspect shipments that are considered medium or high risk.

In addition, the Maghreb partner should allow broker guarantees to cover potential duties and taxes while goods are in transit through a country. This element is essential if businesses are to take advantage of the improved transportation measures. When goods are diverted or lost, the

---

17. The Ecotech agenda was created to support the Bogor Goals for open trade and investment. Six priorities were identified: developing human capital, fostering safe and efficient capital markets, strengthening economic infrastructure, harnessing technologies of the future, promoting environmentally sustainable growth, and encouraging the growth of small and medium enterprises (Yamazawa 2000).

issuer of the guarantee would compensate the host country for duties or taxes that ought to have been paid.

Conclusion

Economic integration in the Maghreb has stalled due in large part to political tensions within the region. Meanwhile the international community has come to view the Maghreb through the twin lenses of terrorism and migration. These facts on the ground and perceptions in the air need to change. Cooperation already exists in regional business activities, in trade agreements, and in diplomatic ties between the Maghreb countries and their major international partners. Initiatives toward regional and global integration should be nurtured. This volume has set forth an array of cooperative measures that the United States and the European Union can pursue with the Maghreb nations to promote integration within the region and more widely. Several of those measures can be accomplished in the short term. In turn, they can foster larger economic reforms in the region, which would, hand in hand with political reforms, greatly enhance the role of the Maghreb in world affairs.

References

Dennis, Allen. 2006a. *The Impact of Regional Trade Agreements and Trade Facilitation in the Middle East North Africa Region.* World Bank Policy Research Working Paper 3837. Washington: World Bank.
Dennis, Allen. 2006b. *Trade Liberalization, Factor Market Flexibility, and Growth: The Case of Morocco and Tunisia.* World Bank Policy Research Working Paper 3857. Washington: World Bank.
World Bank. 2006. *Is There a New Vision for Maghreb Economic Integration?* World Bank Report 38359. Washington.
Yamazawa, Ippei. 2000. *Asia Pacific Economic Cooperation (APEC): Challenges and Tasks for the Twenty-First Century.* New York: Routledge.

About the Contributors

Guillaume Alméras is a partner at BGV Consulting in Paris, where his fields of expertise are international banking and development finance. His past work experience includes management of start-up financial institutions in emerging-market countries. He was the international project manager at Natixis, one of the major French corporate banks. He is also an expert in design and implementation of financial-sector reform and programs in developing countries. He obtained a postgraduate degree in humanities from the Ecole Normale Supérieure in France.

Omar Aloui is a professional economist and manager of a leading consulting firm in food policy and agricultural studies based in Rabat, Morocco. He earned his doctorate in applied economics from Pierre Mendès France University of Grenoble. He is also trained in applied maths and demography. He is associated with universities in Morocco as a visiting professor (Rural Territorial Development Master) and with international training bodies in Morocco and West Africa. He is frequently consulted as a food policy expert by international donors and as an agricultural economist by international private investors. He also contributes regularly to economic publications for students.

Mohamed Hedi Bchir is principal country economist at the African Development Bank in Egypt. He was economic affairs officer, dealing with trade policies and studying the impacts of trade policies for African countries, at the United Nation Economic Commission for Africa in Ethiopia, Addis-Ababa. From 2001 to 2005 he was research fellow at the Centre d'Etudes Prospectives et d'Information Internationales, where he has been developing the MIRAGE model of the world economy. He has published a number of papers related to global modeling and trade agreements assessment and on the effects of the Barcelona effects on North African economic integration. He also developed the database on bound import duties, which is now integrated in the MAcMap database. He received a PhD in macroeconomics from Paris 1 University (Sorbonne).

Hassan Benabderrazik has broad experience as consultant on economic development issues in Morocco and the Maghreb. He founded and directed, from 1985 to 1998, the consulting group AgroConcept, which led him to specialize in the analysis of macro and microeconomic issues, including farming, fishing, trade, energy, and transport. He has conducted studies for private investors, both Moroccan and foreign, Moroccan state bodies, and international organizations such as the World Bank. As secretary general of the Moroccan Ministère des Affaires Générales from 1999 to 2001, he gained practical experience in formulating and implementing policies, negotiating with international agencies such as the World Bank. As secretary general of the Ministry of Agriculture from 2001 to 2004, he led negotiations with the European Commission on a key sector of the Moroccan economy. He lectures at the Institut National des Statistiques et de l'Economie Appliquée. He earned advanced degrees from the Ecole Nationale de la Statistique et de l'Administration Publique in Paris in 1980 and from the Centre Européen pour le Développement in Bari (Italy).

Antoine Bouët joined the International Food Policy Research Institute in February 2005 as senior research fellow in the Markets, Trade, and Institutions Division to conduct research on global trade modeling, trade policies, regional agreements, and multilateral trade negotiations. He was professor of economics at University of Pau (France) and scientific adviser at the Centre d'Etudes Prospectives et d'Informations Internationales–Paris (CEPII), where he developed the MAcMap database of world market access and participated in the development of the MIRAGE model of the world economy. He has carried out research on market access, global trade modeling, the economics of trade retaliation, and the relationship between trade policy and research and development. He has been director of the Centre d'Analyse et de Traitement des donnees economiques in France (1996–2004) and chairman of the European network Research on International Economics and Finance (2002–04). He was GTAP Research Fellow in 2005. He received a PhD in international economics from Bordeaux University.

Claire Brunel is a research assistant at the Peterson Institute for International Economics, where she works on trade issues, particularly regarding North Africa, North America, and the European Union. Before joining the Institute, she worked at the European Commission in the Economics and Financial Affairs DG, for BNP Paribas in macroeconomic studies, and for Schroeder Salomon Smith Barney in mergers and acquisitions. She obtained a bachelor's of science degree in mathematics and economics from Georgetown University and an MPhil in economics from the University of Oxford.

Dean DeRosa is principal economist at ADR International Ltd. and a visiting fellow at the Peterson Institute for International Economics. He has been an economist with the International Food Policy Research Institute, International Monetary Fund, Asian Development Bank, and US Department of the Treasury. He holds a BA degree from the University of Washington and a PhD from the University of Oregon, both in economics. He is author of *Regional Trading Arrangements among Developing Countries: The ASEAN Example* (1996), contributor to a number of the recent Peterson Institute Policy Analyses on prospective US free trade agreements, and coauthor of several journal articles on aspects of international trade, foreign investment, and economic development.

Betina Dimaranan joined the Markets, Trade, and Institutions Division of the International Food Policy Research Institute (IFPRI) as research fellow in July 2007. She currently conducts research on global trade modeling, multilateral and regional trade agreements, and on the impacts of biofuels policies on developing countries. Prior to joining IFPRI, she was a research economist and the database administrator of the Global Trade Analysis Project (GTAP) in Purdue University. She has conducted research on trade and development topics that include trade liberalization under the Uruguay Round, food and agriculture markets in the Asia-Pacific region, China's and Vietnam's accession to the World Trade Organization, reform of OECD domestic support, and the impacts of growth of China and India on developing countries. She managed the construction of the GTAP5 and GTAP6 databases and edited two volumes that document the global database, more recently *Global Trade, Assistance and Production: The GTAP6 Data Base*. She received a PhD in agricultural economics from Purdue University. She is a 2008 GTAP Research Fellow.

Stuart E. Eizenstat heads the international practice of Covington & Burling LLP. His work at Covington focuses on resolving international trade problems and business disputes with the US and foreign governments, and international business transactions and regulations on behalf of US companies and others around the world. During a decade and a half of public service in three US administrations, Ambassador Eizenstat has held a number of key senior positions, including chief White House domestic policy adviser to President Jimmy Carter (1977–81), US ambassador to the European Union, undersecretary of commerce for international trade, undersecretary of state for economic, business, and agricultural affairs, and deputy secretary of the Treasury in the Clinton administration (1993–2001). Ambassador Eizenstat has received seven honorary doctorate degrees from universities and academic institutions. He has been awarded high civilian awards from the governments of France (Legion of Honor), Germany, Austria, and Belgium, as well as from Secretary of State Warren Christopher, Secretary of State Madeleine Albright, and Secretary of the Treasury Lawrence Summers. He is a graduate of the University of North Carolina and of Harvard Law School.

Mustapha Faïd is president of SPTEC Conseil, a Paris-based consulting firm specializing in oil and gas issues. He has more than 30 years of experience in the oil and gas industry. He was appointed general manager of Observatoire Méditerranéen de l'Energie from February 2007 to June 2008. Previously, he worked for 20 years for Sonatrach, where his last position was executive vice president of marketing and business development and member of the Board and of the Executive Committee, between 1989 and 1994. He was one of the organizing members of two top-level annual conferences in Paris, the International Oil Summit and the International Gas Summit, which have become essential international meetings on the energy scene. For several years he was a lecturer at the Institut Français du Pétrole. He also participates actively as speaker and facilitator in several international symposiums, conferences, and seminars. He holds a doctor-engineer in industrial chemistry degree from Pierre et Marie Curie University in Paris, an engineering degree in oil refining from the Algerian Petroleum Institute in Algiers, and a bachelor's degree in physics and chemistry from the University of Algiers.

Francis Ghilès, a leading European expert on the Maghreb, is a senior fellow at the European Institute of the Mediterranean, specializing in security, energy, and broader political and economic trends in North Africa and the Western Mediterranean. During his distinguished career as a journalist, he spent 18 years writing for the *Financial Times* and also freelanced for a number of newspapers including the *New York Times*, *Wall Street Journal*, *Le Monde,* and *El Pais*. He has published numerous articles in French, English, and Spanish and is a frequent commentator in print and broadcast media. He has lectured in universities, think tanks, and defence institutions on both sides of the Atlantic and the Mediterranean and in Japan. He studied at SciencesPo, Grenoble and earned advanced degrees at the University of Keele and St Antony's College, Oxford.

Gary Clyde Hufbauer has been the Reginald Jones Senior Fellow at the Peterson Institute for International Economics since 1992. He was the Marcus Wallenberg Professor of International Finance Diplomacy at Georgetown University (1985–92), senior fellow at the Institute (1981–85), deputy director of the International Law Institute at Georgetown University (1979–81); deputy assistant secretary for international trade and investment policy of the US Treasury (1977–79); and director of the international tax staff at the Treasury (1974–76). He has written extensively on international trade, investment, and tax issues. His publications include *Economic Sanctions Reconsidered*, 3rd edition (2007), *US Taxation of Foreign Income* (2007), *Toward a US-Indonesia Free Trade Agreement* (2007), *US-China Trade Disputes: Rising Tide, Rising Stakes* (2006), *The Shape of a Swiss-US Free Trade Agreement* (2006), *NAFTA Revisited: Achievements and Challenges* (2005), *Reforming the US Corporate Tax* (2005), *Awakening Monster: The Alien Tort Statute of 1789* (2003), *The Benefits of Price Covergence* (2002), *The Ex-Im Bank in the 21st Century* (2001), *World Capital Markets* (2001), *Fundamental Tax Reform and Border Tax Adjustments* (1996), and *US Taxation of International Income* (1992).

Abderrahmane Hadj Nacer is a distinguished specialist in banking, finance, and economics in North Africa. He ran the department of economic affairs at the presidency of Algeria from 1985 to 1989, where he drafted the blueprint on economic and industrial reform. He played a key role in enacting these reforms when he was appointed governor of the central bank of Algeria in 1989. He has held a string of senior banking positions in France and North Africa: adviser on Muslim Country Affairs at Banque Lazard Frères & Cie (1992–94); CEO of GP Banque (Société Marseillaise de Crédit Group) Paris (1994–97); CEO of Union Bank, Algeria's first private bank (1995–97); CEO of HBC Holding Paris since 1995; adviser to the president of Natexis Banques Populaires (1998–2002); and founding partner of IM Bank (Tunisia) since 2002. A graduate of the Ecole Polytechnique (Algiers), he earned doctorates from the University of Lille and the Catholic University of Louvain.

Marcelle Thomas joined the International Food Policy Research Institute in 1988 and is now a research analyst in the Markets, Trade, and Institutions Division (MTID). As part of her ongoing work at MTID, she has joined the team on globalization and trade, applying the MAcMap dataset of trade protection indicators and the MIRAGE global computable general equilibrium model to assess the impact of bilateral and regional trade agreements on developing countries. She received a BS degree in mathematics and an MA degree in economics from North Carolina State University.

Index

African Bank for Development and
Trade, 15
African Development Bank (AfDB), 133,
134
AFTA (ASEAN Free Trade Area), 18
as gravity model indicator, 50, 50t, 52
Agadir Agreement, 8t, 9f, 15, 157
Agreement on Investment and Trade in
Services (CACM), 21
agribusiness. *See also* food industries
under Agadir Agreement, 15
employment in, 5
under Euro-Med Partnership, 14,
152–53
global trade in, 27, 28t–29t
intraregional trade in, 27, 30t–31t
in Mirage model analysis, 73–76, 75t,
77t, 83
recommendations, 99, 158–60, 159t
revealed comparative advantage,
32–33, 34t–35t
agricultural indicators, 153–54, 154t
AIA (ASEAN Investment Area), 19–20
Air Algérie, 146
Air France, 146
air safety regulation authority, 98
air transport, 98, 141–42
fifth freedom rights to, 169, 169n
infrastructure, 145–46
reforms, 143, 146, 163
Algeria
agricultural sector, 153–56, 154t, 157,
161t
arms sales to, 93–94
banking sector, 125, 126t, 127, 137
privatization of, 98, 127, 136
emigrant remittances, 133
energy consumption, 102, 102t, 111

energy reserves, 94, 106, 107t
energy trading, 119–20
EU association agreement with, 13, 13n,
40n, 152
food consumption, 154, 155t
geography and population indicators,
25, 26t, 111, 112t
logistics performance ranking, 144, 144t
merchandise trade balance, 112–14, 114t
pipelines, 96–97
tariff regime, 40, 41t, 42–43
terrorism in, 3–4
transportation sector, 139–48
US economic ties with, 164, 165t
Western Sahara dispute, 1, 4, 10, 94
Algeria-Morocco border, closure of, 10,
10n, 89, 139, 144, 147
allocation efficiency gains, 88, 90
al Qaeda, 95
al Qaeda in the Islamic Maghreb (AQIM),
3–4
AMU. *See* Arab Maghreb Union
antiterrorism measures, 4–5, 21, 95, 99
APEC (Asia Pacific Economic
Cooperation), Ecotech agenda, 169,
170n
Appel de Tanger for Maghreb unity, 94
AQIM (al Qaeda in the Islamic Maghreb),
3–4
Arab League, 11, 11n, 40n, 51n
Arab Maghreb Union (AMU), 7–11, 8t, 9f
econometric analysis of (*See* gravity
model analysis; Mirage model
analysis)
economic performance and, 11, 12t
failure of, reasons for, 139, 157
revitalization of, 10–11, 51, 163–71
tariff regime, 40n

CGE (computable general equilibrium) model. *See* Mirage model analysis

Chile, Mexico, Australia, and Singapore (CMAS) FTAs, 49–50, 50*t*, 52

China, 95, 98, 152

Clean Development Mechanism (CDM), 120

climate change, 97, 99
   agricultural productivity and, 5
   sustainable development and, 120

climate zone, 25, 26*t*

CMAS FTAs, 49–50, 50*t*, 52

coal consumption, 104, 105*t*
   demand projections, 117*t*, 118

COMESA, 8*t*, 9*f*, 16, 16*n*

comparative advantage, revealed, 32–33, 34*t*–35*t*

competition, imperfect, in Mirage model, 81, 81*n*

complementary policies, dynamic modeling of, 81–84, 90

computable general equilibrium (CGE) model. *See* Mirage model analysis

conformity assessment, 14*n*

consumer credit, 131–32

consumer price policies, 154

Continuous Assisted Quotation (CAC40), 98, 136

credit access, 128–32, 137, 138

Crédit Populaire, 127

cumulation, forms of, 14, 14*n*

currency convertibility, 98, 136

customs clearance, electronic data interchange for, 140, 143, 170

customs reforms, 143–44, 170

Dakar rally, 4

Darfur, 15

debt, public, 130, 130*t*

debt markets, 129–30

desalination plants, 123

development banks, 132, 133, 135

distributional effects, Mirage model analysis of, 89

Doing Business 2008 (World Bank), 168

Dubai Ports World, 143

dynamic Mirage model analysis, 81–90, 85*t*–88*t*
   domestic investment, 84
   services trade, 82, 83*t*
   trade facilitation, 82–84

Eastern Europe, business climate in, 168

Ecofin Council, 135

econometric techniques. *See* gravity model analysis; Mirage model analysis

Economic and Technical Cooperation (Ecotech) agenda, 169, 170*n*

economic growth
   banking sector and, 137
   energy sector and, 112, 113*t*
   gravity model analysis of, 61–67, 66*t*
   infrastructure and, 140
   rates of, 94

economic performance, 5
   effect of AMU on, 11, 12*t*
   international comparison of, 23, 24*t*
   terrorism and, 23

economies of scale, 150–51

Ecotech (Economic and Technical Cooperation) agenda, 169, 170*n*

EDI (electronic data interchange), 140, 143, 170

efficiency gains, 88, 90

Egypt
   banking sector, 125, 126*t*, 127
   energy reserves, 106
   financial-sector reforms, 125–27
   QIZ agreement, 168

EIB (European Investment Bank), 15, 132, 133, 135

electricity
   alternative sources of (*See* nuclear power; renewable energy)
   consumption of, 105–106, 106*t*
   demand projections, 116–18, 117*t*
   intraregional trading in, 110*t*, 110–11, 119

electricity markets, integration of, 21, 97, 122–23, 169, 169*n*

electronic data interchange (EDI), 140, 143, 170

El Khalifa, 127

ELTAM line, 119

emigrant remittances, 128, 132–35
   banking sector and, 134–35, 137
   uses of, 134

emigration, 94–95, 98, 99, 166–67, 171

employment, gravity model analysis of, 61–67, 66*t*

energy consumption, 102*t*, 102–106
   demand projections, 116–18, 117*t*
   by energy type, 103*f*, 103–106
   population growth and, 101, 111, 112*t*

energy intensity, 112

energy resources, 106–108, 107*t*

international comparison of, 23, 24*t*
link between trade and, 59, 60*b*–61*b*
versus other regional initiatives, 19*t*,
    19–20, 22
services trade and, 36, 43
terrorism and, 5
Foreign Sovereign Immunities Act, 165
Framework Agreement on the ASEAN
    Investment Area, 19
France
    Continuous Assisted Quotation
        (CAC40), 98, 136
    emigrant remittances from, 133
    Union for the Mediterranean proposed
        by, 166
free trade agreements (FTAs). *See also*
    specific agreement
    agricultural exception clauses, 158
    econometric analyses of (*See* gravity
        model analysis; Mirage model
        analysis)
    "plus" scenarios for, 52, 58
    services trade liberalization, 36, 43
freight. *See* shipments; transportation
    sector
FTSE (Financial Times Stock Exchange)
    index, 98
full cumulation, 14, 14*n*

GAFTA. *See* Greater Arab Free Trade Area
Galsi pipeline, 122
GDP growth, 1
    effect of AMU on, 11, 12*t*
    gravity model analysis of, 61–67, 66*t*
    international comparison of, 23, 24*t*
    Mirage model analysis of, 89
    versus other regional initiatives, 18, 19*t*,
        22
    transportation sector and, 140
General Agreement on Tariffs and Trade
    (GATT), 36, 82–83
    Enabling Clause, 167, 167*n*
Generalized System of Preferences (GSP),
    48, 165, 165*t*
generational transition, 94–95
geographical decomposition, Mirage
    model analysis, 72–73, 73*t*–74*t*
geography of Maghreb region, 25, 26*t*
Germany, Union for the Mediterranean
    proposed by, 166
globalization, regional effects of, 152
Global Trade Analysis Project (GTAP 6.2)
    database, 70–72

global warming. *See* climate change
GNP (gross national product)
    energy sector and, 112, 113*t*
    ratio of market capitalization to, 129,
        129*t*
gravity model analysis, 2, 45–68
    basis and dataset, 45–48, 47*t*
    estimation results, 48–50, 50*t*
    integration scenarios, 50–53
    simulation results, 53–67, 54*t*–57*t*
        FDI impacts, 56*t*–57*t*, 59–61
        output, employment, and growth
            impacts, 61–67, 66*t*
        trade impacts, 58–59
Greater Arab Free Trade Area (GAFTA),
    8*t*, 9*f*, 11–13
    agricultural sector, 157
    tariff regime, 13, 40*n*, 51*n*
Groupe Banque Populaire, 127–28
Groupe Salafiste de la Predication et du
    Combat (GSPC), 3
GSP (Generalized System of Preferences),
    48, 165, 165*t*
GTAP 6.2 (Global Trade Analysis Project)
    database, 70–72

harbors. *See* maritime transport
Harmonized System (HS), 72
Heckscher-Ohlin model, 150
HIV (human immunodeficiency
    virus), 14
Horizon 2020 project, 136
horizontal trade, 150–51
hub-and-spoke opportunities, 145
human capital, 25, 26*t*

Ibn Khaldun, 100
iceberg costs, 83
IDB (Inter-American Development
    Bank), 21
immigration. *See* emigration
imperfect competition, in Mirage model,
    81, 81*n*
imports, 27, 28*t*–29*t*
    gravity model analysis of, 59, 62,
        64*t*–65*t*
    protection of (*See* tariffs)
income, real, Mirage model analysis of,
    79*t*, 80–81
India, 95, 98, 152
industrial sectors, in Mirage model
    analysis, 73–76, 75*t*, 77*t*
information-sharing agreement, 4, 21

National Bank of Egypt, 127
National Société Générale Bank, 127
natural gas
  consumption, 104, 104t
    demand projections, 117t, 118
  pipelines, 89, 96–97, 104, 108–10
    energy demand and, 118
    energy trading and, 119–20, 122
  reserves, 106, 107t
    dependence on, 5
    intraregional trade, 108–10, 119, 122
natural resources, 25, 26t. *See also* energy
    sector
  food industries and, 151, 159
  global trade in, 27, 28t–29t
  intraregional trade in, 27, 30t–31t
Neighborhood Investment Facility (EIB),
    135
new trade theory, 150–51, 151t
nonperforming loans, 131, 138
nontariff barriers (NTBs), 42–43
  under GAFTA, 13, 40n, 51n
  Mirage model analysis and, 73n
North African Dow Jones index, 138
North American Free Trade Agreement
    (NAFTA), as gravity model indicator,
    46, 46n, 49–50, 50t, 52
Norway, foreign direct investment,
    38–39, 39t
nuclear power, 121, 123

Office Chérifien des Phosphates, 141
Office National de l'Electricité, 97
Office National des Transports (Morocco),
    141
oil
  consumption, 103, 103t
    demand projections, 117t, 118
  reserves, 106, 107t
    dependence on, 5
    intraregional trade, 108, 109t, 119
open skies policy, 98, 143
origination rule. *See* rules of origin
output, gravity model analysis of,
    61–67, 66t

Palestine Liberation Organization, 93
Pan Am Flight 103 bombing, 10, 13–14
Pedro Duran Farell Pipeline, 96, 108–10
per capita income, 5
  effect of AMU on, 11, 12t
  international comparison of, 23, 24t
Permanent Secretariat for Economic
    Integration (SIECA), 20

petroleum. *See* oil reserves
"plus" scenarios, for bilateral FTAs,
    gravity model analysis of, 52, 58
Polisario Front, 4, 10
political economy, 2, 3–6, 93–96, 171
  of energy sector, 94, 124
  versus other regions, 18, 20
  of US-Maghreb relations, 164
population, 5, 23, 24t, 25, 26t
  energy consumption and, 101, 111, 112t
ports. *See* maritime transport
poverty, Mirage model analysis of, 89
power grid, trans-Maghreb, 169, 169n
power plants, 96–97, 104, 123
processed food industries, 154, 155t, 156
proximity, 150, 158
public debt, 130, 130t
public goods, regional, 151, 158, 159t

qualified industrial zone (QIZ) program,
    168, 168n

railway transport, 98, 139, 141
  infrastructure, 145
  reforms, 142
RCA (revealed comparative advantage),
    32–33, 34t–35t
real income, Mirage model analysis of,
    79t, 80–81, 85t–88t, 88
regional banks, creation of, 11, 98, 135–36,
    137
regional initiatives. *See also* regional
    integration; *specific initiative*
  international comparison of, 2, 19t,
    21–22
regional integration
  attempts at, 7–16, 8t, 9f
  benefits of, 2
  compared with other regional
    initiatives, 2, 19t, 21–22
  recommendations for, 2, 163–71
  sector-specific, 96–99
regional public goods, 151, 158, 159t
regulatory harmonization, 2, 99, 169–70
  versus other regional initiatives,
    19, 22
Renault-Nissan, 146
renewable energy
  consumption of, 105, 105t
  demand projections, 117t, 118
  reserves of, 106–108
  sustainable development and, 120
research and development, energy sector,
    121

Other Publications from the Peterson Institute

The Political Economy of Korea-United
States Cooperation*   C. Fred Bergsten
and Il SaKong, editors
February 1995   ISBN 0-88132-213-X
International Debt Reexamined*
William R. Cline
February 1995   ISBN 0-88132-083-8
American Trade Politics, 3d ed. I. M. Destler
April 1995   ISBN 0-88132-215-6
Managing Official Export Credits: The Quest
for a Global Regime*   John E. Ray
July 1995   ISBN 0-88132-207-5
Asia Pacific Fusion: Japan's Role in APEC*
Yoichi Funabashi
October 1995   ISBN 0-88132-224-5
Korea-United States Cooperation in the New
World Order* C. Fred Bergsten/Il SaKong, eds.
February 1996   ISBN 0-88132-226-1
Why Exports Really Matter!* ISBN 0-88132-221-0
Why Exports Matter More!*   ISBN 0-88132-229-6
J. David Richardson and Karin Rindal
July 1995; February 1996
Global Corporations and National
Governments   Edward M. Graham
May 1996   ISBN 0-88132-111-7
Global Economic Leadership and the Group of
Seven   C. Fred Bergsten
and C. Randall Henning
May 1996   ISBN 0-88132-218-0
The Trading System after the Uruguay Round*
John Whalley and Colleen Hamilton
July 1996   ISBN 0-88132-131-1
Private Capital Flows to Emerging Markets
after the Mexican Crisis*   Guillermo A. Calvo,
Morris Goldstein, and Eduard Hochreiter
September 1996   ISBN 0-88132-232-6
The Crawling Band as an Exchange Rate
Regime: Lessons from Chile, Colombia,
and Israel   John Williamson
September 1996   ISBN 0-88132-231-8
Flying High: Liberalizing Civil Aviation
in the Asia Pacific*   Gary Clyde Hufbauer
and Christopher Findlay
November 1996   ISBN 0-88132-227-X
Measuring the Costs of Visible Protection
in Korea*   Namdoo Kim
November 1996   ISBN 0-88132-236-9
The World Trading System: Challenges Ahead
Jeffrey J. Schott
December 1996   ISBN 0-88132-235-0
Has Globalization Gone Too Far?   Dani Rodrik
March 1997   ISBN paper 0-88132-241-5
Korea-United States Economic Relationship*
C. Fred Bergsten and Il SaKong, editors
March 1997   ISBN 0-88132-240-7
Summitry in the Americas: A Progress Report
Richard E. Feinberg
April 1997   ISBN 0-88132-242-3
Corruption and the Global Economy
Kimberly Ann Elliott
June 1997   ISBN 0-88132-233-4

Regional Trading Blocs in the World
Economic System   Jeffrey A. Frankel
October 1997   ISBN 0-88132-202-4
Sustaining the Asia Pacific Miracle:
Environmental Protection and Economic
Integration   Andre Dua and Daniel C. Esty
October 1997   ISBN 0-88132-250-4
Trade and Income Distribution
William R. Cline
November 1997   ISBN 0-88132-216-4
Global Competition Policy
Edward M. Graham and J. David Richardson
December 1997   ISBN 0-88132-166-4
Unfinished Business: Telecommunications
after the Uruguay Round
Gary Clyde Hufbauer and Erika Wada
December 1997   ISBN 0-88132-257-1
Financial Services Liberalization in the WTO
Wendy Dobson and Pierre Jacquet
June 1998   ISBN 0-88132-254-7
Restoring Japan's Economic Growth
Adam S. Posen
September 1998   ISBN 0-88132-262-8
Measuring the Costs of Protection in China
Zhang Shuguang, Zhang Yansheng,
and Wan Zhongxin
November 1998   ISBN 0-88132-247-4
Foreign Direct Investment and Development:
The New Policy Agenda for Developing
Countries and Economies in Transition
Theodore H. Moran
December 1998   ISBN 0-88132-258-X
Behind the Open Door: Foreign Enterprises
in the Chinese Marketplace   Daniel H. Rosen
January 1999   ISBN 0-88132-263-6
Toward A New International Financial
Architecture: A Practical Post-Asia Agenda
Barry Eichengreen
February 1999   ISBN 0-88132-270-9
Is the U.S. Trade Deficit Sustainable?
Catherine L. Mann
September 1999   ISBN 0-88132-265-2
Safeguarding Prosperity in a Global Financial
System: The Future International Financial
Architecture, Independent Task Force Report
Sponsored by the Council on Foreign Relations
Morris Goldstein, Project Director
October 1999   ISBN 0-88132-287-3
Avoiding the Apocalypse: The Future
of the Two Koreas   Marcus Noland
June 2000   ISBN 0-88132-278-4
Assessing Financial Vulnerability:
An Early Warning System for Emerging
Markets   Morris Goldstein,
Graciela Kaminsky, and Carmen Reinhart
June 2000   ISBN 0-88132-237-7
Global Electronic Commerce: A Policy Primer
Catherine L. Mann, Sue E. Eckert, and Sarah
Cleeland Knight
July 2000   ISBN 0-88132-274-1

The WTO after Seattle Jeffrey J. Schott, ed.
July 2000 ISBN 0-88132-290-3
**Intellectual Property Rights in the Global
Economy** Keith E. Maskus
August 2000 ISBN 0-88132-282-2
**The Political Economy of the Asian Financial
Crisis** Stephan Haggard
August 2000 ISBN 0-88132-283-0
**Transforming Foreign Aid: United States
Assistance in the 21st Century** Carol Lancaster
August 2000 ISBN 0-88132-291-1
**Fighting the Wrong Enemy: Antiglobal
Activists and Multinational Enterprises**
Edward M. Graham
September 2000 ISBN 0-88132-272-5
**Globalization and the Perceptions of American
Workers** Kenneth Scheve/Matthew J. Slaughter
March 2001 ISBN 0-88132-295-4
World Capital Markets: Challenge to the G-10
Wendy Dobson and Gary Clyde Hufbauer,
assisted by Hyun Koo Cho
May 2001 ISBN 0-88132-301-2
Prospects for Free Trade in the Americas
Jeffrey J. Schott
August 2001 ISBN 0-88132-275-X
**Toward a North American Community:
Lessons from the Old World for the New**
Robert A. Pastor
August 2001 ISBN 0-88132-328-4
**Measuring the Costs of Protection in Europe:
European Commercial Policy in the 2000s**
Patrick A. Messerlin
September 2001 ISBN 0-88132-273-3
Job Loss from Imports: Measuring the Costs
Lori G. Kletzer
September 2001 ISBN 0-88132-296-2
**No More Bashing: Building a New
Japan–United States Economic Relationship**
C. Fred Bergsten, Takatoshi Ito, and
Marcus Noland
October 2001 ISBN 0-88132-286-5
Why Global Commitment Really Matters!
Howard Lewis III and J. David Richardson
October 2001 ISBN 0-88132-298-9
**Leadership Selection in the Major
Multilaterals** Miles Kahler
November 2001 ISBN 0-88132-335-7
**The International Financial Architecture:
What's New? What's Missing?** Peter Kenen
November 2001 ISBN 0-88132-297-0
**Delivering on Debt Relief: From IMF Gold
to a New Aid Architecture**
John Williamson and Nancy Birdsall,
with Brian Deese
April 2002 ISBN 0-88132-331-4
**Imagine There's No Country: Poverty,
Inequality, and Growth in the Era
of Globalization** Surjit S. Bhalla
September 2002 ISBN 0-88132-348-9
Reforming Korea's Industrial Conglomerates
Edward M. Graham
January 2003 ISBN 0-88132-337-3

**Industrial Policy in an Era of Globalization:
Lessons from Asia** Marcus Noland
and Howard Pack
March 2003 ISBN 0-88132-350-0
Reintegrating India with the World Economy
T. N. Srinivasan and Suresh D. Tendulkar
March 2003 ISBN 0-88132-280-6
**After the Washington Consensus:
Restarting Growth and Reform
in Latin America** Pedro-Pablo Kuczynski
and John Williamson, editors
March 2003 ISBN 0-88132-347-0
**The Decline of US Labor Unions and the Role
of Trade** Robert E. Baldwin
June 2003 ISBN 0-88132-341-1
**Can Labor Standards Improve under
Globalization?** Kimberly A. Elliott
and Richard B. Freeman
June 2003 ISBN 0-88132-332-2
**Crimes and Punishments? Retaliation
under the WTO** Robert Z. Lawrence
October 2003 ISBN 0-88132-359-4
Inflation Targeting in the World Economy
Edwin M. Truman
October 2003 ISBN 0-88132-345-4
**Foreign Direct Investment and Tax
Competition** John H. Mutti
November 2003 ISBN 0-88132-352-7
**Has Globalization Gone Far Enough?
The Costs of Fragmented Markets**
Scott Bradford and Robert Z. Lawrence
February 2004 ISBN 0-88132-349-7
**Food Regulation and Trade:
Toward a Safe and Open Global System**
Tim Josling, Donna Roberts, and David Orden
March 2004 ISBN 0-88132-346-2
**Controlling Currency Mismatches
in Emerging Markets**
Morris Goldstein and Philip Turner
April 2004 ISBN 0-88132-360-8
**Free Trade Agreements: US Strategies
and Priorities** Jeffrey J. Schott, editor
April 2004 ISBN 0-88132-361-6
Trade Policy and Global Poverty
William R. Cline
June 2004 ISBN 0-88132-365-9
**Bailouts or Bail-ins? Responding to Financial
Crises in Emerging Economies**
Nouriel Roubini and Brad Setser
August 2004 ISBN 0-88132-371-3
Transforming the European Economy
Martin Neil Baily and Jacob Kirkegaard
September 2004 ISBN 0-88132-343-8
**Chasing Dirty Money: The Fight Against
Money Laundering**
Peter Reuter and Edwin M. Truman
November 2004 ISBN 0-88132-370-5
**The United States and the World Economy:
Foreign Economic Policy for the Next Decade**
C. Fred Bergsten
January 2005 ISBN 0-88132-380-2

WORKS IN PROGRESS

**Australia, New Zealand,
and Papua New Guinea**
D. A. Information Services
648 Whitehorse Road
Mitcham, Victoria 3132, Australia
Tel: 61-3-9210-7777
Fax: 61-3-9210-7788
Email: service@dadirect.com.au
www.dadirect.com.au

India, Bangladesh, Nepal, and Sri Lanka
Viva Books Private Limited
Mr. Vinod Vasishtha
4737/23 Ansari Road
Daryaganj, New Delhi 110002
India
Tel: 91-11-4224-2200
Fax: 91-11-4224-2240
Email: viva@vivagroupindia.net
www.vivagroupindia.com

**Mexico, Central America, South America,
and Puerto Rico**
US PubRep, Inc.
311 Dean Drive
Rockville, MD 20851
Tel: 301-838-9276
Fax: 301-838-9278
Email: c.falk@ieee.org

**Asia (*Brunei, Burma, Cambodia, China,
Hong Kong, Indonesia, Korea, Laos, Malaysia,
Philippines, Singapore, Taiwan, Thailand,
and Vietnam*)**
East-West Export Books (EWEB)
University of Hawaii Press
2840 Kolowalu Street
Honolulu, Hawaii 96822-1888
Tel: 808-956-8830
Fax: 808-988-6052
Email: eweb@hawaii.edu

Canada
Renouf Bookstore
5369 Canotek Road, Unit 1
Ottawa, Ontario K1J 9J3, Canada
Tel: 613-745-2665
Fax: 613-745-7660
www.renoufbooks.com

Japan
United Publishers Services Ltd.
1-32-5, Higashi-shinagawa
Shinagawa-ku, Tokyo 140-0002
Japan
Tel: 81-3-5479-7251
Fax: 81-3-5479-7307
Email: purchasing@ups.co.jp
*For trade accounts only. Individuals will find
Institute books in leading Tokyo bookstores.*

Middle East
MERIC
2 Bahgat Ali Street, El Masry Towers
Tower D, Apt. 24
Zamalek, Cairo
Egypt
Tel. 20-2-7633824
Fax: 20-2-7369355
Email: mahmoud_fouda@mericonline.com
www.mericonline.com

**United Kingdom, Europe
(*including Russia and Turkey*), Africa,
and Israel**
The Eurospan Group
c/o Turpin Distribution
Pegasus Drive
Stratton Business Park
Biggleswade, Bedfordshire
SG18 8TQ
United Kingdom
Tel: 44 (0) 1767-604972
Fax: 44 (0) 1767-601640
Email: eurospan@turpin-distribution.com
www.eurospangroup.com/bookstore

**Visit our website at:
www.petersoninstitute.org
E-mail orders to:
petersonmail@presswarehouse.com**